DIVREI ISH

SELECTED
ADDRESSES and ESSAYS
ON JEWISH LIFE AND JEWISH EDUCATION

ALVIN I. SCHIFF

*Published on the Occasion of
The 80th Anniversary
of the Board of Jewish Education
of Greater New York*

FOREWORD BY
ELIE WIESEL

BOARD OF JEWISH EDUCATION
OF GREATER NEW YORK
An Agency of UJA-Federation

The printing of this volume was made possible through the generosity of the Alvin I. Schiff Endowment Fund of the Board of Jewish Education of Greater New York.

ISBN: 0-88384-143-6

Dedicated to the Future

Danielle Aliza
David Jeremy
Marc Adam
Yonatan Shmuel

בני בנים הרי הם כבנים. (יבמות סב:)
"Children's children are like one's own children." (Yebamot 62b)

The most reliable criterion for determining the potential of Jewish continuity is the level of Jewishness of one's grandchildren — the guarantors of the Jewish future:
עתיד שכולו תכלת,
"a future that is all sky-blue."

ON THE TITLE OF THIS VOLUME

DIVREI ISH — דברי אי"ש

In Jewish tradition acronyms and acrostics have been employed frequently by writers, particularly by the *paytanim* — the liturgical poets of the Middle Ages. Over the years, the authors of scholarly works, halachic treatises, responsa, Hebraic literature and Biblical and Talmudic commentaries have been identified by the initials of the authors' names. The use of acronyms continues until this day.

The title of this book — Divrei Ish — literally means, "The Words of A Man" or "The Sayings of A Man." Dr. Schiff, in his writings, memos and letters regularly uses the acronym אי"ש—Ish, deriving from the first letters of his given names and family name אברהם יצחק שיף. Hence, the Hebrew acronym אי"ש—Ish and the title Divrei Ish.

CONTENTS

ON PERSONNEL

FOCUS ON THE BOARD OF JEWISH EDUCATION OF GREATER NEW YORK

FROM DEEP DARKNESS TO GREAT LIGHT

2

FOREWORD

Colleague, comrade in arms, and friend, Alvin Schiff is close to me. His passion for Jewish education is contagious and fruitful; he has invested in it his energy and fervor. The New York Jewish community owes him a lot; its educational network has developed, thanks to his efforts and his creative imagination, at a pace that cannot but arouse enthusiasm.

I have known Dr. Alvin Schiff for years. We have collaborated more than once, on more than one project, but always within the framework of Jewish education.

It was, it still is, his obsession. To combat ignorance, to help others discover the beauty and depth of the Jewish ethic, the adventure that constitutes Jewish history with its inexhaustible riches, the sense of responsibility that flows from it; a Jewish child, a Jewish adolescent, who is not steeped in this heritage, risks withdrawing from it, and consequently, being lost to his or her people. That is why education is, for a Jew, the most urgent of priorities; it always has been.

In Judea and Babylonia, in Provence and Spain, at the time of the Gaonim, and later in Eastern Europe, the emphasis was placed on the duty to teach children the sad or glorious bonds they most forge for themselves through language and knowledge, ties with family and community extending back to Rabbi Akiba and Isaiah, until Abraham.

"Veshinantam lebane'ha" is a Biblical commandment. It is incumbent upon us to teach children Torah, in the broadest and noblest sense of the term. It is not by accident that of all the titles accorded to Moses, it is that of "Rabeinu" that we retain: he is the teacher par excellence. And we are all his disciples.

3

In Heder, in the Yeshiva or Yeshiva k'tana, it is as a disciple that the young Jew penetrates the enchanting universe of the Law and its Commentaries. He learns how to rejoice on on Shabbat, how to prepare for the Festivals, and weep for the victims and martyrs of persecutions. To be a Jew is a way of life that envelops one's entire being.

Once upon a time, in Poland or Romania, parents preferred to go hungry in order to save enough money to pay their children's tutor. That was the dream they had in common: not that their children be rich or well-established, but that they be good Jews, that is to say, conscious of their obligations as Jews, and of their privileges.

If so many Jewish children in New York have been able to fulfill the dreams of their parents, it is to Alvin Schiff that they are indebted.

Elie Wiesel

PREFACE

Reducing thoughts to writing — rendering oral expression in written form — is in good Jewish tradition. Besides the Bible, the prime examples of that tradition are the recorded compilation of the Oral Law and the voluminous commentaries on the Bible and Talmud.

Jews were recognized early in their history as people who respected the printed word. Accordingly, our sages cautioned us to be exceedingly careful when committing ideas to writing.

חזקה על חבר שאין מוציא מתחת ידו דבר שאינו מתוקן. (פסחים ט')

The fear of not presenting a thought in perfect written form has discouraged many would-be-authors from appearing in print.

Post Talmudic Jewish history is punctuated by a plethora of writings ranging from scholarly halachic discussions and profound philosophic treatises to ordinary descriptions of everyday life. Over the past several decades, this literature has been enriched by the contributions of many American Jewish writers on a wide variety of Jewish topics. I am honored that this selection of my statements, addresses, memos and *divrei Torah* over the last forty years will now be part of this growing library of American Jewish literature.

While presented on a variety of occasions in many different settings, they all deal with the theme of Jewish continuity which is essentially their unifying principle. More specifically, they all relate to the theory and practice of Jewish education in which I have been engaged for forty-five years.

The publications committee for this volume tried to select items that do not repeat themselves. But, given the nature of my Jewish communal involvement and my considered points of view about the need to enhance Jewish life and maximize the effectiveness of Jewish education, accomplishing this is almost impossible. In this regard, the reader will understand that the repetition of one or more ideas is not only inevitable, but is an integral part of my role in Jewish education.

I am indebted beyond words to the lay leadership of BJE and to the members of the publications committee who painstakingly saw this compilation through completion.

Alvin I. Schiff
אי"ש

— I —

A WAY OF LIFE — PERSONAL CREDO

*Prepared as a matter of
personal record, upon assuming full-time
Chairmanship of the Department
of Education at the
Ferkauf Graduate School of
Humanities and Social Sciences,
Yeshiva University, September 1965*

My Jewish credo is the credo of my faith; it is also my American credo; it is my human credo, too. My commitment to Judaism encompasses my belief in the God of Israel, my engagement with the people of Israel and my involvement with the Land of Israel. It embraces, also, my commitment to the American society and to all mankind.

Judaism possesses a mystifying polarity. It is knowledge and feeling, contemplation and experience, prayer and study. It is *halachah* and *aggadah,* doctrine and creativity. It is a land and a people, statehood and diaspora. It is being oppressed and becoming free, joy and sorrow. It is ritual and ethics, particularism and universalism. It is miracle and expectation, recorded history and the

7

mystery of survival. It is the holy and the ordinary, the this-worldly and other-wordly. Judaism is the weekday and the Sabbath.

Judaism is all these and more. It is the unbroken chain of Biblical tradition, Talmudic tradition, Rabbinic tradition and contemporary Jewish life. It is the undefinable, indescribable spirit of a people with common roots, common history and common destiny.

I believe that the Jewish people is greater than all its constituent groups, that the historic, national-religious cement that unites us is more enduring than the current ideological schisms that divide us. I have no taste for sectarianism, be it of the right, of the left or of the center. I object to extremism, be it in the name of piety or under the banners of liberalism or compromise. I am part of Klal Yisrael. I interact with the Jewish community socially, professionally and intellectually. My belief in the concept of Klal Yisrael motivated me, in 1963, to establish the Oceanside Jewish Forum, and subsequently the Jewish Community Council of Oceanside in which all Jewish organizations in Oceanside - religious, philanthropic, Zionist, fraternal and social — participate.

I believe that Judaism is a way of life. It cannot be expressed solely via personal, home ritual or synagogue-initiated or synagogue-oriented activity. Judaism is a moral and ethical tradition. This is its universalistic heritage, although it cannot be represented exclusively in universal terms. Judaism is an ethnocentric and spiritual tradition. This is its particularistic heritage. The combination of both is absolutely essential to the Jewish way of life.

I am proud to be different. The difference is that I am Jewish. This feeling of distinction obligates me in a very special way to put forth my strength for Jewish causes. My sense of difference bolsters my self-image. Yet, my Jewishness is not flaunted; it is as natural as my breathing. I am revolted by Jews who try to hide their Jewish identity and by those who attempt to hide behind their Jewishness.

I have deep emotional commitment to the Jewish people. As a Jew I still feel deep pain — almost psychosomatic in its impact — about the European Holocaust. I will never be able to forgive the people who allowed the bearers of the Amalekite standard to ravage barbarously. In memory of the six million who perished and for the heroes of the Warsaw ghetto uprising, I perform the Seder Ritual of Remembrance on Passover Eve after the third of the four ceremonial cups of wine, just before the door is opened for the symbolic entrance of the Prophet Elijah.

I feel special kinship to our brethren behind the Iron Curtain. This year, after the Seder meal begins, I will place a matzah on the table — not to be eaten so that our children ask why — to express my oneness with the religio-cultural plight of Soviet Jewry.

I identify strongly with the Jewish State. Israel's accomplishments are my accomplishments. I take particular pride in them — as if I had wrought them with my own hands. Israel's difficulties and troubles are a source of real anxiety to me.

I have intellectual commitment to Judaism. The combination of observance of Jewish tradition and study of Jewish lore are a major source of my personal fulfillment. I perceive this union — knowledge and practice — as a *conditio sine qua non* for meaningful Jewish survival. The threefold ideal of Jewish life — the People of Israel, the Torah of Israel and the Land of Israel — is best expressed via this dual interdependent medium. I believe that intensive Jewish education is the key to insuring true Jewish living. More than that, in Jewish tradition Torah study is a mode of worship; and so it should be even in America.

I view the problems and prospects of America — the struggle for civil rights, the war on poverty, the fight against immorality and drug addiction — through Jewish spectacles. And, through Jewish eyes I observe the portent and promise of the human race — the cold war, the population explosion, the emerging new nations, and the tedious trek toward world peace.

I am against war because war is bad, and because it is offensive to the spirit of Judaism which holds supreme the dignity and worth of every human life. I am for equal job opportunity and for equal educational opportunity for all Americans because these are a person's inalienable rights and because the achievement of equal opportunity is the fulfillment of a basic Judaic tenet.

I believe that Judaism transcends time. It has been able to accommodate to and can harmonize with all eras of human progress — the age of reason, the era of industrialization, the space age and the future, supermodern periods of scientific advancement — without compromising its essence.

For me, Judaism is my way of life.

WITH
OUR
SOURCES

– 2 –

ON OUR MODERN
JEWISH HERITAGE

Presented at
Federation of Sisterhoods
89th Anniversary Meeting
New York, N.Y.   May 1985

Jewish Heritage

This month is what Jewish Heritage is all about.

Today is the 26th day of the Hebrew month of Nisan — five days after the holiday of Passover. Today is also the eleventh day of the Omer.

Tomorrow is יוֹם הַשׁוֹאָה וְהַגְבוּרָה — the day of remembrance of the catastrophe which befell the Jewish people at the hands of the Nazis and their collaborators, the day of remembrance of the deeds of courage and heroism of our brothers and sisters in Europe.

Tonight we will gather in many synagogues around the country to memorialize the six million Jewish martyrs and observe the 42nd anniversary of the Warsaw Ghetto Uprising.

Next Wednesday is the יוֹם הַזִּכָּרוֹן לְחַלְלֵי צָהַ"ל — Remembrance Day for Israel's fallen soldiers.

Sunday is Rosh Hodesh — the Jewish New Moon — the beginning of the new Hebrew month of Iyar. Sunday, too, is the day of the Salute to Israel Parade in New York.

And next Thursday we celebrate יוֹם הָעַצְמָאוּת — Israel Independence Day — the 37th birthday of the Jewish State.

What a dose of heritage in such a brief period of time!

What a rich calendar of bitter-sweet events!

What does this bittersweet heritage mean to American Jewry? Will Jewish youth be prepared to appreciate it and observe it? Will we be able to preserve our "modern" heritage?

Before responding to these questions, permit me to share some thoughts and feelings about the bitter and the sweet, about tragedy and hope, about gloom and opportunity, about death and life, about the Holocaust and Israel.

The Bitter

גֶעדֶענק! זְכוֹר! Remember!

The Holocaust bids us never to forget. How can the people who experienced the Shoah ever forget? How can one who hears about the extent of the tragedy that befell European Jewry ever forget?

How can we forget the millions of innocent Jews whose lives were snuffed out so mercilessly in the hellish death camps of Poland? How can we ever forget the one million children who died *al Kiddush Hashem?*

Millions of words have been written and spoken about the Holocaust. But, never enough. Hundreds of monuments all over the world have been dedicated in memory of the victims of Nazi bestiality. But nothing can ever be conceived by the human mind or spoken by the human mouth or made by the human hand to describe adequately the degree and scope of Nazi brutality and inhumanity and the extent of the suffering of our people. Nor will we mortals ever be able to comprehend or measure the nature of the heroism and martyrdom of the heroes of the Warsaw ghetto.

In our annual commemoration of the Holocaust period it would be well to recapitulate some of the ugly, bitter events of this time. On January 30, 1933, Adolph Hitler was appointed Chancellor of Germany. By April of that year, there was a boycott of Jewish shops and businesses in Germany. Two years later, the infamous Nuremberg Laws were enacted, and two years after that — in July 1937 — the Buchenwald concentration camp was opened.

The infamous Kristallnacht pogroms took place in Germany and Austria on November 9 and 10, 1938. Two hundred synagogues were destroyed, 7500 Jewish shops were looted, and 30,000 male Jews were sent to concentration camps. And two years after Kristallnacht, the Warsaw ghetto with its 500,000 Jewish inhabitants was sealed off. Shortly thereafter the rapid process of extermination began.

- Thousands of Jews were butchered in Romania;
- 34,000 were massacred in Babi Yar;
- 19,000 were murdered in Odessa;
- 340,000 were liquidated in Chelmno;
- 250,000 were killed in Sobibor;
- 700,000 were slaughtered in Treblinka;
- 3,000,000 were burned alive in the crematoria
  of Auschwitz-Birkenau;

And, the story of extermination continued until the end of World War II.

While we memorialize the victims of the Holocaust at this time, we must remember that the bitter taste of history during the last five decades was not limited to the Shoah. Two million Soviet Jews have been trapped since the end of World War II in a totalitarian, anti-Semitic country *where* it is impossible to live and *from where* it is impossible to leave. Soviet anti-Semitism and anti-Zionism is rampant. The Soviet government has methodically tried for years to sever Soviet Jewry from its cultural heritage. By and large, the Jews of the Soviet Union suffer quietly. Many of them try to live as Jews, as Elie Weisel depicted so movingly in his *Jews of Silence.* In the Soviet Union, Jewish activists are sent daily to labor camps. Hebrew teachers are arrested for "anti-Soviet activity." Jewish study groups are raided regularly and their books confiscated; and, the number of refusniks grows and grows.

Also, the story of the oppression of Jews in Arab lands must be told at this time. Hundreds of thousands of Jews living in Moslem countries found themselves unwelcome during the World War II period, suffering degradation and threats to life and limb and to their Judaic heritage. Then, there are the Ethiopian Jews, once numbering in the hundreds of thousands. Now, this community of as few as 25,000 brave souls physically lives in intense poverty and disease and spiritually faces feverish missionary activity and a Marxist government's policy of forced assimilation.

Finally, the Land of Israel was destined to soak up the blood of many of its most valiant sons in the wars of defense in 1948, 1956, 1967 and 1973. They died so bravely trying to vouchsafe freedom and security for the inhabitants of Israel — largely, immigrants from the hell of Europe and the oppression of Arab countries.

The Transition from Bitter to Sweet

Jewish tradition, as ancient as the first Seder immediately following the Exodus from Egypt some 3200 years ago, teaches us to appreciate the sweet after tasting the bitter. During the Seder we express this remarkable ability by eating *moror* and drinking wine, by eating matzoh and by feasting, by dipping the *moror* into *haroset* and by leaning as we eat and drink. This binary experience is summed up pithily in the Hagaddah: "The Lord brought us out of slavery into freedom, out of sorrow into happiness, out of mourning into joy, out of darkness into light, out of bondage into redemption. So let us sing a song of praise to the Lord. Halleluyah."

The Sweet

The post-Holocaust sweetness is epitomized by the miraculous establishment and vouchsafing of the State of Israel. And now we celebrate 37 years of Jewish statehood — with all the problems and disappointments, struggles and anxieties, hopes and opportunities, accomplishments and blessings that represent the birth pangs and growing pains of a free Jewish nation on its own land.

So dramatic! So pulsating! So alive! And so exciting!

May 1945 — the war in Europe is ended. The post-war exodus to Palestine begins.

1945, 46 and 47 — Jews enter Palestine legally and illegally.

November 1947 — the United Nations Assembly votes Palestine partition plan.

May 1948 — the *New York Times* headline announces: "Zionists Proclaim New State of Israel. Truman Recognizes It and Hopes for Peace."

May 12, 1949 — Israel wins a seat in the U.N. by a vote of 36-12. And we become a nation among nations.

With the ingathering of exiles from dozens of lands, Israel becomes a melting pot of cultures as East meets West and West meets East. The miracle of the Hebrew language spreads as Hebrew becomes the *lingua franca* of the new State.

And then there is Operation Magic Carpet.

Do you remember the magic of the מַרְבַד הַקְּסָמִים?

The incredible airlift of Yemenite Jews in 1948 actually began while the Israel War of Independence was in full swing. The odds against such an operation succeeding or even taking place at all were unbelievably high.

But the Yemenite Jews (not unlike their Ethiopian brothers and sisters this past year) with their utter determination, indomitable spirit, remarkable courage and unswerving faith, and with the dedicated assistance and guidance of the Jewish Agency, made their way to Israel, after a perilous 200 mile long journey on foot from Yemen's capital city of Sana to the country of Aden, through parched deserts, rocky mountains and precipitous passes.

No hurdle seemed too great for our Yemenite brethren.

In Aden — through a long, complicated process, including extensive medical examinations and inoculations — they were miraculously airlifted "on the wings of eagles" to Lydda Airport in Israel.

Time moves on swiftly.

June 1967 — after two eventful decades of growth and challenge, the lightning-fast Six-Day War unites Jerusalem as the capital of Israel. The spirit of Jews everywhere was uplifted by the swift victory and incredible show of military prowess. We were so proud of Israel, of Israel's young men and women in the service of their people. We remember vividly Golda Meir's heartfelt comment about the war, "More than our boys being killed," she said, "I am terribly distraught that we had to kill Arabs in order to achieve our security." Such is the soul of a Jewish mother.

Then, another decade of challenge and change.

October 1973 — Yom Kippur War took its heavy toll of lives. The tiny Jewish State again demonstrated its military might and the courage and bravery of its young soldiers.

March 1979 — Egypt and Israel sign a formal treaty ending a state of war after 30 years.

More challenge and change.

Winter 1985 — we are witness to another saga of courage and heroism — Operation Moses, our most modern Exodus, the liberation of Ethiopian Jewry.

For this, in the words of the Haggadah, "we give thanks and praise the One who brought about all these miracles for our ancestors and for us (in our own day)."

The Challenge

And now, to answer the questions. What does the bittersweet heritage mean to American Jewry? Are we going to be able to preserve it?

While there is a noticeable growth of young, committed Jews in America and a great increase in the number of Jewish children and youth receiving an intensive Jewish education — witness the growth of the Jewish day schools and yeshivot — there is a frightening deterioration of Jewish commitment in the general Jewish population.

The statistics about apathy, intermarriage and assimilation are not a fantasy. When the president of Israel says that every *minute* we lose *one* more Jew, he's not dreaming. Lou Lehrman just happens to be an example of what is happening in many communities.

The overall picture of Jewish education is not any rosier. Consider that there are about 1 million Jewish children in America, ages 2-18. If the present trend continues, 400,000 of them will receive no Jewish education whatsoever.

But we must not despair. There is a great awakening among Jewish communal leadership. Federations are seriously considering ways to assist Jewish outreach programs, and ways to increase financial support to Jewish education. The World Leadership Conference that took place in Jerusalem last June is an example of the new awareness of top echelon Jewish lay leaders, heretofore not involved in Jewish education, beginning to give serious attention to the challenge of preserving the Jewish heritage through Jewish schooling.

Simply put, they're running scared. They want to make sure that their grandchildren and great grandchildren will have a Jewish community in which they can grow up and which they can support.

Synagogue leadership — rabbis, educators and lay leaders — are working harder to improve their respective school programs, recruit more children, reach more Jewish families, and teach them more effectively.

JWB has just completed an ambitious study on Maximizing Jewish Educational Effectiveness in Jewish Community Centers and is now beginning to implement the recommendations of the Study.

While Jewish commitment and involvement has precariously deteriorated during the last 20 years, the Jewish community, to borrow a phrase from the Bible, seems to be "girding its loins" for the future and working all the harder to preserve our heritage. We can do it. We've met the challenge in the past. We can meet it now. Meet it we must — and turn the bitter into sweet.

— 3 —

THE JEWISH SPECTRUM: TEKIAH, SHEVARIM, TERUAH

September, 1986

The Jewish New Year is not only a time of personal introspection, but it is also an appropriate time to examine the quality of Jewish life in our community, metropolitan New York, and around the nation. Despite disclaimers from various quarters to the contrary, this Jewish New Year, 5747, as in the New Years of the past decade, we are facing a serious erosion of Jewish life.

The threats to the American Jewish community are increasingly apparent. Witness the apathy of many Jews to organized Jewish life, the increase of intermarriage, and the decline of the percentage of Jews contributing to UJA/Federation (only one family in six contributes to the UJA Federation Campaign in Greater New York) as well as the limited number of Jewish children receiving any kind of formal or informal Jewish education. Given the current trend of enrollment, only 60-65 percent of all Jewish youths of school age will be exposed to any kind of formal Jewish schooling during their lifetime.

The weakening of Jewish life is painfully evident during the High Holy days. In the past, the vast majority of Jews attended synagogue during this season. But times have changed drastically.

20

According to recent surveys, only one-half of the American Jewish population can now be found inside a synagogue on the High Holy days. In fact, a study completed last year about the Los Angeles Jewish community reveals that a mere 26 percent are members of synagogues.

In the past, we were reasonably assured that almost all Jews would gather to hear a Jewish message at this time of year. The impact of the message varied according to the ability of the speakers and sermonizers and the receptivity of the listeners. But, at least, there was a chance to influence the minds and hearts of the majority of Jews about their Jewishness.

These Jews were also exposed to intense efforts by the rabbi and lay leaders to inspire them toward greater Jewish commitment. More often than not, one of the sermons dealt with the topic of *talmud torah* — Jewish education. Frequently, appeals were made for pupil recruitment and for fiscal support to the congregational school or to the local Jewish educational institution. Now, because of the severe drop in synagogue attendance, many Jewish families cannot be reached at all. And if parents do not consider it important enough to be in a synagogue this time of year, how can we hope to influence their children, who are not enrolled in any type of Jewish schooling?

Three levels of Jewishness now exist among American Jewry. One group does not attend synagogue at all during the year, and is completely out of our reach. Another group is made up of those adults for whom Rosh Hashanah and Yom Kippur will be their sole contact with Jewish life.

At the other end of the Jewish spectrum are those Jews for whom participation in High Holy Day worship is a natural part of their ongoing Jewish involvement: daily or weekly synagogue attendance, active membership in Jewish organizations, occasional visits to Israel, and ongoing support of Jewish causes.

The three levels of Jewishness may be compared to the three sounds of the shofar: TEKIAH — a steady continuous blast; SHEVARIM — three fragmented, plaintive bleats; and TERUAH — nine fidgety, trembling vibrations.

The clear, unswerving tone of the *Tekiah* bespeaks a wholesome Jewish self-image and points confidently toward the future of the Jewish family, while the halting, choppy notes of the

Shevarim represent an unsure Jewish self-portrait and a doubtful Jewish tomorrow. The nervous, percussion-like sounds of the *Teruah* express the quickening erosion of Jewish identity and flight from Judaism, with no Jewish continuity in sight.

This constellation of Jewish behavior suggests the need to develop and nurture three differing modes of communication with Jews in our community — for the "Tekiahs" who are committed to the perpetuation of Judaism, and whose children are the recipients of a sound Jewish education; for the "Shevarim" who are marginally committed, and whose children are generally exposed to a mild smattering of Jewish schooling; and for the "Teruahs" whose families have virtually no relationship with the Jewish community.

All these Jewish groups are a concern to the Board of Jewish Education of Greater New York. Each category of Jews implies a specific challenge — a special opportunity.

We have always viewed the age-old biblical commandment "You shall teach your children diligently" both as a parental obligation and as a communal responsibility. Traditionally, the Jewish home played a major role in the Jewish education of its children. There they learned how to live Jewishly and become imbued with the spirit of yiddishkeit. Parents who were not able to provide formal instruction either engaged tutors or sent their children to a school. In such cases, the teacher served *in loco parentis.* In educational terms, we would say that the home excelled in dealing with the affective domain of Jewish schooling.

But these times have long gone. What is needed now are unique responses to the different levels in Jewish life. As the central agency for Jewish education in metropolitan New York, we feel a responsibility to each and every part of the Jewish community.

For the Jewishly-committed, we need to advocate for and help to obtain and provide programmatic and fiscal support for the various formats of intensive Jewish education. This we try to accomplish through a variety of services for teachers, principals, students and parents, helping intensive Jewish educational formats, particularly yeshivot and day schools, maintain their levels of achievement.

Secondly, we need to help increase the involvement of marginal Jewish families in Jewish life and Jewish education. Many of these persons are those very adults for whom High Holy Day services are their only involvement in Jewish life. In order to learn how to reach them and their families more effectively, the Board of Jewish Education is now engaged in a major ethnographic study of Jewish supplementary education. The findings will help develop responses to questions relating to this population.

And finally, we have a responsibility to the unaffiliated — as a resource to those groups and individuals working to integrate unaffiliated Jews into the Jewish community. These include a variety of Federation agencies, particularly the Jewish community centers now engaged in maximizing the effectiveness of their Jewish educational approaches.

We realize the difficulty of adequately addressing this three-fold challenge. Fortunately, we have outstanding partners in this sacred undertaking — the world renowned philanthropists, Mr. and Mrs. Joseph Gruss; and the recently merged Federation of Jewish Philanthropies and United Jewish Appeal. Their combined sponsorship and support of the Fund for Jewish Education and the special programs initiated and financed by Joseph Gruss and his wife, all administered by BJE, make it possible for the Jewish community to respond meaningfully to the three all-important challenges of modern Jewish life.

In Solomonic terms, the triple threaded responsiveness is the best guarantee that the fabric of Jewish life will be held together eternally.

— 4 —

FREEDOM AND JEWISH CONTINUITY

Dvar Torah prepared for
UJA-Federation
Domestic Affairs Division Assembly
February 9, 1987

Freedom, we Jews have learned throughout our history, is a very precious commodity. The momentous occasion of our freedom from slavery is portrayed dramatically in the Exodus of our ancestors from Egypt. This moving story about which we read in our synagogues during this coming Sabbath raises many interesting questions.

The Israelites could have reached Israel from Egypt in a matter of weeks, certainly within several months of travel. But, we are told that "God did not lead them by the way of the Philistines, although it was nearer." And so our forebears wandered for forty years in the wilderness. Why? There are many answers.

The one offered by a 12th century Spanish biblical exegete is the source for my Dvar Torah today. "One must wonder," said Ibn Ezra, "why 600,000 men did not stand up and fight the Egyptians. The answer: The Israelites had, from their youth, learned to fear

24

Egypt. Those leaving the land of bondage had to learn how to live as free people."

Needed were forty years to educate a new generation of Israelites who would be able to appreciate their freedom and create a new standard of living for themselves.

My friends, this message is also the message for our times.

We live in a blessed land of freedom. In a free society, people make choices — social, vocational, moral and religious choices — to be or not to be productive members of the society; to become active members of the Jewish community or to opt out of it.

UJA/Federation has to help Jewish parents and children make the right choices — to use their freedom in the right way, Jewishly. It takes Jewish education — lots of quality Jewish schooling — to accomplish this. It is up to us to acquire the skills of Jewish living and transmit them to our young. This challenge places upon our shoulders a grave responsibility.

Will we use our freedom to guarantee Jewish continuity? to assure that our children will take our place as leaders of the Jewish community?

Cultural pluralism — the earmark of our free society — has a double effect on Jewish life in this country. It enables us to live freely as Jews. At the same time, it makes it possible for our children and grandchildren to lose, without pain or difficulty, all signs of Jewishness and to disappear into the growing mingling crowds of the majority culture.

Jewish education is the only antidote to this danger. It asks Federation leadership: "Are you ready to provide the necessary support to Jewish educational programs and services so that our freedom will continue to be a blessing to us as *Jews* and Americans?" Are you prepared to make Jewish education your number one priority? Will you have the courage to shift priorities when faced with the difficult process of allocations?

Given the growing awareness among our UJA/Federation lay and professional leadership about the importance of quality Jewish schooling, I am convinced that the answer will be a resounding yes!

Let us turn the blessings of freedom into the promise of Jewish continuity and the promise into reality by the quality and quantity of our support for Jewish education.

We don't have to wander forty years to appreciate freedom. It is ours to enjoy! Let's use it to our collective best advantage.

We're on the right track. I hope we're running hard enough and fast enough!

— 5 —

NEEDED: JEWISH LEADERSHIP

Dvar Torah,
Hanukkah eve, Shabbat Miketz,
Presented at Board of Directors' Meeting
Board of Jewish Education
of Greater New York
December, 1990

The current world situation, particularly relating to the security of Israel and the Jewish people is the most critical since World War II. Given these troubled times, strong leadership is needed to unite world Jewry to respond to common challenges. The coincidence of *Parshat Miketz* with Hanukkah provides us with a dual glimpse of leadership in the persons of two namesakes.

Following in the footsteps of his father Mattityahu, Yehudah Hamaccabee — according to *Sefer Hamaccabim* — fought against Antiochus with confidence and gladness since he attributed his potential for victory "not in the multitude of a host, but in the strength from Heaven." Yehudah was infused with religious zeal to overcome the Syrians. The key to his success was his ability to inspire his brothers and followers and unite them toward a single goal.

The hero of our sidrah is Yehudah, the son of Ya'akov. Unlike his brother Reuven, he was able to convince Ya'akov to allow him to take Binyamin with him to Mitzrayim — an action which changed the course of Jewish history. Why did Ya'akov listen to Yehudah and not to Reuven? They both pleaded with Ya'akov and both tried to instill in him the confidence that they would return from Egypt with Binyamin. Both claimed that they will bring punishment upon themselves if they will not succeed. Avot D'Rabbi Natan, in commenting on Yehudah's plea *anochi eh-ervennu meeyaddee tevakkshennu* — "I will be surety for him; from my hand you shall demand him" — underscores the significance of the word *anochi* — "I." Yehudah pledged that he personally will be guarantor. On the other hand, Reuven's pledge was, "You can kill my two sons if I do not bring him back to you." Yehudah was ready for the ultimate punishment to *himself.* The *Torah Temimah* stresses this point as well. *Yehudah arrav atzmo.*

Another explanation is offered by the 19th century Italian scholar Benamozegh in his commentary on the Torah — *Aim Lamikrah.* In his plea, Yehudah emphasized that if he will not succeed in returning with Binyamin *ve-hattatee le-cha kol hayamim* — "I will have sinned against you forever." Bearing the blame forever — in this world and in the world to come — is the ultimate punishment. Yehudah was ready to sacrifice his peace of mind in *olam hazeh* and in *olam habba* for not returning Binyamin.

Yehudah's pre-eminence as a leader is noted in various places in the Torah. Ya'akov's *berachah* to Yehudah contains many references to his leadership qualities — "Yehudah, you are the one; to you your brothers will do homage." Ya'akov speaks of his ability to overcome difficulties and crises: *karra ravvatz k'aryeh* — "He kneels down and rests like a lion." From this blessing, the *Hiddushei Ha-rim* notes, "This is the quality of Yehudah. Even when he falls and kneels, he is still strong like a lion. He does not fall prey to *yeeush* (despair); he does not give up; but, he admits his wrongdoing, his weakness (as in the case of Tamar) and immediately gets up, does *teshuvah* and is ready to overcome difficulties."

According to the Ramban, Yehudah's leadership was recognized by Moshe Rabbainu when he selected Yehudah, and not his older brothers to lead *b'nai Yisrael* in the journey toward *Eretz Yisrael.* "Moshe placed the tribe of Yehudah in the East to travel first because Yehudah is the unquestioned leader . . ." The Ramban emphasized Yehudah's ability to motivate and work with Torah leadership and gain the necessary support from the financial resources of the people.

This is precisely what is needed today — Jewish leadership with ability to motivate greater support for Torah and for the needs of world Jewry and Israel. Over and above these needs, is the need for unified leadership in Israel and the Diaspora. The problem is that Israel has too many spokesmen, each presenting a different point of view. Recently, when asked if the U.S. will support Israel in the current crisis, a U.S. official replied "which Israel?" American Jewry also needs a unified voice. Our divisiveness often speaks louder than our common purpose.

It might take a miracle to develop the leadership that will unite us. But, that's exactly what celebrating Hanukkah is all about. In the spirit of the Midrash, may the statement *mah she-eera l'avot eera l'vanim* become a reality in our time — *bayammim hahem, bazman hazeh.*

— 6 —

THE CRUCIAL PARTNERSHIP
FOR JEWISH SCHOOLING

Presented at Joseph S. and Caroline Gruss
Excellent Teachers Fund Recognition Assembly
Federation of Jewish Philanthropies
March 18, 1986

In *Bamidbar,* the Book of Numbers, we read that when the Israelites left Egypt they journeyed in a special formation — each tribe under its own flag. Leading the march toward Canaan were the tribes of Judah, Issachar and Zebulun. ראשונה יסעו: "They shall travel first — at the head of the camp" says the Biblical text.

This formation has symbolic meaning for all time. Neither Judah, nor Issachar, nor Zebulun were Jacob's oldest sons. By what virtue were their tribes chosen to lead the journey through the wilderness? Why this combination of leadership?

The combined attributes of Judah, Issachar and Zebulun represented the priority needs of the Israelites as they were about to become a free nation in their own land.

Though not the eldest, Judah was the acknowledged leader of *B'nai Yisrael.* Judah's leadership was meaningless, however, without the partnership of Zebulun and Issachar. So integral to Judah's leadership were these tribes that, when the census of the Israelites on the journey from Egypt was taken, they were included as part of the tribe of Judah. And for good reason. חז״ל tell us זבולון עוסק בפרקמטיא that Zebulun was crucial to Jewish survival because he engaged in commerce and with his philanthropy rendered support to Issachar. Issachar was vital becuase he was involved in Torah learning.

Together Zebulun, the man of action, the philanthropist, and Issachar, the teacher-student-scholar, expressed the ideal partnership of Jewish education without which Jewish life could not prosper.

Nachmanides — the Ramban — the 13th century Spanish philosopher, biblical exegete and physician, summarized this necessary threesome of Jewish leadership in simple terms.

יהודה בעל מלוכה, ועליו שבט יששכר שהוא בעל תורה,

ועליו מטה זבולון שהוא בעל עשירות.

"Judah, the leader, supported by Issachar, the Torah scholar, supported. in turn, by Zebulun, the philanthropist."

The greatest challenge to Jewish communal leadership in America is to make this combination a vibrant reality in Jewish life.

Mr. and Mrs. Joseph Gruss, Federation leadership and Torah education represent this combination in our community. As the paradigm of the Zebulun concept, Mr. and Mrs. Gruss, through their insight and generosity, help vouchsafe the Jewish future as they recognize that the work of יששכר — Torah teaching — is indeed a Godly profession.

בשעות ידועות ביום יושב הקב״ה ומלמד תינוקות של בית רבן.

G-d, Himself, we are told, spends several hours a day teaching young children.

And so, this Excellent Teachers assembly at Federation is a real expression of the יששכר-זבולון-יהודה partnership for Jewish continuity. To be sure, this partnership today proclaims, in the words of the anonymous poet:

"No printed word nor spoken plea,
Can teach young hearts what man should be,
Nor all the books on all the shelves,
But what the teachers are themselves."

חילכם לאוריתא!

More power to you in the teaching of Torah and in the support of Torah teaching.

– 7 –

MAN'S RESPONSIBILITY —
TIKKUN OLAM

Dvar Torah on Shabbat Breishit
November 1, 1986

This Shabbat we read the first sidrah of the Torah. And, as we read it, we celebrate the creation of the world. Indeed, the physical world is wondrous and awesome, with breathtaking nature, unbelievable potential for development, and extraordinary, incredible opportunity for humankind.

Yet, when we look at the world today, we observe a universe filled with greed, destruction, oppression, and terrorism. And we ask ourselves, "Couldn't God have created a better world? Couldn't He have perfected creation?" After all, we are informed in the 27th verse of the first chapter of Breishit, וַיִּבְרָא אֱלֹקִים אֶת הָאָדָם בְּצַלְמוֹ "God created man in His own image." Shouldn't the image of God be more perfect? Shouldn't God's ultimate creation have been created with perfection?

Our sages thought of this question as well. We are told that the Talmudic sage, Rabbi Yohanan asked, "Why was man created in the image of God? In response to his own question, he said: "The story of God's creation of man can be likened to a king who ruled over a

WITH OUR SOURCES 33

country. The king decided to build a new city, and he began building it. One day he called together all the inhabitants of the city and in their presence he appointed one of his officers to rule over them. And he said to his officer, 'Until now, I have been dealing with all the needs of the city, with each detail and every facet of city life. From now on, I'm giving all this responsibility to you.' Said Rabbi Yohanan, "God created man in His image, and gave him the responsibility of making it a better place in which to live."

To be sure, God took the first steps in creating a good world. But He didn't complete creation. He left it up to man to perfect the world. Indeed, when we recite kiddush each Friday night, we recognize this fact as we quote from Chapter 2: "On the seventh day God ceased from all His work which He created, *to make*" — אֲשֶׁר בָּרָא אֱלֹקִים לַעֲשׂוֹת . . . The verb form לַעֲשׂוֹת *(la'asot)* "to make" seems extraneous here.

According to Ibn Ezra, the word *la'asot* means that God gave man the power, the ability — *la'asot* — to do, *to make,* to improve upon His creation, after God ceased creating.

This, then, is the challenge to our generation. It is the challenge to the synagogue, to the Jewish school, to our families, to the Jewish community at large, and the challenge to Israel — to work as hard as we can to strive to achieve תִּקּוּן עוֹלָם — Tikkun Olam — to try to improve the imperfect world that was created by God. We cannot slacken in our efforts to achieve perfection. The *Mitzvah* is in the trying.

May we have the individual and collective will and the strength to bring about *Tikkun Olam*. After all, that is why man was created.

— 8 —

THE FIFTH QUESTION
PESAH 5751

Prepared March 18, 1991
Distributed to Jewish Schools
in Greater New York

Why is this night of Pesah different from the Seder nights of other years? During all Seder nights heretofore, we ate our matzah and drank four cups of wine, reclined during the meal and asked the four questions. And now, in 5751 we do the same thing — but with a difference. The difference is the Persian Gulf War.

Why is this night different from all other nights? It is different because the world has learned another lesson about tyranny. it learned that being a Haman or a Hitler doesn't pay. The world learned about the dangers of allowing a modern Haman to develop to the point where he can wreak havoc relentlessly. It learned what Israel had been trying to convey to freedom loving peoples for over a decade. Were it not for Israel's destruction of Iraq's nuclear plant in 1981, who knows how much devastation Saddam Hussein might have caused, not only in Israel and the Middle East, but in other parts of the world as well.

The difference between tonight's Seder and previous Seder

experiences is that tonight we give special thanks to Israel for having destroyed the nuclear capability of Iraq. We express our deep gratitude to the United States of America and its armed forces for turning back the would-be-Pharaoh/would-be-Hitler of our times. And with more knowledge about the potential destructive elements in the Middle East, we pray for peace — for a safe and secure Israel. We pray that Israel's neighbors sincerely join in an effort to bring about peace in the Middle East. Let there be *shalom al Yisrael.*

— 9 —

TORAH LEARNING AND PEACE

Presented at the 80th Anniversary
Cocktail Reception
In Honor of Dr. Alvin I. Schiff
Board of Jewish Education of Greater New York
January 29, 1991

What subject is appropriate tonight?

1) Tu B'shevat — the New Year for Trees? Tomorrow is Tu B'shevat. There **is** a relationship between Tu B'shevat and Jewish education. In Jewish tradition, Torah and Torah study are referred to as an *Etz Haim* — a tree of life.

2) Support for Jewish education? This is a crucial subject, appropriate **at all times** for the Jewish community.

But both of these themes — Tu B'shevat and support for Jewish education — pale in the face of the Persian Gulf War which engulfs the whole world even though it is being waged only in the Middle East. And it affects Israel so terribly, so severely.

Yet, after more careful reflection we must conclude that even at this time — particularly at this crossroad in our history — we must rally for Jewish education. Indeed, there is a significant connection

36

between Jewish education and the war and our striving for peace.

The Talmud helps to underscore the connection.

אמר רבי אלעזר אמר רבי חנינא: תלמידי חכמים מרבים שלום בעולם;
שנאמר: "וכל בניך לימודי ה' ורב שלום בניך". אל תקרי בניך אלא בוניך.

"Disciples of the wise increase peace in the world, for it is said, 'And all your children are learned in the ways of God (literally students of the Almighty) and there will be abundant peace to your children.'

"Do not read the word *Ba nayich*, your children, but *Bo nayich*, your builders."

Children who study Torah are indeed builders of peace.

We, leaders of the Jewish community, have a primary obligation to our young builders — the builders of Jewish life, builders of American society and builders of the future of the Jewish community. To be sure, they are also partners in the building of Israel.

It is obvious that through knowledge and understanding we can help bring about peace. Not an easy task, not a quick process — but a necessary responsibility of Jewish communal life — one we dare not shirk, one we must not shirk.

It is a responsibility that those of us here share happily and willingly. That is why I am so personally grateful to the volunteer lay leaders of BJE, UJA-Federation and the larger Jewish community for your respective roles in helping build Jewish life.

That is why Zevulun Hammer called me today and asked that I convey his warmest wishes for the success of BJE's 80th Anniversary dinner. That is why I'm so thankful to BJE leadership for this very special reception.

"שלום רב לאוהבי תורתך"

"There will be abundant peace for the lovers and supporters of Torah" ends the section of the Talmud I quoted earlier.

May abundant peace be our lot.

May your own efforts be crowned with success. After all, our Zaides and Bubbies would say תורה איז די בעסטע סחורה. Undoubtedly, supporting Jewish education is the best investment in our future. It is the investment that pays the highest dividends, the investment with the richest rewards — Jewish continuity and shalom.

May we succeed together.

– 10 –

THE LIVING SIDDUR

Originally written as a cantata
for the graduation ceremony
of Hebrew School of Congregation Beth Sholom,
Lawrence, N.Y.   June 12, 1952.

PRELUDE TO PRAYER

Did you ever feel so happy that you wanted to proclaim your happiness? You wanted to laugh, to cry, to shout. You needed some way to express your emotions.

But, somehow you felt that no one could realize your joy as you did. No one could fully share it with you.

Did a tense feeling ever grip you? You were sure no one could understand it; and you could not describe it to anyone. Yet, you had a burning desire to do something, to clench your fists, stretch your arms, shut your eyes, run around the block, or shake yourself. You didn't know exactly what, but you *did* want to express your feeling in some way, to someone.

There is Someone near you at such times, Someone who understands exactly how you feel, Someone to whom you can express yourself. That Someone realizes your moments of happiness and your feelings of sadness; that Someone always understands your every mood.

Not everyone may feel so elated; not everyone may have experienced such moods of tenseness; not everyone feels joy and gratefulness or gloom and grief in the same way.

Yet, we all feel thankful some time or other. We feel sad or letdown at times. There are moments when we are satisfied or when we are wanting; when we wish to give praise or to make a request.

We are human, all of us. We all have experiences; we all have emotions; we all feel the need to express them.

God is about us always, ever willing to hear us. Certainly we can express ourselves to Him. Our only vehicle of communication with Him is PRAYER.

Our prayer may be simple — yet, to God, sublime. It may be short, yet in reality far reaching.

Through prayer we can soar high above the loftiest clouds — reach out to the farthest ends of the earth. We can penetrate the thickest forest and explore the darkest cave, even traverse the deepest canyon. Prayer can throw us back into the deep past and project us far into the distant future.

Haven't you often wondered about prayer? How does it lift us up and fling us high across the highest mountains? How does it comfort us and bring us relief? Haven't you often given thought to the origin of the prayer book? How has the Siddur become so hallowed to our people?

Let us take a guided tour through the Siddur and see for ourselves why it has been the fountain of inspiration and source of aspirations of our people for over 2,500 years?

II

MODEH ANI — GRATITUDE FOR LIFE

You wake in the morning after a good night's rest. You open your eyes. The bright sun communicates with you through its streams of warmth and light. Night is done. The day breaks and you take your place among the free and living.

You don't wonder about that great mystery — the return of life at daybreak. You take it in your stride. Yet, if you stop to think of the miracle of life — the miracle of living protoplasm in a bulk of flesh and bones; if you pause to contemplate the miracle of sight, of hearing, of speech, of sense of smell, of touch, and if you take a moment to perceive the wonders of nature around you; then you begin the morning with a prayer of thanks to your Maker — the Maker of all these miracles.

"I am grateful to Thee, the living and eternal King for having restored my soul this morning."

מודה אני לפניך, מלך חי וקים,

שהחזרת בי נשמתי בחמלה,

רבה אמונתך.

III

MAH TOVU — ISRAEL IS BLESSED

The prayers of the Siddur have their origin in Bible times and in historical situations varied yet singularly significant. Moses had led the Israelites through the wilderness for nearly forty years. They were to undertake final conquest of their homeland. They were fresh from victory over the Amorite Kings and now settled on the border of Moab. Balak, King of Moab and his people were filled with dread. The Israelites, however, merely wanted peaceful passage through the land of Moab and not a war. Nevertheless, we find Balak inciting the neighboring people of Midian, saying, "This multitude will consume us and all that is around us like an ox licks up the grass of the earth.

Balak sent messengers to Balaam, who was famed throughout the east as a soothsayer whose curse was irresistible.

"Behold," his message read, "there is a people that has come out of Egypt. They cover the face of the earth and they now encamp against me. Come now, I pray thee, curse this people for they are too mighty for me. Perhaps I shall prevail and smite them and drive them out of the land, for I know that he whom you bless is blessed and he whom you curse is cursed."

After much deliberation and repeated communication with Balak, Balaam accepted the invitation, but not without undue warning from God not to curse the Israelites.

When he finally prepared to use his mystical powers, Balaam

stood on top of Mount Peor and viewed the camp of the Israelites. So impressed was Balaam with the multitude, the power and the unity of Israel, that he found it impossible to curse them. Those below were the people who had been freed from human bondage, the people who received the Toah; they were a people with a mission — with a purpose. How could he squelch the yearning of this chosen people to be free in their own land and to do God's will. Balaam could but break into unstinted blessing of Israel. With Godly inspired elequence, he declared:

"How goodly are thy tents, O Jacob, thy dwelling places, O, Israel"

מה טבו אהליך, יעקב,
משכנתיך, ישראל.

IV

ADON OLAM — GOD'S UNIVERSALITY

About 900 years ago a great man of the spirit lived in Spain. He was Solomon ibn Gabirol, poet, linguist, composer and religious philosopher. In his lifetime, he saw nature's greatness and wondrous variety. It moved him to express his absolute trust in God. He sang of God of the Universe, as Ruler, Friend, Guardian and Redeemer. He sang:

"To God there is no beginning and no end. He existed before all things were formed and will remain when all is gone."

Gabirol's poem *Adon Olam* has become one of the most popular hymns in our Prayer Book. The beauty of its form, the easy rhythm of its verse and the tender passion of its contents refresh our spirits. No wonder that *Adon Olam* is sung in so many and varied melodies.

אדון עולם אשר מלך
בטרם כל יציר נברא
לעת נעשה בחפצו כל
אזי מלך שמו נקרא.

V

ASHREI — GREATNESS AND GOODNESS

It is 10 degree weather, the wind howls, the piercing mixture of hail and snow beats viciously against the window panes of your home.

Inside your warm oil-heated house you sit comfortably, not touched by nature's cold ferocity.

Have you wondered during those moments how fortunate you were to be the recipient of God's warm and cozy blessings?

King David — master of the pen and harp, in his 145th Psalm, provides us with a beautiful prayer which celebrates God's greatness and goodness:

טוב ה׳ לכל ורחמיו על כל מעשיו.

"The Lord is good to all and His tender mercies are over all His works"

פותח את ידך ומשביע לכל חי רצון.

Thou openest Thine hand and satisfiest every living thing with favor . . ."

VI

EXODUS FROM EGYPT

There have been moments in the lifetime of every one of us when we have given up hope for some cause, only to hear of an incident that brings new hope to us and inspires us to greater levels of faith.

Such is the story of our miraculous exodus from Egypt. It stirs our imagination. It fires us with new spirit. After 400 years of bondage a free people emerges to conquer its own promised land. And the Siddur, in the language of the Bible, relates this story:

"And the Lord saved Israel that day out of the hand of the Egyptians — and Israel saw the great power which the Lord put forth against the Egyptians, and the people believed in the Lord and in Moses His Servant."

And together with Moses and the children of Israel we sing a song of praise to the Lord —

"Who is like unto Thee, O Lord, amongst the mighty. Who is like unto Thee, glorious in Holiness, revered in praises, doing marvels."

מי כמכה באלים, ה׳,
מי כמכה נאדר בקדש,
נורא תהלות, עשה פלא.

VII

LAND OF ISRAEL — THE HOPE OF A PEOPLE

You may ask — what really is the key to our survival? How can a people have so much stamina? How can they overcome so much tragedy? The destruction of their homeland, the burning of their Holy Temple, 2,000 years of exile, aimless wandering, degrading poverty, indescribable persecution, blood libels, gas chambers, concentration camps, crematoria.

Whence do our people derive their stubborn will to persist, to go on, to live as a nation? Whence do they draw that unbending fortitude, that superhuman zest for life, that persistent endurance, unequaled in the history of mankind?

Turn your eyes to the Siddur. Leaf through its worn pages. There you will find the source of our daily inspiration and see the words that fanned the flame of hope in the hearts of our people. The very hope that has enabled us in our lifetime to witness the rebirth of our people in the Land of Israel.

תקע בשופר גדול לחרותנו
"Sound the great horn of our freedom"

"O, bring us in peace from the four corners of the earth and make us go upright to our land"

והביאנו לשלום מארבע כנפות הארץ
ותוליכנו קוממיות לארצנו.

The Siddur is filled with references to Israel as it is replete with reminders of our exodus from Egypt. Within its well-worn covers our eternal dream of renaissance looms forth to pierce through the dark pages of our history.

VIII

ONE GOD, ETERNALLY OURS

Close your eyes for one moment.

Picture a large, fierce, well-trained army besieging a small peace-loving country. Its mighty forces aim to snuff out all life in this little country. However, they meet with stubborn resistance. Though it is small and weak in numbers, this little nation overwhelms its powerful aggressors with its undaunted spirit. The scheming, determined attackers soon begin to strike at the roots of the resistance. They are determined to crush the spirit of this stubborn little people.

Those mighty fearless hordes are the aggressive Roman legions. The small peace-loving nation is Israel, and that obstinate, undying spirit is the belief in one God fortified by the study and observance of His Laws.

The Roman Conquerors decreed that no Jew be found studying the Torah or observing Jewish ritual. Violation of this decree meant cruel torture and certain death.

Nevertheless, under the leadership of Rabbi Akiva, the Jews continued to study the Torah and abide by its precepts — and defend their country against the aggressor.

Rabbi Akiva was captured by the Romans. He was sentenced to die. As the Roman executioner was tearing his flesh with fiery combs of iron, Akiva recited the prayer of eternal faith.

שמע ישראל, ה׳ א-להינו, ה׳ אחד.

"Hear, O Israel, the Lord our God, the Lord is One."

ברוך שם כבוד מלכותו לעולם ועד.

"Blessed be His name whose glorious Kingdom is forever and ever."

ואהבת את ה׳ א-להיך בכל לבבך ובכל נפשך ובכל מאדך.

"And thou shalt love the Lord, Thy God, with all thine heart, with all thine soul and with all thine might."

With incredible calmness, Akiva told his weeping followers — "All my days I have longed for this hour. I have loved God WITH ALL MY HEART, and I have loved Him with ALL MY MIGHT, now I can love Him WITH ALL MY SOUL — with my whole life."

So great was Akiva's love of God! This same undying love was expressed via martyrdom numerous times since the death of Akiva. The Jew through the ages has loved God with his heart's last drop of blood, and has given up his dearest inclinations, even life itself, for his Maker. That is why we proclaim the Shema with every fiber of our being.

Can we overestimate the significance of this prayer? Can we overemphasize the importance of the Shema to Jews everywhere? Can we ever give too much of ourselves to understand its full meaning? And now, as ever, we pray to the Almighty:

"O, Guardian of Israel, guard the remnant of Israel and suffer not Israel to perish — who say "Hear, O Israel, the Lord, our God, the Lord is one."

שומר ישראל, שמור שארית ישראל
ואל יאבד ישראל, האומרים שמע ישראל.

This was the prayer of our brethren in the horror camps of Europe as they were marched into the crematoria and gas chambers. This, too, is our prayer today.

IX

ISRAEL UNITED

Have you ever stopped to wonder how a people scattered over the face of the globe, living for centuries in the far corners of the earth, and dwelling in surroundings as different as day is from night, and subject to varied environmental pressures and influences can exist as *one* united people?

Certainly this is as great a mystery as Jewish survival itself.

Yet, this is paradoxically an obvious mystery.

Jewish unity transcends time and space just as God's oneness transcends these worldly elements.

Your name is Cohen and you live in Lawrence, L.I. Ezra is a dark-skinned Jew. He lives in Casablanca. Your speech is unlike his, your dress is different, your mannerisms are not at all similar; even your color differs. You live in a comfortable sunlit home. He dwells in the squalor and filth of a mellah. Yet you are one and the same people. You both hold the same hallowed Siddur in your hands. You both read its consecrated words just as they were originally written in the Bible.

שמע ישראל, ה׳ א-להינו, ה׳ אחד.
Hear, O, Israel, the Lord our God, the Lord is One.

Both of you are Israel. Both of you call one on another to hear your proclamations that your God is One. He unites you with a singleness of purpose. Together you are witnesses of his Oneness.

And you say to one another —

"And thou shalt love the Lord thy God with all thine heart, with all thine soul and with all thine might."

As blood is essential to human life, our belief in one God and his Torah is the common source of our inner strength and spiritual unity. This belief is the life blood of the Jewish people.

And that is precisely what those Roman war lords wanted to snuff out. They aimed to break that spiritual link that connects us. They tried to crush the tie between us and God. They forbade belief in one God, the God of Israel. They knew that as long as there will be a Jewish spirit, the Jew cannot completely be annihilated. They realized that when the soul thrives, the body, no matter how weak or emaciated, will live on too.

X

THE HOLY SABBATH

Our Sabbath prayer takes us back to the Middle Ages, to the time of the Talmud and to the Bible era.

We usher in the Sabbath on Friday eve as the bridegroom welcomes his bride. With Rabbi Shlomo Halevi, 16th century composer of the famous *L'chah Dodi* poem we sing:

לכה דודי לקראת כלה, פני שבת נקבלה.

"Come friend, let us welcome the Sabbath bride."

With Rabbi Chanina, a Talmudic scholar we sing:

"Come, let us go out to meet the Sabbath Queen."

בואו ונצא לקראת שבת המלכה.

On Sabbath morn we stand at the foot of Mt. Sinai with our ancestors as Moses proclaims God's words:

ושמרו בני ישראל את השבת,
לעשות את השבת לדרתם ברית עולם.

"And the children of Israel shall keep the Sabbath, to observe the Sabbath throughout their generations, for an everlasting Covenant. It is a sign between Me and the children of Israel forever, that in six days the Lord made the heavens and the earth, and on the seventh day He rested, and ceased from his work."

XI

THE SIDDUR AND OUR DAILY LIVES

The Siddur is an open eternal invitation from God to man to get together and talk things over.

It is invitation to put on *tefillin,* to wear a *tallis,* to place a *mezuzah* on our door posts.

The Siddur is an everlasting reminder to the Jew, to be thankful for God's bountiful blessings, for the food we eat, for the homes we live in, for the clothes we wear.

It reminds us to be ever grateful for our health and for the Bill of Rights that characterizes the freedom of our great bastion of Democracy — the good old U.S.A.

The Siddur is the whole drama of our earthly existence. We open it for birth, we read from it in marriage, and we turn to it in death.

The Siddur is our daily companion.

We use it in times of joy and in moments of sorrow.

It is the prayer of an old teary-eyed woman beseeching the welfare of her family.

It is the prayer of a child asking for good health.

It is the prayer of a young successful businessman thankful for his good fortune.

It is the prayer of a college graduate grateful for the honors she received.

In sorrow we turn to God and pray:

אבינו מלכנו. חננו ועננו כי אין בנו מעשים
עשה עמנו צדקה וחסד והושיענו

"Our Father, our King! Be gracious unto us and answer us, for we have no good works of our own; deal with us in charity and kindness and save us."

In happiness we declare in the eloquence of the Psalmist:

הריעו לה׳ כל הארץ. עבדו את ה׳ בשמחה, באו לפניו ברננה

"Shout for joy unto the Lord, the whole land. Serve the Lord with joy. Come before Him with exulting."

In gratitude we proclaim —

מודים אנחנו לך . . .
על חיינו המסורים בידך ועל נשמותינו הפקודות לך.
ועל נסיך שבכל יום עמנו, ועל נפלאותיך וטובותיך
שבכל עת, ערב ובקר וצהרים

"We give thanks unto thee and declare Thy praise for our lives which are committed unto Thy hand, for our souls which are in Thy charge and for Thy miracles which are daily with us, and for Thy wonders and Thy benefits which are wrought at all times — evening, morn and noon."

The Siddur welcomes us to come together and listen to the reading of the Torah.

As the Ark of the Torah is opened during our synagogue services on Mondays, Thursdays, on Sabbath days and festivals, we recite the biblical passage concerning The Holy Ark of Old:

ויהי בנסע הארן ויאמר משה:
קומה ה' ויפוצו אויביך וינוסו משנאיך מפניך

"And it came to pass, when the Ark set forward (and the children of Israel broke camp) that Moses said: 'Rise up, O Lord, and Thine onemies shall be scattered and they that hate Thee shall flee before Thee'."

When the Torah is taken out of the Ark — we declare with the prophet Isaiah —

כי מציון תצא תורה, ודבר ה' מירושלים.

"For out of Zion shall go forth the Torah, and the words of the Lord from Jerusalem."

As we close the Ark after reading the Torah, we sing as Moses sang when the Holy Ark, bearing the Ten Commandments, came to rest —

"Return, O Lord unto the tens of thousands of families of Israel"

And with King Solomon, we sing of the Torah —

עץ חיים היא למחזיקים בה ותמכיה מאשר.
דרכיה דרכי נעם וכל נתיבותיה שלום.
השיבנו, ה', אליך ונשובה,
חדש ימינו כקדם.

"It is a tree of life to them that grasp it, and of them that uphold it everyone is rendered happy. Its ways are ways of pleasantness and all its paths are peace. Turn us to You, O God, and we shall return; renew our days as of old."

The Siddur helps us atone for our sins. Through our prayers for forgiveness we derive strength to correct our wrongdoings. We approach God as a child comes to his loving father.

סלח לנו, אבינו, כי חטאנו.

"Forgive us, O our Father for we have sinned; pardon us, O, our King, for we have transgressed; for Thou dost pardon and forgive."

To the Jew, the Siddur is all this, and more.

To the world, the Siddur is the eternal proclamation of G-d's universality. We all hope and pray that the time will come when peace and happiness will rule the world. In that day shall the Lord be One and His name One.

ונאמר: והיה ה׳ למלך על כל הארץ,
ביום ההוא יהיה ה׳ אחד ושמו אחד.

THE
COMMUNITY
AND
JEWISH
EDUCATION

— II —

THE JEWISH SCHOOL AND SOCIETY

Keynote Address,
Twentieth National Conference
on Jewish Education

Johannesburg, South Africa
July, 1983

Shavua Tov. Gut vach. Goei aand.

I must say, I feel very much at home here. You see, I'm a Litvak, and as my wife will attest, I'm a Litvak all the way. Since most South African Jews have Lithuanian antecedents, this makes me feel like a member of the family.

At this moment I feel like the precocious Bar Mitzvah boy who loved chocolate and, for a Bar Mitzvah gift, was taken on a tour of a chocolate factory. While standing on the catwalk of the huge plant viewing the luscious looking warm brown liquid below, he was overcome by the odor and slipped. As he was falling into the vat of delicious chocolate, he raised his eyes heavenward and exclaimed, "Oh Lord, let my mouth be worthy of this auspicious occasion."

I'm a chocolate lover, and I love speaking about education, particularly about Jewish education. My prayer tonight is: let my words be worthy of this important gathering.

This 20th National Conference takes place at an auspicious time. On Monday, coinciding with the last day of the conference, we celebrate a wonderful, little-known Jewish holiday — *Tu B'Av,* the 15th day of Av. Since it comes just six days after Tishah B'av, this festival is a kind of antidote to the period of national mourning. The Talmud tells us לא היו ימים טובים לישראל כט״ו באב וכיום הכיפורים. The 15th of Av and Yom Kippur were considered the best days of the Jewish year. There are many reasons given for the observance of Tu B'av. The reason that has most relevance to our conference is that the 15th of Av was the day when the Israelites stopped dying in the wilderness, an indication that the 40 years of wandering were over. They were about to enter Israel — one of the most momentous occasions in Jewish history. The Tu B'av festivities in the time of the first and second Commonwealths were exceedingly joyous as they commemorated the end of the Israelites' long, arduous strife-ridden journey (following their Egyptian bondage) and the beginning of national freedom in the land of their forefathers.

South African Jewry is known for its passion and commitment to Israel, to Jewish life and to Jewish education. And when you face challenges in your community, you come together to develop collective responses to them in the hope that you can leave the problems behind and begin a period of greater progress, not unlike our ancestors who left behind the troubles and frustrations of the wilderness to enter the land of promise. In a word, you are determined to turn problem into promise and I am pleased to participate with you in this effort.

Since I'll be speaking twice on th same subject, I plan to raise questions, underscore problems and cite challenges in tonight's plenary keynote address. Tomorrow I will develop the theme further.

My frame of reference, of course, will be the United States. When I refer to American society and the American Jewish community, I would hope you will make the appropriate comparisons and inferences regarding South Africa and your Jewish community here.

Societal Change

"The School and Society" — a very crucial topic, especially in our turbulent times. The word that best describes our society today is "change" — rapid change, to be sure. The nature of the speed of change taking place brings to mind a story told by a scientist not too long ago. He said that his grandfather used to ride in a horse-drawn carriage but was afraid of the automobile, and that his father drove a car but was scared to death of flying. He then added that he goes around the world in a jet plane and doesn't think about it at all, but is quite concerned about travel in space. Then he stopped for a minute and said that his five-year-old son would love to travel in space but is scared to death of horse-drawn carriages.

The theme of the opening session of our conference is most apprpriate because the dazzling array of societal changes directly and indirectly affects schools — political change, economic change, social change, familial change, demographic and cultural change and technological change.

Nuclear proliferation, the escalation of the arms race and the threat of nuclear annihilation contribute to uneasiness and anxiety and, in the extreme, to an increase in the use of drugs, alcoholism and other addictions.

Children exposed to thousands of hours of television viewing prior to entering school and continuously thereafter are greatly influenced by television's power to control time, attention and cognitive habits. Moreover (according to Neil Postman), the effect of this technology is the "disappearance of childhood" and the blurring of the line between adult and child in our society. Since television in South Africa is a rather recent phenomenon, its effect may not yet be so visible or glaring. But, if it takes hold as it did in America, you can be sure it will have a pronounced effect on childern and youth.

Interactive telecommunications will also have a profound influence on both the cognitive and social development of the young. Computers and systems approaches to learning being used in the schools *emphasize the product* rather than the *process of learning.* In terms of their impact on education, technological advances and their application to instruction can best be compared with the invention of the printing press.

In the United States, changes in the distribution of population cohorts and declining birthrates result in declining school enrollments and greater numbers of people over 65 years of age. Austerity budgets along with spiraling costs have hindered educational decision-making. Moreover, disillusionment with and loss of confidence in its educational institutions reduced public support for schools during the last decade. Parenthetically and interestingly, the most recent Gallup poll, the findings of which were just released last week, shows a sudden change in public attitude toward the public school and a desire to provide more financial support to the schools. This is a result of the rapidly growing governmental awareness the past year about the needs of education (I will dwell upon this phenomenon in my address tomorrow) and about the need to raise teacher requirements and provide higher salaries to teachers. Indeed, the governors of the states have initiated legislative changes and hundreds of district boards of education have begun to implement programs to meet these needs. This movement is beginning to change radically public opinion in the United States.

The two-income family, the single-parent family, and the lack of stability in family life also affect the child and the school. Other significant social changes are reflected in a return to fundamentalist values, on the one hand, and moral relativism on the other.

In the U.S., the 1982 and the 1984 Gallup Polls found that discipline remains the major concern of parents. No wonder! Just consider the permissiveness of the modern home and the growing autonomy of children. Pupil mobility, discontinuity from the past and questionable future have produced the "now" generation which has instant gratification as its credo.

And, then, there is the widening gap between the rich and the underclass; and the growing crime rate and the fear of crime.

All these societal changes have serious implications for the school.

Open Society and the Jew

For Jews, for the Jewish community, the challenges of the general society in which we live are further compounded. To be sure, the challenge of the open society to Jews, Judaism and Jewish education is not new. It actually began 200 years ago with the French Revolution. As Ahad Ha'am, the early twentieth century philosopher of Zionism, noted in a penetrating essay, "Imitation and Assimilation," all minorities in Western (or open societies) have no choice but to imitate the larger environment in which they live.

A recent study of American Jewish identification begins with two questions: "How well are American Jews getting along as

Americans?" "How well are American Jews getting along as Jews?" At this conference we might ask: How well are South African Jews doing as South Africans? How well are the South African Jews doing as Jews? Two simple, seemingly innocuous questions — but full of uncertainty, challenge and blessing.

The answer to the first question is rather simple. South African Jews, like American Jews, have made it economically. Recently an Afrikaaner leader, Louis Pienaar, was quoted in the Anglo-Jewish press as saying that the Afrikaaners realize the important contribution of South African Jews to the economy of South Africa. This statement, as well as the anti-Semitic caricature of Jewish financial power, the image of the Jews as the "Hoggenheimer," is a reaction to the fact that South African Jews as a whole are economically successful.

And you have made it culturally and intellectually as well. But here lies the problem of Jewish progress in a modern society.

Tradition of Jewish Education Endangered

In America, for example, Jewish education became an important problem in Jewish life from the moment Jews were transplanted to the North American continent. The task was monumental — relating the Jewish school to the development of American Judaism and to the larger American society. And the resources needed for this were never equal to the task.

From the start, the open, free, untraditional American setting threatened the development of Jewish education. In the first instance, the increasing diffusion of Jewish intellectuality among the various arts and sciences, and among numerous academic and professional concerns, deprived Jewish education of a cadre of Jewish educators of quality.

Secondly, the theory and practice of voluntarism Jewish life deprived the Jewish education enterprise of a secure base of on-going support. Although the American Jewish community generally recognized the value of Jewish schooling, local Jewish communities, for the most part, did not assume adequate responsibility for their respective educational programs.

As a result of these two conditions — the transposition of intellectual and cultural interests by a large majority of Jews, on the one hand, and the lack of real organized community support on the other — Jewish education was left to the rather meager resources and designs of individual Jews and small groups of concerned leaders.

And so here we are, in these turbulent, critical times, faced with ever-growing problems in Jewish education — problems which are not really the making of the Jewish educational establishment. Essentially, these fall into two categories: issues relating to Jewish communal responsibility, and problems pertaining to the educational program.

In viewing Jewish life in North America against the backdrop of rapid social change in the larger environment, one is struck by the unresponsiveness of a significant segment of Jewish communal leadership toward adequate support of Jewish schooling. The underlying reason for this condition, in large measure, is that the leadership of the Jewish community does not feel a sense of urgency about the failures and problems in this area. It does not feel about its Jewishly "disadvantaged" children as many leaders of our general society feel about the need for more effective education for the disadvantaged minorities.

There is a direct relationship between America's prosperity and its educational growth. While the United States is a consumer oriented society, education, since 1957 (in response to Sputnik) has been considered not as a consumer product, but as an investment in the future. By contrast, the Jewish community views Jewish education almost entirely as a consumer service. To its credit, Federation leadership is increasingly aware of the need for massive support for Jewish education. Such support, to be sure, means either a major reordering of priorities or the uncovering of large new resources to meet the critical challenges of Jewish education.

Think now of how the following conditions can affect the Jewish school in America. Consider, too, whether or not they apply or are liable to apply to the Jewish community and the Jewish school in South Africa.

Given the current trends in the Jewish community in America, by the end of this decade:

- One out of every three Jewish children will be brought up by only one natural parent;

- One out of every three children born to a Jewish

mother or Jewish father will have a non-Jewish parent;

- One out of every two Jewish college students who marry at the end of the 1980's will marry out of the faith;

- One out of every five married Jewish couples will have no children;

- One out of every three couples will have only one child;

- One out of every two Jewish families will not be affiliated with a synagogue or with any Jewish organization;

- Two out of every five Jewish children will receive no Jewish education;

- Two out of every five Jewish children will receive no Jewish education and will not have a Bar or Bat Mitzvah.

When I made these projections about the Jewish community in a public address last year, they were published in a variety of newspapers in the United States and Canada. As a consequence, my office was deluged by telephone calls and letters (over 700, to be sure) from rabbis, communal professionals and lay leaders, underscoring the validity of the projections in their own personal experience.

Regarding intermarriage, I'm given to understand that this is becoming increasingly problematic in South Africa. More and more spouses are coming to the Bet Din to be converted. The question is how many more do not seek conversion at all.

The contrast between the contemporary Jewish family and the Jewish home of the past is dramatic. The Jewish home has always been held up as a model of family togetherness and generally thought to be impervious to negative influences. Open society and Western affluence, however, have taken their toll on the Jewish family.

However, the picture is by no means all bleak. Those same Jewish values that have characterized Jewish home life, motivating individuals toward outstanding academic, professional and cultural accomplishment, are still evident in many family settings.

There are many signs of Jewish vitality in the Jewish community as well: the increased *Jewish* awareness among Jewish communal leaders; the growing communal support for Jewish education; the continuing record of support for humanitarian causes, particularly for Israel; the growing *Jewish* agenda of many national and local Jewish organizations.

It is important to note that the history of Jewish education in America is marked by many positive accomplishments, including: the development of the Jewish day school as a major mode of Jewish schooling; the building of impressive Jewish educational facilities; the introduction of modern instructional strategies and the creative use of media; the production of innovative teaching and learning materials; the convening of exciting educational conferences and workshops; the development of a wide variety of American-Israel programs such as teenage and family tours, summer and year-long study in Israeli educational institutions, and teacher education projects and cooperative curriculum activities.

American Jewish education has many bright spots. However, despite all the progress that has taken place in Jewish education, the Jewish community in America may soon lose this instrumentality as an effective method for transmitting Jewish heritage and Jewish values. It may lose *the* institution most needed for Jewish continuity.

Yes, the vitality of the Jewish community is overshadowed by the increasing apathy of Jews and the declining Jewish populations.

It is unfortunate but true, that with the exception of some Jewish day schools and yeshivot, Jewish parental commitment to Jewish schooling is generally less than supportive. The overwhelming majority of Jewish parents do not really associate themselves with the goals of the Jewish schools which their children attend, and do not provide the necessary home reinforcement for Jewish schooling. Researchers in public and private education have demonstrated that academic effectiveness is doomed without support from the home and the community, and that family background affects pupil achievement more than any school factor.

If Jewish studies and values are to be transmitted effectively, parents must become active partners in the education of their children. Quite simply, without the involvement and commitment of the Jewish family, Jewish education *is* doomed. I will have more to say on this subject tomorrow. Suffice it to say for now that schools and families must together face the challenge of society. It takes two to tango. Neither the school nor the family can make it Jewishly alone — one without the other.

And it is Jewish communal leadership that must assure that school and family work together to achieve a common purpose. Furtunately, the South Africa Jewish community has the characteristics of both Zebulun and Issachar — committed lay leaders and dedicated professionals. Your communal leadership is known throughout the Jewish world — via the activities of the United Communal Fund, the Jewish Board of Deputies, the South African Board of Jewish Education, to mention just a few organizations. The South African Jewish community holds the record of the highest per capita contributions to Israel — and this is without the benefit of tax deduction.

The unique history and role of your Board of Jewish Education make it possible for you to make the needed responses to the challenge of society. The Board succeeded in developing a marvelous network of day schools. You have the resources of a Yeshiva College [elementary and secondary school] and the teacher faculty program — and a committed rabbinate. Moreover, you have unique connections with Israel, building constantly upon your traditional Zionist commitment and experience. Of course, you are aware of the specific educational challenges to your community. Let me mention them before I sign off tonight.

Ask yourselves: Are the goals of your school clear? Without clear-cut Jewish purposes, schools cannot hope to achieve maximum Jewish identification in the changing society in which we live.

Do you have commitment to excellence in Jewish studies as well as in secular studies? Are you doing your utmost to upgrade Judaic instruction? Do schools manage to convey effectively why Judaism is rewarding to both pupils and parents? In his recent visit to Cape Town, Dr. Seymour Fox correctly identified this message as a paramount challenge in our sophisticated modern society. Do the curriculum and extracurricular activities encourage the understanding and appreciation of yiddishkeit?

You know the answers to these questions. Changing the status quo, modifying the role of the Hebrew Matriculation Syllabus, changing school schedules and course work, and increasing the hours of Jewish studies are not easy to accomplish. But deep down, committed Jewish leaders know the need for insuring that schools are responsive to the challenge of Jewish continuity in today's world.

To be sure, if the findings of Professor Allie Dubb's Survey of attitudes of King David matriculants made a decade ago still hold true, the students want more Judaism, they want to study Jewish ethics and Jewish philosophy and Jewish history. And, I might add, with the right kind of instruction, Talmud can be a most valuable addition to the curriculum.

Our American experience indicates that an intensive Judaic curriculum in the day school in no way impedes progress and achievement in general studies. The time devoted to Jewish studies in American Jewish day schools ranges from 15 to 25 hours a week and averages about 20 hours weekly.

Attention to the affective domain — maximizing the Jewishness of the school environment — is critical in modern society. Do the schools take advantage of the full day to create a positive Jewish climate? Do they exploit Israel sufficiently as a resource, as a catalyst, as a place to study and experience Jewishness?

Do pupils continue their Jewish study after they graduate? Research has shown that high school has a cumulative effect as it reinforces the learning of elementary school. Post-secondary school, however, goes beyond the cumulative impact as it provides the much needed "multiplier effect," that additional reinforcement that helps guarantee adult Jewish identification. Does the South African Jewish community succeed in motivating students to continue Jewish studies after matriculation in South Africa? in Israel?

Finally, ask yourselves, are you giving sufficient attention to recruiting new, talented South African Jewish Studies teachers?

Are you giving adequate consideration to ways of recognizing and rewarding superior teacher performance?

In the United States, the most recent Gallup opinion poll findings, released just last week, show that the American public favors merit pay by a margin of two to one. What is interesting about American opinion regarding merit pay is that, for the first time, the major teachers' unions are not fighting this suggestion, but are waiting to see the outcome of new state and district experiments with merit pay for superior performance.

What is your position in regard to this crucial matter? What works well in the profit sector may well be one of the keys to increasing the quality of instruction in Jewish schools.

Just as I began with a story about a Bar Mitzvah boy, let me end with one about a Bat Mitzvah girl.

Once upon a time, in a small town in ancient Greece, there was an oracle getting on in years. In this town, a little Bat Mitzvah age girl thought it was time for a change and wanted to replace him as oracle. In those days, the way to become an oracle was to ask a difficult question and stump the incumbent oracle.

She decided to do just that. She thought and thought and conceived the following plan. She would go into the forest and catch a tiny bird and bring the bird to the oracle in her cupped hands, and she would ask the oracle, "Sir, what do I have in my hands?"

In his wisdom, the oracle would say, "My little girl, you have a bird in your hands." "Yes, I do," she would answer, "but tell me sir, is it dead or alive?"

"If the oracle says alive, I'll crush it to death," she thought. "If he says dead, I'll open my hands and let it fly away."

And so it came to pass, the Bat Mitzvah girl caught a little bird in the forest and brought it to the oracle. To the question, "What do I have in my hands?" he answered, "A little bird."

Then, with a gleam in her eye, the Bat Mitzvah girl asked, "Tell me, sir, is it dead or alive?" The oracle thought for a moment and was about to answer. Then, in his wisdom, he emoted, "Young girl, the answer to that question lies in your hands."

Will South African Jewish schools meet the challenge of modern society? I'm sure they will because the answer to this question lies in your collective hands.

— 12 —

THE ROLE OF
COMMUNITY AND SYNAGOGUE
IN JEWISH EDUCATION

Address, Twentieth National Conference
Johannesburg, South Africa
July, 1983

Yehoram Gaon, the Israeli singer, tells a story of a South African man who visited New York. He met a Japanese man carrying two large suitcases and wearing an unusual watch. Besides keeping time, day of week, day of month and year, it was able to take a pulse beat, show temperature and humidity and do a host of other things.

"How much is the watch?" asked the South African visitor. "Give me $50 and you can have it," answered the Japanese man. "Only $50?" "Yes, only $50!" was the retort. The visitor quickly handed him a $50 bill and in return the Japanese man gave him the watch and the two heavy suitcases. "What are these for?" asked the visitor. "Oh," said the Japanese, "the suitcases contain the batteries for the watch."

The challenge posed in this session has to do with the support system for Jewish education. How much baggage should the Jewish community carry in order to make Jewish education truly effective? What kinds of batteries should it supply to Jewish education so that schools can operate effectively?

As a frame of reference for our discussion, I'd like to share with you the findings of a study completed last month in New York. This study is an example of the (potential) role of society and the impact of changes in the general society on Jewish education. Here, again, my perspective is the American Jewish community. In reality, the same kind of social forces are at play in both the American and South African Jewish communities.

Never before in American history has there been so much concern evidenced about education as during the last two years in the United States. During this brief period of time some thirty major national studies and reports on education have appeared. At the Board of Jewish Education of Greater New York we wanted to determine how the Jewish community felt about the recommendations in these reports.

Consequently, we surveyed a broad segment of the community: day school teachers and principals, supplementary school teachers and principals, parents and lay leaders in New York and nine other cities.

Out of the thirty-two recommendations included in our survey instrument, there were four suggestions that respondents felt were *absolutely essential,* and two others that were judged *extremely important.*

The four *absolutely essential* recommendations are "increase local funding for schools," "increase national funding for schools," "increase significantly the base salary of all entering teaching personnel," and increase significantly the base salary of all current teaching personnel." Almost 100 percent of all the respondents — lay and professional alike — feel these are *sine qua non* conditions for upgrading Jewish education.

The two recommendations perceived as *extremely important* are "improve academic leadership and supervision," and "devise ways to honor teachers."

The findings of this study ring out loud and clear. They proclaim: the Jewish community must make Jewish education a priority. We must provide much more support to it. We must guarantee that we can recruit and retain qualified teaching personnel and we must make sure that the Jewish studies program receives the best kind of supervision possible.

Making Jewish education a priority is measured by the dollars we spend for it, by the financial support we give to it, by the salaries we pay and by the status we accord to teachers and principals of Jewish studies.

In the world at large, society blames schools for lack of pupil achievement. "Society holds schools responsible for everything that goes wrong," says a leading American educator. But isn't it true that schools reflect the moral values and quality of life of society and not the other way around? Moreover, the public gets the kind of schools it wants.

"Whatever Lola wants Lola gets," says one of the hit songs of a major American Broadway production *Damn Yankees*. This is true for Jewish education as it is for schooling in the general society. The Jewish community gets the kind of schools it wants.

And we can't blame the students either for not giving serious enough attention to Jewish study, to Jewish values and to Jewish observances. One American educator makes the point this way. With tongue in cheek he said, "We have these marvelous buildings, this splendid equipment, magnificent curriculum, expert teachers and administrators, then, damn it all, the parents send us the wrong kids." However, he noted, "It is time we gave up that cop-out and accepted children as they are delivered to us."

In order to guarantee Jewish continuity, the Jewish community has added responsibility concerning the way parents "deliver" their children to our schools. I'll expand upon this subject later in my talk.

Reacting to the recent spate of national reports on public education, Harold Howe II, former U.S. Commissioner of Education, wrote, "Suddenly, corporate barons, presidential candidates, university presidents, governors, and legislative leaders in Congress and in State capitals have mounted a crusade to improve schools. Will the governors, the corporate leaders and the others who are now fanning the fires of educational reform be willing to stay with that important task over time?"

In response, Howe said, "The kinds of changes now being

recommended will not come easily or quickly because *they challenge vested interests*. It is essential that the interest of groups outside education be sustained and, particularly, that business leadership remain supportive, since one necessity for educational improvement is more *money* to support that improvement."

Howe's blunt analysis and recommendation apply with particular force to Jewish education.

There has been a great awakening in the Jewish community — especially among Jewish communal leaders — about the need for quality Jewish education. The changes in communal attitude regarding the importance of the Jewish school can best be illustrated by the Jewish community's position vis-à-vis Jewish all-day education — the brightest and most promising aspect of Jewish cultural and religious life in America.

It is hard for us now to imagine that, as late as the 1960's, major Jewish leaders — including educators and leaders of ideological movements — opposed the Jewish day school. Still gripped with the *melting pot* ideal of America (which has been replaced so dramatically by the concept of *cultural pluralism),* these men and women of good will fought vigorously against the day school because they believed it was *un-American* and would have an adverse effect upon the Jewish community.

How wrong they were! They themselves are not the first to recognize the fallacy of their thinking. The growth of the Jewish day school has been truly remarkable, expecially when we consider that orthodox Jews developed it against a backdrop of opposition and doubt from the rest of the community.

In South Africa, you can be proud of your community's role in establishing day schools. If we include the preschool enrollment, about two-thirds of all South African Jewish children of school age attend Jewish day schools.

In the United States, many communities have been blessed with private business leaders who have facilitated and supported the growth of this vital institution. This brings me back to Harold Howe's plea regarding the absolute need for "groups" outside education, particularly business leadership," to be supportive of education. (In essence, this is the first suitcase of batteries Jewish education needs.)

Howe probably doesn't know it, but the idea of partnership between business and education — between philanthropy and schooling — is as old as the Jewish people. Jewish tradition recognized that if Jewish life is to continue, this partnership must be an absolute priority.

Jewish life in medieval and contemporary times in Europe and North Africa, where the overwhelming majority of Jews lived, was replete with examples of this partnership. Witness the volume of Responsa and *Takanot Kehillot* — the communal regulations — and the minute books of the *Hevrot Talmud Torah* outlining the respective roles of the *gabbaim* and *parnassim* (the communal leaders) and the *melamdim* (the teachers). These kinds of partnerships provide interesting models for making Jewish education a priority communal concern even today.

The greatest challenge to Jewish communal leadership is to make this combination a vibrant reality in Jewish life. And, this, as Howe notes for American education, is not easy to accomplish because, to use his words, it "challenge(s) *vested interests.*"

The problem in the *Jewish* community is that the "vested interests" are good humanitarian concerns. And who can argue with support for humanitarian causes? Nevertheless, if the American Jewish community is unable to raise substantially more dollars for its variety of local, national and global causes, including Israel, there will be no alternative but to change priorities in Federation allocations. Without dramatically increasing the salaries of teachers, we will have no teachers. Certainly we will not have high-caliber teachers or quality education, even in our day schools and yeshivot. And, without effective Jewish education there will be no committed Jews to support humanitarian causes.

This past spring, one of the leading day schools in the country interviewed thirty-five candidates for *one* Jewish studies high school position and found all of them unqualified. Another leading day school just couldn't find anyone to apply for such teaching jobs. Talented young people are simply not choosing to enter a profession that is low paying, offers little or no security, provides few if any benefits, cannot guarantee professional growth opportunities, and offers little in the way of communal appreciation and social stutus.

Commenting on the same problem in general education, Walter Cronkite, a prominent television commentator, recently said:

"Imagine any self-respective doctor working for that kind of money ($22,000, the average annual income of teachers)! You don't have to be a *masochist* to be a teacher, but it certainly helps." Imagine any self-respecting *Jewish* professional working for the kind of money we pay teachers in Jewish schools! ($16,000 is the average annual salary of full time teachers.)

The information reported to my office regarding the "mission impossible" of the two day schools I just cited prompted me to write an editorial for the Spring issue of *Jewish Education* magazine entitled, "Warning, this building may soon be closed!" The possibility of this happening to many Jewish day schools is real — *very real.* The only way to change the situation is to change the priorities of Jewish communal fund allocations and to find more individual supporters.

This brings us to the next suitcase of challenges, which can best be labeled "reach and teach." Unless we *reach* our children, we can't *teach* them!

In speaking of the failure of public schools, David Seeley, former executive of the New York State Public School Association, underscored the fact that education is virtually an "undeliverable merchandise" for many children because they are not motivated sufficiently to want to learn. The problem, he notes, is that teachers work too hard at teaching, while pupils don't work hard enough at learning. He concludes that you can't teach children. You can only "learn" them.

The only way that this can happen is through the encouragement, help and motivation children receive in their homes. Then, and only then, will good teachers be able to do the rest of the job.

This clearly points the way to a Jewish communal and synagogue priority — forging alliances between schools and parents. Our primary emphasis in Jewish schools has been — and rightly so, logic dictated — on children. However, it is clear now that we must change our emphasis and target our educational efforts at the *families* of our students, particularly at those families whose Jewish commitment and affiliation are marginal. Unless these parents are turned on to Jewish education; unless they associate themselves fully with the goals of the school which their children attend; unless they become knowledgeable partners in the Jewish schooling of their children, Jewish education simply cannot be effective.

Yesterday I spoke about the fact that most Jews have transposed their traditional intellectual and cultural interests and support for *Jewish* study to the arena of secular learning.

This transposition made possible the rapid upward professional academic and economic mobility of immigrant Jews in a free society. But, at the same time, it threatens the quality of Jewish life continuity.

Children realize early in their school years that their parents *highly value* general and professional education. They also readily perceive that their parents feel that Jewish study is of no real consequence other than leading to a perfunctory Bar or Bat Mitzvah ceremony. And, so, the Jewish school is saddled with the burden of trying to motivate children to take seriously that which their families dismiss as not particularly vital or relevant to their adult lives.

While the family is the primary shaper of Jewish identity and commitment, powerful influence can be exerted by the social setting in which the child is placed — especially by peers. This calls for developing and nurturing alternative environments *in loco parentis.*

Research in education has amply demonstrated the power of the learning climate. One of the advantages of the day school is its all-embracing (7-9 hours a day) environment. The Jewish day school provides an opportunity for total immersion in a Jewish atmosphere. Appropriately utilized, this significant amount of time in a Jewish environment can create conditions necessary to motivate Jewish learning and practice.

For Jewish supplementary schools, *alternative environments* must be developed through weekend retreats and Shabbatonim — which have a proven track record of success. In addition, Jewish educational summer camping and a summer or year-long experience in Israel must become a regular part of Jewish schooling.

These recommendations are not new by any means. But they have not been taken seriously by *enough members* of the Jewish community. They must become priority concerns.

So important is the "alternative environment" approach that I have suggested substituting — for grades 4 and up of the supplementary school — one weekend in a Shabbaton setting for a week of school — eliminating three formal school sessions each month. (In some South African supplementary schools this will mean canceling five school days.) Instead, pupils will spend nine weekends — Friday afternoon through Sunday afternoon — in a Jewish environment, interacting with committed high school and college students who serve as Jewish models for them. They will eat together, sing and dance together, play and pray together and learn together.

The total number of hours they will be together in a Jewish atmosphere during one year of such a program will be double the amount of school time in a full year of sessions in a congregational school.

Providing sufficient "time on task," an exciting atmosphere, models of Jewish commitment, and opportunities for Jewish socialization are the earmarks of such an approach. But it costs money. And this brings us back full circle to the challenge of making Jewish education an absolute communal priority.

Reaching students also means reaching out to them in non-school settings, as the title of this session — "Beyond the School" — implies. This is best expressed by building bridges between formal and informal education; by developing and strengthening alliances between schools and youth organizations; by introducing informal Jewish educational activities into the school and formal Jewish study into youth group settings. This kind of integration can go a long way in achieving the confluence of cognitive and affective learning so necessary for assuring the behavioral results of Jewish education.

The synagogue should naturally have a special place in the scheme of Jewish education. In America, its educational role is synonymous with the Jewish supplementary school or congregational school, or Hebrew school or Heder, as you call it.

Supplementary Jewish education in America began in the late 1800's and early 1900's as either private *hadarim* or communal Talmud Torahs, largely unrelated to the synagogue. During the 1920's and 1930's, the communal Talmud Torah (which was initially developed as a communal response to educating the children of the poor) was the dominant form of Jewish education. With the move of Jews to suburbia and the development of synagogues which sponsored their own schools, the communal Talmud Torah all but disappeared by 1960 — leaving the supplementary school — with some notable exceptions — a congregational institution.

On the surface, this development — the congregationalization of supplementary school — seemed to augur well for its potential. However, the synagogue school never materialized into an effective Jewish educational instrumentality.

The reasons for this are seemingly well known: insufficient number of hours of instruction; part-time teachers; the after public school nature of the program, specifically the late afternoon hours of classroom attendance; competition with social, recreational and personal concerns; and non-continuation after Bar or Bat Mitzvah.

However, the underlying reasons, the overriding causes for the failure of this form of Jewish education in America are — strange as it may seem — the lack of real commitment on the part of the synagogue leadership to the school program. This led Dr. Alexander Dushkin, the renowned educational leader, to suggest that the congregational school, even in its heyday, was the "step-child of the synagogue." This is amply demonstrated by the relatively low status of the members of the lay education committees and the professional educators in the synagogue hierarchy.

Another major factor leading to the failure of supplementary schools is the influence of an unsupportive home and environment.

Many parents are either marginally Jewish or do not fully associate themselves with the philosophy and purposes of their respective synagogues. You well know that synagogue membership does not guarantee religiosity or Jewish commitment. This means that many parents do not fully appreciate the instructional aims of the school or understand sufficiently the content of the instruction to which their children are exposed. This leaves their children insufficiently motivated for effective learning, and lessens the possibility that the Jewish school can have a lasting influence.

While it may be true that under certain conditions the Jewish school has an effect which might be independent of familial background and other socializing influences, it seems clear that without significant home involvement in the process of Jewish education, the conditions for maximizing the effectiveness of Jewish schooling cannot be fulfilled. And when schooling has an effect independent of the family, it often creates a serious problem at home — the disruption of *shalom bayit*. The very success of the school frequently alienates children from parents who are untouched by the influence of the school.

The role of the home will be discussed in more detail by

Professor Seymour Fox. Suffice it to say, in the context of our discussion, that the synagogue must interface with the home and help bring about the congruence of school values and home values necessary for effective learning. In order to make this a reality the synagogue must develop teaching and learning strategies that involve the whole family.

What synagogues need — what the Jewish community requires — therefore, in order to provide effective Jewish schooling for children, are full-time Jewish family educators to replace the part-time congregational supplementary school teachers. Supplementary Jewish education for children must be transformed into an education program for the entire family.

This means reorienting the roles of all synagogue personnel. Each of them — rabbi, cantor, teachers and principal — needs to become a full-time Jewish family educator, instructing children in classroom settings, leading informal educational groups, working with family members in their homes, and providing individualized tutelage, Jewish family counseling and referrals as needed to parents and children alike.

The Jewish family educators would work in teams — plan and organize their work and establish their goals at the beginning of each semester, trimester or bimonthly or monthly period. To be sure, this approach requires the restructuring of the synagogue, the congregational school and the curriculum of instruction as well as the retraining and training of personnel.

It will not be easy to induce the necessary modifications into the synagogue structure. Nor will the individual rabbis, rabbinic groups or lay leaders take easily to what amounts to a structural and programmatic revolution in the synagogue. But, there may be no other viable alternative for the synagogue school.

The concept of Jewish family education can work as well for the day school. In fact, one day school in New York is currently experimenting with this idea. How to integrate family outreach activity into the day school program is an exciting challenge.

Finally, an important dimension of the role of society and synagogue in Jewish schooling is expressed in the attitudes and actions of the adult community.

In the society at large, educators are urged to bring education into concert with the goals of society. In Jewish terms, this means the Jewish community must have goals worthy of emulation by Jewish educational institutions. In our modern age — in an open society — for the Jewish school to succeed there must be a congruence of school values, community values and home values. Simply stated, we have to get our values together. Jewish tradition has much to offer in this direction.

Throughout Jewish history, Jews were expected to be lifelong students of the Torah. Jewish learning in the home, in the school, and in the community was the very plasma of Jewish life. It was the soul of a people and the guarantor of continuity.

From here flows a crucial challenge to the Jewish community and synagogue. What kinds of students of Torah are the adult Jews? What kinds of role models are adult Jews for schools and for students?

"If gold rusts, what shall iron do?" asks the English poet, paraphrasing a well-known Talmudic statement. Ask yourselves, are you a learning community? Are your families learning families? Can schools succeed if there is discontinuity between their values and those of the parents and community?

The responses you make to these questions and to the other challenges I have posed will indicate the kind of batteries you carry in your suitcases — the kind of communal and synagogue support you give to our most precious commodities — our Jewish school children.

— 13 —

EDUCATING JEWS TOWARD KNOWLEDGE AND COMMITMENT

Presented at
UJA/Federation Communal Planning Committee
Meeting on Priority Setting
March 16, 1988

I welcome this opportunity to talk about the future of the Jewish community.

The Talmud stresses that Jewish children, properly educated, are the guarantors of the Jewish future. More than that; in our times, Jewish education is the guarantor of the future contributors to the Jewish community — contributors of both substance and self to Jewish continuity. Jewish children of today, with sound Jewish educational backgrounds, will be the contributors to the UJA/Federation Campaign of tomorrow. Some of these children will become the next generation of Jewish communal leaders.

There will always be some poor and near-poor in New York. There will always be some homeless people among us. There will always be individuals requiring health care and social and psychological guidance. And there will always be an aged population to serve. But, there is no assurance that, without proper Jewish education, that there will always be Jews to serve, or Jews to provide services to the poor, the homeless, the ill, the troubled and the aged.

Let's face it. We now have the chance of a lifetime. The Jewish community is at a crossroad. We dare not ignore the danger signs that beckon us to do everything in our power to insure Jewish survival.

Jewish education — the transmission of Jewish knowledge and the formation and reinforcement of Jewish identity — is a primary *Jewish* communal responsibility. For the *Jewish* dimension of Jewish communal service there is *no* government funding and *no* public financial support. This responsibility — guaranteeing quality Jewish education experiences to Jewish children, youth, families and adults — falls squarely and fully upon the shoulders of the Jewish community.

In addition to Jewish education, Jewish communal leadership has to respond to all kinds of human, social and health needs of the Jewish population. The support of UJA/Federation to agencies which respond to these needs is crucial. But, of all the services made possible by UJA/Federation assistance, one service function requires special attention — indeed, the highest priority consideration — because it, and it alone, addresses our Jewish future. How viable the Jewish community will be in the year 2000 and beyond, depends upon how we succeed in educating the next generation of children and youth and how effectively we impact the Jewishness of Jewish families and young adults in the 1990's.

It is to this task we must *all* give our priority attention and support. It is a task that highlights both our challenge and our opportunity. ! חילכם לאוריתא

May we go *together* from strength to strength.

— 14 —

ON MARKETING, EVALUATING
AND FUNDING JEWISH EDUCATION

*Excerpts from paper
presented at the Jewish Federation
Council of Los Angeles
October 28, 1988*

INTRODUCTION

King Solomon advised us *davar be'ito ma tov* — "a timely thought is always in place." I want to thank you for your invitation. I want to thank you for bringing me here to the Dodgers' *simchah*. Their destruction of the Oakland A's was music to my ears for what the A's did to my Boston Red Sox. In this light, I'd like to begin with an athletic *dvar Torah*. The text is Kirk Gibson. Look at Kirk! He couldn't run; he could hardly walk; he could barely lift his arms; he was in great pain; and then boom!

Kirk was like much of what Jewish education is today. Beset by serious problems, difficulties and challenges, what we have is great potential. The Jewish community has what it takes to turn around the game of Jewish education. We have to find ways to let the potential explode à la Kirk Gibson. And that's why we're here today. And, why you're involved as Jewish communal leaders in a most vital joint enterprise . . .

The Talmud helps me justify *my* reason for being here. *Yoter me'ma sheha-egel rotzeh linok, ha-parah rotzah l'hanik* — "more than the calf wants to suck milk, the cow wants to give it." And, this cow always wants to give milk. My problem is whether my *halav yisrael* is the kind of milk you want, and the kind you need. I have developed my remarks according to Steve Huberman's insightful suggestions. Steve suggested that I speak on three topics: marketing Jewish education; evaluating Jewish education; and funding Jewish education à la New York's Fund for Jewish Education. Three separate subjects, but interrelated.

MARKETING JEWISH EDUCATION

Do you remember Sputnik, 1957? Do you know that Sputnik was one of the most important turning points for education in America? Until 1957, education in America was considered as a consumer good. (It's still considered like a consumer good by many Americans.) After Sputnik, when we realized we had to compete with the Russians and we had to help universities do the kind of research that was necessary to compete effectively with them, Americans began to view education as an investment. We had to invest significantly in education — in higher education and in research — to produce the effects needed to compete with the Russians in the arenas of science, defense and military strategy.

Marketing *Jewish* education requires Jewish communal leaders to change the concept of Jewish education from that of a consumer good purchased by parents to an activity in which Jewish communal leadership must invest heavily.

Marketing Jewish education speaks to two audiences. First, it speaks to the people that have the means to make it succeed. This audience must find ways to make Jewish education a communal priority. Jewish communal leadership must support it as a priority with the same urgency that Blacks consider their problems and with the same urgency that Jews for Jesus freaks and missionary groups invest millions and millions of dollars on missionary activities to Jews. Do we invest that kind of Jewish communal money to make Jews out of Jews? If we want to market Jewish education effectively, the providers have to be seized with a feeling of urgency about the need to make the necessary changes in Jewish education and to provide the necessary support to make them possible.

The second audience is composed of the consumers and clients. Some people call this kind of marketing "recruitment." Others refer to it as reaching out to children and parents. I would like to share with you an outreach program developed by the Board of Jewish Education of Greater New York 14 years ago.

Recruiting Students

According to our best estimates, 35% of the Jewish school population, 5-18 years of age, would not be exposed to formal Jewish schooling. We decided to use Madison Avenue techniques to reach unaffiliated Jewish families with children. We weren't reaching them through synagogue bulletins, through Center bulletins or through local newspapers. "Let's reach them through the major newspapers, television, and radio," we said. Accordingly, we mounted a media recruitment campaign during the first two weeks of September 1973. You may remember some of our full page ads in the *New York Times*. "If you're Jewish, chances are, your grandchildren will not be Jewish." "When your child hears the word 'shofar' this Rosh Hashannah, will he think it's the person who is going to drive his parents to a concert?" We developed some forty messages over a period of 12 years. Between 1973 and 1985 the recruitment campaign brought into the Jewish school system in Greater New York approximately 10,000 Jewish children.

Unfortunately, we had to terminate it because it became financially prohibitive. In retrospect, the campaign was able to reach enrollment in Jewish schools of some 10,000 children who may never have been exposed to formal Jewish schooling without it.

Marketing Bureau Services

There is another dimension to marketing Jewish education. Steve Huberman asked "How do you market the services of the Board of Jewish Education of Greater New York?" First, lay and professional leadership of the bureau must believe fervently that Jewish education is the top Jewish communal priority. Second, the services must be designed to respond to specific needs. When I assumed the professional helmsmanship of the Board of Jewish

Education of Greater New York, I proposed that we transform it from an organization that dispenses general services to an agency that provides specialized services. If specialization is good enough for medicine and good enough for law, then it should be good enough for Jewish education. Accordingly, we developed a service approach based almost entirely on the concept of specialization. As a result, we now have eight specialized centers and a variety of other specialized programs. The areas of specialization include, among others, early childhood, family, media, micro-computer, outreach, special education, management assistance, government relations, curriculum materials development, testing, resource development and social planning. Specialized in-service programs for educators are provided through our Principals' Center in conjunction with Harvard, Columbia and the University of Pennsylvania, and through our five Teachers' Centers.

The effect of specialization has been remarkable. In the early 1970's, for example, fifty early childhood teachers and directors would participate in an annual early childhood education conference. In 1988, 1,800 early childhood teachers and directors are regularly involved in workshops, institutes and conferences. During each of the last several years we had to turn away three to four hundred early childhood educators who wanted to pay $35 to participate in the annual all-day conference simply because we had no room. There is no synagogue in New York that has enough space for the plenary sessions, exhibits, workshops and seminars. We don't have the money to spend on hotel facilities — nor would we. What is the key to marketing Early Childhood Education services? Heightened specialized quality programming and staffing!

Another example of marketing bureau services. Fifteen years ago there were literally no schools that requested media assistance from BJE. To be sure, most Jewish educators were threatened by the idea of hardware in their classrooms. In the 1987-88 school year, BJE provided 3,700 media consultations and previews. If we had sufficient funds we could have responded to many more requests for media assistance. What is the secret to this marketing success? A highly specialized quality program and quality staff!

In the 1970's, Jewish communal leaders in New York did not think that *Jewish* special education was an activity that should be funded by Federation. By and large, they believed that children with special needs should be served only through *general* education and that the Jewish community's responsibility for retarded Jewish youth and learning disabled children does not extend beyond the provision of human services. The marketing challenge here was huge. Nothing succeeds like success. A highly skilled specialized staff and innovative programming now generate about a million dollars a year in outside grants for Jewish special education in addition to the $100,000 per year budgeteed through UJA-Federation funding.

Our Teachers' Centers are another example of creative marketing. In 1976, we established our first Teachers' Center in a 10' x 10' room in Long Island. Presently, we have five Teachers' Centers, two of which are university-based. In Nassau County, Long Island, a former Jewish Community Center now serves as our Teachers' Center in that area.

This past year, 1,600 teachers spent 60,000 hours *voluntarily* in the Teachers' Centers.

What does all this say about marketing education services? It says that if you develop appropriate specialized quality responses to real needs you heighten school and community awareness of these needs and actually create a demand for service that responds to them.

The marketing challenge essentially relates to specialized responses to the felt needs in the field. The appropriate responses market themselves.

EVALUATING JEWISH EDUCATION

My next topic deals with evaluation. There are two major dimensions of education. One relates to the cognitive domain, the other to the affective domain. The first suggests that we evaluate knowledge. The second posits that we assess attitudes and involvement. Public education invests heavily in testing pupil knowledge and recording achievement scores. Throughout the various state systems and local districts testing in all grades and all subjects has become a fetish.

To be sure, the testing programs in general education provide useful information about aspects of pupil progress. However, evaluation relating solely to the cognitive domain has its limitations. When we evaluate subject achievement, we do not appraise the child's total progress. We don't examine where he or she is going. We only evaluate what children have been taught, not what they are able to learn; and not their attitudes to learning and to life, for which school should be preparing them.

Besides assessing individual pupil progress, evaluation also means appraising the effectiveness of a school and a school system. Assessing the effectiveness of education is a favorite pastime of the American people. In every generation new knowledge is added to our battery of information about school evaluation. This past decade and a half is no exception. The 1970's and 1980's are highlighted by Effective Schools Research activity that has added many new, creative ideas to the way we think about educational effectiveness.

Effective Schools Research and Jewish Education

A quick insight into some of the contributions of Effective Schools Research to our understanding of good educational practice seems in order, particularly since Jewish education does not occur in a vacuum. What are some of the findings of Effective Schools Research that can inform our evaluation of Jewish schools?

To begin with, there is now unanimity about definitions of an effective school in public education. Some findings of Effective Schools Research are well supported; others are more speculative. Therefore, one cannot be totally conclusive about effectiveness. However, the consistency in the research findings across most of the studies suggests that there is general agreement about the key elements of good schooling.

Effective Schools Research demonstrates that a limited number of organizational-programmatic characteristics or correlates consistently obtain in effective schools and are absent, in whole or in part, in the ineffective ones. While it is uncertain whether they are causal or not, the correlates are helpful to our understanding of school effectiveness. Essentially, they tell us that a good school has:

1) a clear focus and institutional mission, and a clearly defined curriculum;
2) strong administrative and instructional leadership;
3) a positive school climate and orderly atmosphere conductive to learning;
4) high expectations by principal and teachers for pupil growth;
5) sufficient and productive student time on task;

6) careful monitoring of pupil progress; and

7) good home-school relationships.

Now, you may say "Let us take these correlates and adapt them to Jewish education. Let us use them as criteria for evaluating Jewish education." Jewish education is a voluntary stystem with much diversity. We cannot necessarily take one group of correlates and apply them equally to all schools.

The Jewish Supplementary School Study

In New York, as in most other Jewish communities on the North American continent, between two-thirds and three-quarters of all Jewish school-age children, 5-18 years old, will receive some formal Jewish education. For most of these children — 70 percent of them — this means supplementary Jewish schooling, 2 to 6 hours per week, 30 to 35 weeks per year, for five or six years.

There has been a growing awareness over the past decade among Jewish lay leadership that this type of Jewish education needs serious attention. What aspects of Jewish supplementary education must be improved? How can we upgrade this form of schooling? These questions have stymied both lay and professional leadership.

To respond to these challenges, the Board of Jewish Education of Greater New York undertook a methodologically rigorous and comprehensive study of the supplementary school. The three-year study included intensive lay and professional involvement, guided by a 15-member lay task force and administered competently by an 11-member professional staff study team. The lay-professional process was a crucial feature of the research.

Setting the State: The Stakeholders

In setting the stage for the Study we realized the need to consider all the *stakeholders* in the Jewish supplementary school. Essentially there are five categories of *stakeholders*.

1. *Consumers* — Pupils exposed to formal and informal education strategies.

2. *Clients* — parents who determine the kind of Jewish education they will purchase for their children.

3. *Transmitters* — all Jewish education personnel — teachers,

principals, rabbis, informal educators, educational consultants and specialists.

4. *Overseers* or facilitators — school committee members who have special roles in assuring that Jewish education is properly maintained, and

5. *Providers* or supporters — trustees of synagogues and school boards, members and professional staff of federation allocation committees, and board members of central agencies for Jewish education.

We determined that it is absolutely necessary for all these stakeholders to be involved in the study.

The Study Sample

The Study Sample included 40 schools — large, medium and small; urban and suburban; Conservative, Orthodox, Reconstructionist and Reform.

The Study Methodology

The Study Methodology comprised two research approaches: a normative survey method (or a modified ethnographic procedure) and a measurement technique, a carefully developed three-part inventory of Jewish knowledge, Jewish involvement and Jewish attitudes — administered after being pilot-tested — to *all* pupils in *all* grades of the participating schools.

Normative Survey Findings

The results of the Normative Survey clearly demonstrated a variety of disturbing realities.

- Jewish education is *not a real* synagogue priority.
- *Rabbis* are peripherally involved in the supplementary school. Most of them lack the necessary training to help make it effective.
- *Principals* are serious about their work. But, synagogue school principaling is just a part-time job. The majority of principals lack sufficient Judaic background and adequate knowledge of supervision and curriculum development for

Jewish education.
- *Teachers* are generally committed to their work. But most of them lack *Jewish* pedagogic skills, and do not have sufficient Jewish knowledge. Eleven percent of the 426 teachers in our sample had no formal Jewish education at all. Teachers have no real institutional commitment, they are not in their respective synagogue schools long enough to make a lasting impact. The teachers in our sample spend an average of six hours per week in a given school. Morever, turnover is great. Two-thirds of them taught in the same school two years or less.
- The overwhelming majority of parents provide little or no home support; nor are they interested. They send their offspring to the synagogue school purely for Bar and Bat Mitzvah.
- And, pupils attend Jewish supplementary school primarily for Bar/Bat Mitzvah. While in most instances they seem well behaved, they are not motivated to learn, nor are they really learning.
- The persons involved with the school have no shared vision of curricular goals. Principals and teachers have the highest curricular goals. Rabbis, lay leaders and parents have the lowest expectations.

There is little or no relationship between the subjects taught and the goals articulated by lay and professional leadership. For example, all the interviewees — principals, teachers, rabbis, lay leaders and parents — felt that the formation of a positive Jewish identity and positive Jewish attitudes is an important goal for the Jewish school. Yet, this aim was far from realized, as we shall see in a few moments.

- The overwhelming majority of schools have no structured curricula. Nor do they regularly follow the curricula prepared by their respective ideological movements.

- The time spent in school is both quantitatively and qualitatively indadequate.

Inventory Findings

The Inventory findings are most revealing the overall increase in Jewish knowledge from the first year of school to the sixth year was *only 10%*. From the second year to the sixth year, Jewish knowledge scores increased *by only 4%*. In all subjects but one there was actually a *drop* in pupil scores from the fifth to the sixth year. Twelve-and 12-1/2-year-olds know less than eleven-and 11-1/2-year-olds. As one of the post-finding consultants said, "Their brains fell out during their pre-Bar-Bat Mitzvah year."

— There was a sharp increase in scores in all subjects by pupils who continued school beyond Bar/Bat Mitzvah and were in their seventh or eighth year of school.

— Jewish involvement of pupils is generally passive. It actually decreased from the second to sixth year of school (by 10%).

— Jewish attitudes of pupils are generally neutral. The Jewish attitudes also decreased from the second to sixth year or school (by 15%).

It is interesting to note that pupils did *not* demonstrate *negative Jewish involvement and attitudes*. All responses involvement and attitudes were pareve — passive or neutral — and went from high passive or high neutral to low passive and low neutral.

School size, ideology, geography and *even numbers of hours of schooling* made no difference in pupils' Jewish knowledge, Jewish attitudes and Jewish involvement.

Conclusions

Schools do a poor job in increasing Jewish knowledge in all subject areas; they show no success in guiding children toward increased Jewish involvement and demonstrate an inability to influence positive growth in Jewish attitudes.

This condition is due to a combination of factors: lack of home involvement and support for Jewish schooling; irrelevant curricular goals; inappropriate school programs; and ineffectual professional personnel, given the needs of pupils and families in the 1980's.

Unless Jewish education of the entire family becomes the absolute priority of the synagogue . . . unless the parents become involved in the Jewish education of their children . . . unless the program is geared to the needs of families . . . and unless all synagogue personnel are able to relate effectively to pupils and their parents, very little or no improvement can take place.

Let me share with you one disturbing feature of supplementary education relating to this latter point. After the study was completed we spent the better part of a year disseminating the findings. All told, we held thirty different city wide and regional meetings in which principals, rabbis, synagogue presidents, school committee chairpersons and parent leaders participated. Between 8 and 50 persons attended each of the meetings. At each regional meeting I asked the question, "In your respective schools how many times a year do the rabbi, principal, school board chairperson, parent leader, teachers and youth director meet together to plan and review progress of the educational program?" There was unanimity of response. Such meetings never or rarely take place.

I suggest you ask the same question in each of the synagogues in the Los Angeles area. How often do all the various stakeholders of each synagogue meet together to develop plans and to review educational progress?

The Findings in the Context of General Education

While there are major differneces between the Jewish supplementary school and the public school, it is instructive to consider these findings and conclusions in light of research in general education which underscore that *family background is the crucial influence on the effectiveness of schooling.*

It is precisely because of this factor — family involvement — that our study makes its major recommendation for the improvement of the Jewish supplementary school.

Transform the thrust of synagogue schools from supplementary schooling for pupils to Jewish family education (including classroom instruction for pupils).

This recommendation suggests the reorganization of the synagogue and the mobilization of the community to provide the necessary support to make this change possible.

Implementing the Recommendations

After having presented the findings and having made recommendations, it was necessary to get all the stakeholders involved in studying the recommendations, refining them, designing strategies for application, developing implementation models, experimenting with these models, validating them, demonstrating how they work, and helping other synagogues replicate them.

Accordingly, BJE initiated the *Supplementary Education Action Plan (SEAP)* process. Upon the completion of the Study Report, we devoted the summer and early fall of 1987 to the development of a detailed set of guidelines for SEAP to help answer the questions: How should the findings be disseminated to achieve the greatest impact? How can we obtain input from all the stakeholders — lay leaders, parents, rabbis, and educators — most efficiently and effectively? What should be their respective roles in SEAP? How can we obtain the necessary support from synagogues for experimentation of the recommendations?

You may ask "Is the New York study applicable to Los Angeles?" Obviously there are differences between communities. However, the answer I will give is the one Professor Harry Passow of Columbia University — one of the country's leading experts in general education — suggested I share with you. In addition to his broad knowledge base in general education, Professor Passow served for many years as chairman of the school board of the largest Conservative synagogue in New Jersey. His advice to communities considering replicating the New York Study is: "Save your money."

I reiterate. "Save your money." The next step for Los Angeles would be to modify the recommendations according to your needs. New York has no ownership on the experimentation process. Here in Los Angeles, Federation, the Bureau and a number of schools might begin experimenting together.

You already have several innovative programs in place: Havurat Noar, Halutz program, Dor Hadash. Why not try to maximize the integration of these programs into the school system and test their impact upon participants? How your community initiates the experimentation is totally up to you. One thing is clear, however. No one can effectively implement a new course of action for the schools. Each school must be fully involved in the planning, development, implementation and evaluation of its own program changes.

I recall learning in my college biology class that when a chick is ready to be born, it breaks its way through the shell. If someone helps crack the shell for the chick, it will die. Like the chick, each school must work at developing the most appropriate response to its own needs.

Some schools might experiment with the Dor Hadash concept for 10 to 13 year olds. Many years ago, I proposed that during the last two or three years of supplementary school one week of classes be eliminated each month. In their stead, one weekend retreat each month (from Friday noon through Sunday noon) October through May might be instituted.

Testing Day School Pupils' Performance

Permit me now to make a brief observation about another kind of evaluation in Jewish education.

In the United States there are no ongoing community-wide testing services. There is, however, one exception. In 1974, the Board of Jewish Education of Greater New York, together with the Yeshiva High Schools Principals Council, (an association of principals of modern Orthodox high schools) developed a uniform high school admissions exam for the 80 modern Orthodox elementary feeder day schools in the Metropolitan New York area. (Together these schools represent about one-half of the all-day school population in Greater New York.)

At the end of each Novermber or beginning of each December every year, all the eighth grade students take one uniform examination for admission into all the yeshiva high schools. Until the inauguration of this service, admissions procedure to yeshiva high schools was like a wild shopping spree. For example, when my daughters graduated elementary day school, they were unsure which high school they wanted to attend and were interviewed and tested in four different high schools. Each admissions procedure was different. Each required the better part of a day. The different kinds of admissions procedures made it very confusing for an elementary school graduate. Now, all eighth graders take the same examination on the same day for admission into any Jewish day high school of their choice. This testing procedure has had a salutary effect upon elementary day schools. It has helped elevate the standards of elementary school achievement.

FUNDING JEWISH EDUCATION

Now to the third theme assigned to me — Funding Jewish
Education. My own personal philosophy is "If you ain't got funding
for schooling, you shouldn't be in the business of education." I feel
strongly about this principle.

One of the first thing I did when I became chief executive
officer of the Board of Jewish Education was to seek funding sources
for schools. I was fortunate to discover Mr. Joseph Gruss — an
unusual person of great wealth and deep, abiding commitment to
Jewish continuity and to Jewish education. As a result of his
involvement in funding Jewish education, the Board of Jewish
Education of Greater Ner York currently administers $12,000,000 of
program support a year to a wide variety of Jewish educational
institutions.

The Fund for Jewish Education (FJE) was created out of an
urgent need to support and enhance Jewish education as a principal
guarantor of Jewish survival. FJE is a tripartite partnership, whereby
Joseph Gruss contributes $1.5 million a year matched by $3 million
from UJA-Federation of Jewish Philanthropies.

During this past year, FJE distributed $5,000,000 to wide-
ranging programs in the Greater New York area. Another $7 million
was provided via special Monument Funds established by Mr. Gruss
and his late wife.

A lay Committee representing Mr. Gruss, UJA-Federation and
the Board of Jewish Education sets policy and determines
allocations. Drawn from many different professions, reflecting all
ideological outlooks, and representing a variety of geographic
locations throughout Greater New York, these diverse, committed
men and women join together to insure that FJE's funds are
expended in the most equitable and cost-effective manner possible.

FJE's goals are to:
— insure the stability of Jewish schools of all
ideologies, including day schools, yeshivot and
supplementary schools;
— provide economic security for career Jewish
educators, in order to attract young, talented
individuals and retain experienced vesteran teachers;
— eliminate health and safety hazards and assure a
secure environment conducive to learning;

— support programs for children with special education needs, including learning disabled and developmentally handicapped;

— provide support for new immigrant students from countries which suppress Jewish religious freedom;

— support outreach programs that touch and teach the minimally affiliated and unaffiliated, and increase the number of children who receive a Jewish education.

School Grants

FJE's grants are distributed in three separate program categories: School Grants, Educator Benefits and Outreach and Special Projects.

Grants-in-aid are awarded to Jewish schools according to enrollment formulas. Special formula variances are given to schools which are crucial to neighborhood preservation or which serve a unique constituency in the community.

Additional grant programs, also based on enrollment formulas, have been developed for schools with large numbers of immigrant students. Grants are also provided to schools with special programs for the learning disabled and developmentally handicapped — recognizing that these costly programs allow the special Jewish child to receive a Jewish education.

Educator Benefits

The Educator Benefits program provides free life insurance coverage in the amount of $75,000 and contributes toward medical and pension benefits of career Jewish educators who teach a minimum of 20 hours per week in day schools and yeshivot, or a minimum of 12 hours per week in supplementary schools. Currently, 4700 Jewish educators receive these benefits.

Outreach and Special Projects

Outreach and Special Projects grants are awarded on a competitive basis for innovative programs proposed by Jewish formal and informal educational institutions. Special priority is given to programs which seek to reach out to marginally affiliated and unaffiliated Jewish youth. All types of Jewish educational institutions are actively encouraged to submit proposals to the Outreach and Special Projects subcommittee. In general, an institution which receives these grants from FJE must provide a significant proportion of its program's cost from its own resources.

New York Benefaction

Although heavily dependent upon the bounty of one individual, the role of UJA-Federation is absolutely critical to JFE and to the Gruss Monument Funds — as fiduciary agent, as contributor of $3 million of matching funds each year, and as facilitator of the lay process, which includes organizing the five FJE committees: plenary, executive and program subcommittees.

While the total communal funding is relatively small compared to the need for financial aid and the total expenditure for Jewish education in New York (over $330 million annually for Jewish formal elementary and secondary education alone), it has an extremely important fiscal and psychological impact on Jewish schooling.

Being blessed with a philanthropist the likes of a Joseph Gruss gives a community an unusual advantage. Before the Gruss-UJA-Federation arrangement, New York did not provide direct subsidies to Jewish educational institutions. Living with the towering effect of one individual means accepting his funding ideas and sometimes compromising with communal processes. However, given the size of his annual contribution to Jewish education via UJA-Federation — now over $7 million — who can complain?

If New York had one or two more such benefactors, and if every Jewish community would have such generous supporters, what a difference it could make cumulatively to the national picture of Jewish education. So, I bring you a "gruss" from New York — that is a yiddish "gruss." May you Los Angeles community be so blessed.

AFTERWORD

In closing, I have attempted to address three topics as requested of me, relying heavily upon my New York experience. The questions and responses regarding marketing, evaluating and funding are essential to the well-being of the various Jewish educational entities in the community. The relationships between each of these three dimensions of Jewish education is obvious. Their importance derives from their potential cumulative impact upon a voluntary system crucial for Jewish continuity. The communal challenge in each area demands sustained efforts as old needs change and new needs emerge. Essential lay leadership qualities required to succeed in effectuating improvements in each area are abiding commitment to Jewish education as a priority and continued strength of resolve to respond to the needs.

A group of Hassidim once came to study with their rebbe and found him weeping. They tried to console him. "Why are you crying?" they asked. "When I was a young man," he said, "I thought I could change the world. So, I set out to try. That's how I learned the world is a very difficult thing to change. Then I turned 30. I decided that it was just as important for me to protect my small corner of the world. So, I invested all my energies in trying to improve my community and my students. That's how I learned that communities and classes of students cannot be made perfect. So, at the age of 40, I set about to change just my family. I spent hours and hours with my wife and children, trying to make my family perfect. But I learned that even families cannot be perfected. When I reached my maturity, at age 60, I realized that there was only one person who would listen to the lessons for which I had been placed in this world to teach. So I set out to perfect myself. But now I know that even that is beyond my powers."

The students were afraid. If the rebbe could not perfect himself, what chance have they? Again, they tried to console him. "Rebbe, rebbe, you are a great man, a scholar, an ethical exemplar beyond compare. What you do is right and just. You should not cry because you are not perfect. Only God can be perfect."

"You don't understand. I'm not weeping because I am sad," said the rebbe. "I'm weeping becuase of the great blessing that God has granted me." "What blessing?" the students asked.

"All through my life I have been faced with great difficulties and challenges," the rebbe answered. "And God has given me strength to try and try and try again to respond to them. That's why I'm crying. I cry out of joy."

The challenges of Jewish education are overwhelming. We may

not succeed in our initial efforts to respond effectively to them. But God blessed us with the strength to try and try again. The effort is worth it. It will result in the blessings of Jewish life.

More power to you!

— 15 —

RETROSPECT AND CHALLENGE
IN JEWISH COMMUNAL EDUCATION

Presented at
the 50th Annual Meeting of the
Board of Jewish Education of Baltimore
March 15, 1972

I'm so pleased *to be here* in Baltimore. This is Henrietta Szold territory, as we used to call Baltimore when we were young Zionists. When I went to the Hebrew Teachers College in Boston we considered the Baltimore Hebrew College (1201 Eutaw Place) a sister institution of high caliber. I recall meeting Dr. Louis Kaplan when he came to visit his son Danny at Camp Yavneh, the Hebrew College camp where I was head counselor 23 years ago. From our conversations, I learned about the characteristics of a vibrant Jewish communal education agency. During this *yovel* — which literally means a horn, a *shofar* — the Baltimore Jewish community has earned the right to blow its own horn. You have much about which to toot.

In the first place, Baltimore contributed to the development of the first central agency for Jewish education. Physician-turned-educator, Samson Benderly, who honed his educational skills in

Baltimore, was imported to New York to organize the first Bureau in 1910. Twelve years later, Baltimore founded its own central agency, which has made significant contributions to the concept and practice of Jewish communal education. And, Baltimore has the distinction of being the first city, outside of New York, to establish a Jewish day school — the Hebrew Parochial School in 1917, — renamed Yeshivat Hofetz Hayim in 1933.

What was the Jewish world like 50 years ago when the Board of Jewish Education in Baltimore was established? Jews had just experienced a most difficult period of adjustment between 1900 and 1920. To be sure, the year 1921 marked the end of a long continuous period of immigration — interrupted only by World War I. The impoverished Jewish immigrants were hardly distinguishable from the huge mass of other immigrants pouring into the United States at a rate of 1,000,000 a year before the First World War. The Jewish immigrants were different, however, in one important way. They differed in their orientation to schooling. They were learning English more quickly than other groups. More Jewish youth were going to college. Moreover, Jews worked harder for economic security, and their upward economic mobility was more rapid.

The beginning of the 1920's marked the decade when Jews started "to make it." They began deserting old congested centers of settlement, earlier and in greater numbers than other ethnic groups. They began to show demographic features characteristic of the middle class earlier than other immigrants, as they began the trek toward becoming a native born population. The Jewish birth rate began to slow down as they acculturated to American society.

The 1920's were days of Zionism, Bundism and Yiddishism; they were the days of the establishment Jewish social organizations. The 1922 American Jewish Yearbook notes: "In the United States during the past twelve months the press reported the founding of ninety-two organizations, thirty-nine religious schools, ninety-nine educational institutions, three mutual benefit societies, seventy-three charitable organizations, one cemetery and nine social clubs."

Jewish community centers began springing up in the 20's. Synagogues tried to become centers of Jewish life, adding meeting rooms, auditoriums and gymnasiums to their sanctuaries. Finally, the 1920's were the days when the national ideological movements began to crystallize into their present form, and the time when the generation gap between immigrants and their children started becoming more visible. Nevertheless, there was, as yet, no evidence of assimilation.

On the international scene, 1921 was a year when the Soviet Union began to intensify its campaign against Jewish religion. Listen to the description in American Jewish Yearbook.

"It is too early to pass judgment on the campaign against the Jewish religion. The situation may be summed up as follows: A recent congress of the Russian communist party adopted a resolution to the effect that one of the aims of the Communists is to revolutionize the human belief in G-d. It was decided to carry on among the masses a campaign for the better understanding of religion, and (against) the spread of religiosity. The campaign against religion is thus universal in Russia. *Among Jews, however, for several reasons, the campaign seems to be much sharper than among other peoples* — employing propaganda and public demonstrations against Jews, requisitioning synagogues. Contrary to all expectations and probably due to various causes, religious feeling has been strengthened among the Jews."

In the early 1920's the civilized world seemed to show some interest in the movement for the establishment of a national home for Jews in Palestine. On May 4, 1922, the Senate of the United States unanimously passed a resolution in favor of the restoration of Palestine as a national home for the Jewish people — this after strenuous effort by the American Jewish community. It is interesting to note the kinds of tensions and countertensions — local and international — not dissimilar to our times, that existed fifty years ago.

Against this backdrop of local and international happenings, several important developments took place to help improve Jewish education.

1. The idea of community responsibility for Jewish education was born. Baltimore was a leader in this regard.

2. The idea of centralized Jewish education service began to take hold. In 1922 central agencies were organized in Baltimore, Philadelphia and Portland, Oregon, following in the wake of the founding of bureaus in New York, Minneapolis, Pittsburgh and Detroit.

3. The establishment of Hebrew colleges became a reality in the

large Jewish communities. Your own college celebrated its golden anniversary about two years ago. Plans for the professionalization of Jewish education were already on the drawing boards in the 1920's.

4. On the school level, two counter forces became apparent. On the one hand, the communal Talmud Torah began to crest in full bloom, only to have a short-lived flourish. In contrast, the congregationalization of the Jewish school began to take root.

5. The 1920's were a time when the theories of progressive education began to impact seriously various segments of the Jewish educational enterprise — with its emphasis on the child and on living experiences.

6. And, the founding of the first Jewish camps took place in the early´ 20's.

But not all was well 50 years ago in most of the Jewish educational system, populated mainly by *hadarim* and private *melamdim,* known as *siddur* peddlers. Listen to the testimony of outstanding pedagogy — a sign on a Jewish educational establishment in a saloon in New York's downtown East Side — which poignantly demonstrates the degrading level of Judaic instruction that was tolerated by the immigrants:

חדר

דא איז דער בערימטער חדר פון די בערימטע פעדאגוגין
מיסטער שאבסאוויטש און מיסטער קרימינסקי

עס ווירד אונטעריכט פון אלף בית ביז בר מצוה מיט א גרוויסארטיגען ספיטש (בר מצוה דרשה) אין ענגליש אידיש אונד לשון קודש. העברעעיש, אידעש שרייבען, עברי, חומש אין רש"י אין גמרה, תנ"ח, עברות בענגליש אדער באידעש און עברת בעברת על פי דיקדיק לויט נאך פארלאנג, אידישע היסטאריעס, רעליגיאן אלעס אופן היימישען שטייגער מיט זעהר ביליגע פרייזען. קומט אונד איבערצייגט אייך. אויך ווערין היר אידישע און דייטשעשע לעטערס געשריבען קיין יוראפ. דא ווירד אויך אבגעשבאכען אין געהיללט א קאנסער וואס די גרעסטע פראפעסאארען קענין נישט אויסהיילען.

רעווערענד שאבסאוויש
בארימטער מוהל און מסדר קידישין

English translation:

HEDER

Here is the famous heder of the famous pedagogs
MISTER SOVSOVITCH and MISTER KRIMINSKY

Here is taught from Aleph Beth until Bar Mitzvah with an outstanding speech (the Bar Mitzvah sermon) in English, Yiddish and the Holy Tongue. Hebrew, Yiddesh (note misspelling), writing, Ivri, Humash, with Rashi with Gemara (misspelled), Tanach (misspelled), Hebrew (misspelled) in Hebrew (misspelled) according to grammar (misspelled) as you require, Jewish history, religion all in a homey (traditional) fashion with very low prices. Come and see for yourself.

Also, here are written Yiddish and German letters to Europe. Here is also exorcized and healed a cancer that the biggest professors are unable to heal.

REVEREND SOVSOVISH (spelled differently than above)
FAMOUS MOHEL AND MARRIAGE PERFORMER
(misspelled)

It is abundantly clear that Jews, rich or poor, who tolerated such poor teaching conditions, subjected their children to woefully inferior educational instruction, the unfortunate results of which are all too well known to us.

Not all teachers were like Mr. Sovsovitch and Mr. Kriminsky. Colorful, painfully touching stories can be told about the early Jewish schools, about recruitment of teachers, about salary payments, about teaching conditions, and about teaching practices, particularly during the Depression years.

The Jewish education profession has changed significantly since those times. To be sure, significant advances have been made in teacher welfare; giant strides have been made in teacher certification and in the professionalization of Hebrew instruction. No comparison can be drawn between the modern Hebrew teacher and his more unfortunate predecessor. However, the Jewish teaching profession is still haunted by the ghost of the *melamed*.

In 1920, 75-85% of Jewish children were not receiving any kind of formal Jewish education. In the early 20's, some leaders of the

New York and Brooklyn Jewish communities organized the Jewish Education Association — a prestigious lay group for the advancement of Jewish education in New York City. Believing that at any time not more than one out of seven of the children of school age in Greater New York was receiving any Jewish training, "the Association set for its aim the stimulation and organization of the community to extend Jewish educational facilities and schools to this vast army of a quarter of a million of Jewishly unschooled children." And at that time, with the exception of a handful of yeshivot, the Jewish day school was but a dream.

We've come a long way since the 1920's. It is not necessary to record all the differences between 1922 and 1972. They are self-evident. One of the major things that has changed is the tempo of life — the pace of change. In the 1920's, a year (even a decade) was the time span to measure events and change. Today it is not even the month or the week, but the day and hour that measure cataclysmic changes in our society and in the world.

It is in this dynamic setting that I see the challenges of the 1970's to Jewish education, particularly to central agencies for Jewish education. The problems and challenges we face now are in large measure the products of seeds sown some fifty years ago. They are, to be sure, an extension or magnification of some of the very tensions and developments initiated five decades ago. I see them as the gut issues of the Jewish community, as the test of the Jewish community's viability. They are either the problem or the promise of our very survival as Jews.

There are four key education challenges to which we must respond with effectiveness if the Jewish community is to thrive fifty years from now. They are: 1) the crisis of role perception; 2) the crisis of polarization; 3) the crisis of construct; 4) the crisis of manpower.

The Crisis of Role Perception

"Who is responsible for what?" is the question that best characterizes this crisis. What are the respective roles of parents (individually and as a group), the synagogue, the independent day school and the community — read Federation? Who speaks for Jewish education? Professionals or lay leaders? Federation executives or Bureau executives? Rabbi or principals? Parents or school boards of directors?

One thing is sure: the role of school is to provide quality education to its children via the effective instruction of trained teachers under the effective guidance of trained supervisors and with the wholehearted support and encouragement of parents.

A key problem concerns the dichotomous views of Federation and the synagogue. The result of this condition is the seemingly never-ending tug of war regarding responsibility for the financial support of Jewish schooling. The real question is how committed are the synagogues and the organized community to Jewish education? The most visible way to demonstrate commitment is for synagogues to maximize their support and for Federation to increase funding for Jewish education, thus encouraging schools and bureaus to fulfill thair obligation to provide quality service to their respective constituents.

To be sure, parents (where they are able) have a primary responsibility for funding the educational experiences of their progeny. The synagogue and the day school — the direct providers of Jewish schooling — have a second-level obligation to finance the programs they sponsor. Beyond these two levels of funding, the organized community has a basic responsibility for the maintenance and enhancement of Jewish education, including the provision of shared services that schools cannot provide for themselves. Jewish education must be viewed by the Jewish community as an investment in our future. The feeling of responsibility for the support of the instrumentality that directly insures Jewish continuity must replace the present Jewish communal attitude that views Jewish education as a consumer good.

We must perceive our Jewishly deprived families with the same urgency as the black community views its disadvantaged population, and as the federal government now considers education as the necessary, fundamental requirement for national security.

The Crisis of Polarization

One of the major problems in the Jewish community is, to use a Yiddish expression, "Yedder ainer macht shabbos far zich." Everyone is doing his own thing. Whether they are child-oriented programs, informal education activities or adult education — eveyone seems to be addressing the challenge in different ways. This problem can best be underscored by the insightful interpretation of our Talmudic sages of a critical statement in the Bible.

After the golden calf was fashioned by Aaron, the high priest, in order to mollify the children of Israel who were impatiently awaiting the return of Moses from the summit of Mt. Sinai, they emoted while pointing to the golden calf, "These are your gods, oh Israel, that have taken you out of the land of Egypt." The obvious question here is "Why the usage of the plural 'gods'?" In truth, notes the Talmud, the Israelites made not one but thirteen calves — one for each tribe, and one master calf to be used as needed. The sin of the golden calf was not the making of an idol. The transgression was that each tribe thought it knew the best way to respond to Moses' lingering absence. None of the tribes would cooperate with others in addressing this problem.

A pluralistic response to a problem is not a sin. However, when unity is needed, when cooperation is required for effective action, individual competing responses constitute a transgression. They impede the development of a potentially significant action made possible only by cooperative endeavor.

Our modern problem of too many responses is twofold: there is inadequate funding to implement all the programs. Moreover, many of the programs often compete with each other and duplicate services.

While it is basic to a voluntary system that each ideological group find responses to its own particular needs, there are always opportunities for intergroup cooperation. In this spirit, the central agency for Jewish education and the ideological movements must find ways for accommodation in the bureau setting within the framework of "unity in diversity."

The Crisis of Construct

It is abundantly clear from research findings in general education over the last decade that school is, at best, a reinforcer of values, attitudes and even behavior patterns acquired at home.

Since a growing number of homes are Jewishly value-free and fewer and fewer parents provide a Jewish ambience for their children, there is a need to create alternative environments to nourish the Jewish behavior of Jewish school pupils. A positive, rich learning climate is an important setting for all learning. It is particularly critical for the Jewish school, which has to do battle with and counteract the negative influence of the home and street.

Clearly, one of the advantages of the Jewish day school is its all-day, full-time construct. To be effective, the day school must provide the alternative environment. This means facilitating the confluence of the cognitive intellectual and affective emotional domains.

As far as the supplementary school is concerned, the Jewish community must support efforts to develop regular (monthly) weekend total immersion programs — "retreats" from Friday noon to Sunday afternoon. These can take the place of one or two weeks of formal classroom study each month for grades 4, 5 and 6.

The problem of the "non-Jewish" Jewish home can be solved in two ways — either by Judaizing the home (this should be given serious consideration) and/or by providing alternative environments via which Jewish youth can experience Jewish life.

The Crisis of Manpower

The ghosts of the "melamed," the "lo yutzlach," the "siddur peddler" have impoverished Jewish education and Jewish life. While the Jewish education profession — if it may so be called — has come a long way, it is beleaguered by its image as a non-profession. If truth be told, neither the current levels of educator remuneration in an economically upwardly mobile Jewish community nor the conditions of employment in the Jewish school have the power to attract bright young people to make careers in Jewish education.

In the first instance, we need new models of Jewish teachers who can create excitement in the classroom, utilize informal educational strategies in the school and relate effectively to parents and peers of pupils.

In order to attract young people who can serve as models, it is critical that parents, schools and community make the necessary investment in educator preservice and inservice and upgrade compensation of effective educators, so that Jewish education can compete with other professions.

There are many young, potentially effective educators now serving Jewish schools. It is the combined obligation of schools and community to make available the necessary professional growth opportunities that will enhance their instructional and supervisory performance.

Moreover, there are many young people who would become Jewish educators, if but the community wills it by supporting their preservice training, enhancing their entry level salaries and guaranteeing their professional growth.

"Glancing back and looking ahead." In retrospect the early 1900's provide us with many nostalgic moments as well as a feeling that all was not so Jewishly positive. The prospect holds the promise of a bright future in which the Board of Jewish Education in Baltimore can play a vital role.

When asked what he considered his best artistic creation, Chagall thought a moment and then replied, "The next one!" Together by our enhanced efforts, we can insure that the next fifty years of Jewish life can be qualititatvely better than the last fifty years by guaranteeing quality Jewish education to our future builders.

Mazel Tov on your Yovel! More power to you!

ISSUES

AND

CHALLENGES

— 16 —

PUBLIC EDUCATION
AND THE JEWISH SCHOOL

*Address given at
a meeting of the National Executive Council
of the American Jewish Committee, Chicago,
Novemeber 2, 1984*

It is here like never before! The great stir about education. As one educator recently noted in a Harvard University symposium, "The rapid fire dissemination of reports has created a sense of urgency within the educational community. There is an eagerness to act . . ."[1] Indeed, as we heard today, and according to all the accounts we have read, the great stir has had national, statewide and local impact. The states are busily involved in finding the most effective ways to bring about dramatic improvements in education.

From my own experience in New York State, as a member of several of the Education Commissioner's Advisory Councils and the Governor's Committee on Education, I can attest to the eagerness of New York's Board of Regents and legislature to act decisively and quickly. Unquestionably, a strong sense of urgency undergirds the new efforts being launched in the name of educational improvement.

How does all the fuss being made about education during the last two years relate to Jewish education? How can the Jewish community most benefit from the spate of reports and the new rush of activity for education? What lessons can we learn from the manifold recommendations regarding public education?

At the Board of Jewish Education of Greater New York we were interested in obtaining answers to questions like these. Consequently, we thought it would be important to determine the extent to which the various segments of the Jewish educational community felt that the recommendations of the reports and studies being issued were relevant to Jewish schools.

To accomplish this, we developed a 32-item instrument which summarized the key recommendations of five of the major national studies and administered it in Greater New York and nine other communities.[2] Forty-seven percent of the 1076 respondents to the questionnaire are professional Jewish educators. Fifty-three percent are parents and lay leaders.

Seven of the 32 recommendations were singled out as having utmost relevance to Jewish schooling. I will refer to these in my discussion.

Essentially, there are four imperatives to be adduced regarding Jewish education from the current developments in general education.

1). Despite the fact that historically Jewish learning and Jewish scholarship have played an important role in Jewish life, Jewish education as a communally-supported venture has not been a priority community concern. Jewish schooling has been relegated largely to the domain of the home and the synagogue and left to special interest groups of intensely motivated individuals seeking to promulgate the study of Torah.

As one of the songs of the Broadway show, *Damn Yankees*, bellowed out, "Whatever Lola Wants Lola Gets," indeed, the Jewish community has the kind of Jewish educational enterprise and level of Jewish education that it has sought. There are a variety of examples of intensive quality Jewish education and many models of poor, ineffective Jewish schooling. The American Jewish Committee, via its Jewish Affairs Committee, over the years, has been partner to and sponsor of forums and research relating to the status and needs of Jewish education in America. The picture emerging from these and other studies and considerations of Jewish education is not rosy. The chief reason for this condition is that Jewish education has not been a priority concern of the organized Jewish community.

Over the past decade many Jewish communal leaders, heretofore unconcerned about Jewish schooling, have evinced a greater interest in Jewish education and its role in Jewish life. Their new attitude has been spurred on and reinforced by realities of the Jewish community: Jewish apathy, declining level of Jewish affiliation, intermarriage, disinterest of their own children in Jewish life, and the gnawing question, who will follow us in Jewish communal leadership?

Hopefully, the effect of the current stir in public education will be to broaden and deepen the sense of urgency within all segments of the American Jewish population, particularly among Jewish communal leaders, about the state of Jewish education and about the need for quality Jewish schooling.

Exploiting the upsurge of interest in public education in order to make Jewish education a priority on the Jewish communal agenda is, then, the first imperative.

2) The second imperative has to do with the profession of Jewish education and the relative roles of professionals and parents regarding the Jewish education of children.

In a landmark report entitled "A Place Called School," its author, John Goodlad, reminds us that "just a few years ago, any serious discussions of how to improve schools . . . was aborted frequently by the explanation that 'everything depends upon the teacher.' The conventional wisdom today in many quarters is that 'eveything depends on the principal.'"[3] There is, as Goodlad notes, some semblance of truth in each of these pronouncements. But, while teachers can exert great influence on children and on the learning process and principals have the power to influence the school climate and the nature of schooling in their respective buildings, each of these statements is simplistic and misdirected. Nevertheless, without effective teachers and principals we might as well close up our Jewish schools.

It is wrong to paint the picture of Jewish education or Jewish schools with a single brush. As you know, there are two major modes of formal Jewish education: the all-day school and the supplementary school. In the former, children receive their total Jewish and general education. Currently, in the United States about one-third of the Jewish pupil population is enrolled in Jewish all-day schools and yeshivot. The supplementary school is just what its name implies. It supplements for two to six hours per week, usually in a congregational setting, the general education a Jewish child receives. It is well known in Jewish educational circles that day school education is a more effective vehicle for Jewish instruction.

This is due to a variety of reasons: the all-embracing day-long Jewish atmosphere; the amount of time devoted to Jewish studies; the presence of full-time career Jewish studies teachers; and the support of parents for this kind of schooling.

Jewish supplementary education is plagued with serious problems — insufficient involvement and support of lay leaders; apathetic parents who send their kids to the congregational school in order to get Bar or Bat Mitzvahed; the lack of sufficient time for instruction; part-time, inadequately prepared teachers and principals; and the lack of continuity beyond age thirteen.

In the public education arena, the Rand Corporation Study entitled "Beyond the Commission Reports" warns that a general shortage of teachers is imminent.[4]

In Jewish education, the teacher shortage is already here full blast. In fact, the Jewish Affairs Committee has issued recently a background paper on this subject.[5]

Day schools and supplementary schools both suffer from the shortage of qualified personnel. Unless something drastic takes place within the next several years to change the current personnel trends we will have no teacher candidates at all, certainly no quality young people who want to become career Jewish educators. Clearly, this points to the need to do those things that will attract talented young persons to teaching: raise salaries, recognize teacher achievement, reward meritorious performance, elevate the social status of Jewish school personnel, and provide teachers with opportunities for professional advancement.

Three of the seven recommendations which were singled out to be extremely relevant by respondents in our BJE Study relate to teachers. These are: "Increase significantly the base salary of all *entering* teaching personnel"; "Increase significantly the base salary of all *current* teaching personnel"; and "Devise ways to honor teachers." No commentary is required here.

Simultaneously with higher status and higher salaries, we should be able to professionalize teaching in Jewish schools along the lines recommended by the Rand Report for the public sector, and incorporate in Jewish teaching those features that help most modern professions to ensure and allow competent performance. We would:

1) make entry requirements more rigorous;
2) provide supervised induction of teachers;
3) encourage autonomous performance;
4) develop peer-defined standards of practice; and
5) assign greater responsibility to teachers with increased competence.[6]

Unlike public education, Jewish education is voluntary. Essentially, each school is a world unto its own. Jewish education is not burdened by the kind of bureaucratic structures we find in public education. Yet, we do not use this to advantage.

Moveover, Jewish schools are small by public school standards. But we don't exploit this condition to personalize and humanize the instructional process. Jewish schools are free to involve parents and community without having to worry about some superstructure in their way.

In a recent issue of *Phi Delta Kappan,* Chester Finn strongly suggests, among others, that schools be encouraged to develop responsible, creative school-level autonomy, or what he calls "strategic independence."[7] In this vein, Goodlad recommends that schools "must become largely self-directing."[8]

Jewish schools are marked by their school-level independence. Yet, do they use their autonomy to greatest advantage regarding teachers, for example? With rare exception, there are no unions in Jewish schools. Education leaders could rather easily initiate innovative career ladder programs and institute plans that reward outstanding performance. Yet, these kinds of initiatives have not been forthcoming.

Regarding the role of principal, it is abundantly clear that in small schools (and most Jewish schools are small) the principal plays an exceedingly important role in setting the objectives of the school program and establishing the tone and quality of school life.

The study conducted by the Board of Jewish Education of Greater New York conclusively demonstrates that teachers, principals, parents and lay leaders alike feel that "improving academic leadership and supervision" is the single most important school-based *educational* challenge the Jewish community currently faces.[9]

Indeed, John Goodlad, in his Study of Schooling, recommends that "each district superintendent take, as first order of business, responsibility for selecting promising prospective principals and developing in them — and in present principals — the ability to lead and manage.[10] This is so very critical for Jewish schools where creative school leadership is so lacking.[11]

The role of parents in Jewish education is crucial. Without parental involvement and family support the Jewish school — particularly the supplementary school — cannot hope to be an effective educational instrumentality. Despite the criticism, in some quarters of the research of James Coleman and Christopher Jencks and their colleagues emphasizing the primacy of the home in instruction, their conclusions about the key role of parents and family in influencing the quality and effectiveness of classroom instruction especially pertain to Jewish schools.[12]

By and large, Jewish schools are not at fault for the quality of what takes place within the school walls. General education has its fierce critics and detractors. The truth is that while school support is often verbalized in our society it is not very evident in the statewide and local appropriations made for the schools. Neither do the schools enjoy the support they require from the home. The Coleman and Jencks research findings strike at the heart of this condition.[13] If there is no will or commitment on the part of the parents, there will be no desire for learning on the part of the students; and what we will have are flat, unexciting, wasted classroom hours — turn-off instead of turn-on.

David Seeley, former President of the New York Public School Association, calls the products teachers try to sell to unwilling pupils from unmotivated homes "undeliverable merchandise."[14] The problem with much of our teaching, he claims, is that teachers teach too hard. Students don't learn hard enough. You can't teach pupils, he concludes. You can only learn 'em.

3) Imperative number three deals with the goals and curricula of Jewish education. Some of the criticism of the reports on public education center on their great emphasis on scholastic achievement to the exclusion of other kinds of learning. It goes without saying that the cognitive domain is a significant concern of Jewish education.

Learning for learning's sake occupies an important place in Jewish tradition. But, for our current Jewish education needs, given the composition of our student population (with the exception of children from Orthodox homes) transmitting knowledge per se is not an overriding goal.

In Jewish schools we are as concerned with the Jewish attitudes and behavior of students as with the knowledge they have gained.

David Cohen of Harvard criticizes the goals set forth in the reports for their overemphasis on solving what he calls the "Toyota problem." The reports underscore the need to improve productivity and efficiency, yet they give little or no attention to teaching children how and why to participate in the democratic process.[15]

Translated into Jewish educational terms, this suggests that Jewish schools should give greater attention to the affective domain — helping children participate in Jewish life by learning *how* to live Jewishly and *why* they should do so.

In the past several years there have been a variety of innovative Jewish curriculum efforts made by various Jewish groups across the country. To date, there is no way of measuring how they are improving Jewish education. What we really need is a greater understanding of what we want to achieve and greater commitment to accomplishing our objectives. This requires commitment and cooperation on the part of lay leaders, principals, rabbis, teachers, parents and pupils.

While they are generally outside the pale of the Jewish community, it is interesting to note that the sectarian ultra-Orthodox and Hasidic groups know exactly what they want to achieve in their schools. Their educational programs are enthusiastically supported by the parents; the professional personnel are singularly committed to the realization of the yeshiva's objectives; and the schools provide ample time to accomplish their aims. Indeed, in their terms, they eminently succeed in realizing their objectives.

4) The fourth imperative relates to the support of the education system. Reacting to the recent spate of national reports on public education, Harold Howe II, former U.S. Commissioner of Education, wrote, "Suddenly, corporate barons, presidential candidates, university presidents, governors, and legislative leaders in Congress and in state capitals have mounted a crusade to improve schools . . . Will the governors, the corporate leaders and the others who are now

fanning the fires of educational reform be willing to stay with that important task over time?"[16]

In response, Howe said, "The kinds of changes now being recommended will not come easily or quickly because *they challenge vested interests.* It is essential that the interest of groups outside education be sustained and, particularly, that business leadership remain supportive, since one necessity for educational improvement is more tax money to support that improvement."[17]

Howe's blunt analysis and recommendation apply with particular force to Jewish education. (Incidentally, the reports offer little advice on how to obtain the huge amounts of money needed to carry out their recommendations.)

Will the Jewish community meet the challenge of more fiscal support?

The BJE Study findings underscore the urgency of the challenge. Every one of the respondents, without exception, views the recommendation to increase communal funding to Jewish schools on both *national and local levels to be "absolutely essential.*[18]

In the context of voluntarism, Jewish schools are, by and large, fiscally dependent upon parents via tuition fees and membership dues, and on the sponsoring groups (the school boards and synagogues), through a variety of fund raising activities.

The major source of *communal* support for Jewish education on the local scene is the Federation. Although not quite keeping up with the increases in grants for all other local needs, Federation allocations to Jewish education increased significantly over the past twenty years to its current level of $45 million. Of this amount, $13 million is allocated to central agencies and $32 million is distributed to educational institutions, largely to Jewish day schools.

To place the amount of local communal support in proper perspective we must realize that the $45 million represents only 7% of the total annual expenditures ($600,000,000) for Jewish education on this continent. Increasing the level of communal funding for Jewish education will require setting new Federation priorities. This upward change in support, as Howe points out for the public sector, will not come easily or quickly because it challenges vested interests.

The problem in the Jewish community is that the vested interests are good humanitarian causes. Nevertheless, if Jewish education is to make its much needed potential contribution to the continuity and enrichment of Jewish life, changes in Federation funding priorities will have to take place. Support of Jewish education must be viewed as an urgent Jewish *communal* responsibility since it concerns the very quality and future of Jewish life.

Increased Federation funding will have to be accompanied by increased support from those parents who can afford it and from synagogues.[19]

Parenthetically, the problem of Jewish school finance in Montreal — a bastion of all-day education — has been greatly alleviated by the significant allocation of funds by the Province of Quebec. This government posture relates directly to the current debate in the United States over the First Amendment and the conflicting interpretations ascribed to the concept of separation of church and state and the idea of accommodation.

National Jewish support to Jewish education is virtually non-existent. Not only is there no national or continental Jewish instrumentality for subsidizing Jewish educational efforts, but the several national Jewish agencies dealing with formal and informal education are supported by local communal funding.

Providing support for Jewish education via a national or continental instrumentality requires the development of an appropriate funding mechanism not unlike the U.S. federal government Title IV and Chapter II programs, or the large private foundations that support secular, cultural and educational endeavors. The time has come for the organized Jewish community to begin considering ways in which it could provide the necessary national leverage to maximize the effectiveness of Jewish education. This is in addition to the need for increasing substantially *local* support for Jewish education.

Louis Rubin notes in the recent issue of *Educational Leadership,* "In the aftermath of the reports, what is abundantly clear is that school improvement must be achieved through local policies."[20] This is equally true for Jewish schools.

However, for Jewish education, national initiatives are also needed. After all, only 370,000 pupils are enrolled in Jewish schools in North America. While spread over the whole continent, the relatively small size of the total Jewish school enterprise lends itself to a concentrated continent-wide stimulus for change and improvement on the local level. Indeed, such an effort is necessary and long overdue.

Essentially, the national initiative should provide matching seed money and guidance to local communities for developing creative responses to their unique educational needs.

In sum, there are many problems that beg to be addressed in Jewish education. Using the current spate of reports and studies in public education as a frame of reference, the most important challenges facing the Jewish community are: creating a sense of urgency about the critical needs of Jewish education; responding quickly and effectively to the critical personnel problems; finding ways to provide greater parental and communal support to Jewish schooling, establishing clear curricular objectives that will yield needed results; providing the time to achieve these purposes; and providing the financial wherewithal to make improvements possible. This latter challenge means increasing significantly local support to Jewish schools and creating a national foundation to fund and guide the development of much needed innovative initiatives.

REFERENCES

(1)   Barranco, John, "Accountable after the politicians have moved one . . ." in "Symposium on the Year of the Reports: Responses from the Educational Community," *Harvard Education Review,* Vol. 54, No. 1, Febrary 1984, p. 6.

(2)   Schiff, A.I. and Botwinick, C., "The Relevance of the Recommendations of Major National Studies on Education to Jewish Schooling;" *Jewish Education,* Vol. 52, No. 2, Summer 1984, p. 7.

(3)   Goodlad, John, *A Place Called School,* New York, McGraw-Hill Book Company, 1984, p. XVI.

(4)   Darling-Hammond, Linda, "Beyond the Commission Reports—The Coming Crisis in Teaching," the Rand Corporation, July 1984.

(5)   Wachs, Saul, "The Jewish Teacher: Professional Status," American Jewish Committee, 1984.

(6)   Darling-Hammond, Linda, *op. cit.,* p. 17.

(7)   Finn, Chester E., Jr., "Toward Strategic Independence: Nine Commandments for Enhancing School Effectiveness," *Phi Delta Kappan,* April 1984, p. 518.

(8)   Goodlad, John, *op. cit.,* p. 276.

(9)   Schiff, A. I., and Botwinick, C., *op. cit.,* p. 9.

(10)   Goodlad, John, *op. cit., p. 277.*

(11)   Schiff, Alvin I., "Focus on the Jewish School Principal," *Jewish Education,* Vol. 43, No. 4, 1980, p. 2.

(12)   Coleman, James S., *Equality of Educational Opportunity,* Washington, Government Printing Office, 1966.
Jencks. Christopher, *Inequality, A Reassessment of the Effect of Family and Schooling in America,* New York, Basic Books 1972.

(13)   ibid.

(14)   Seeley, David. *Education Through Partnership: Mediating Structures and Education,* Cambridge, Mass., Ballinger Publishing Co., 1981.

(15)   Cohen, David, "The Condition of Teachers' Work" in *Harvard Education Review,* Vol. 54, No. 1, Feb. 1984, p. 12.

(16)   Howe, Harold II, "Education Moves to Center Stage: An Overview of Recent Studies," *Phi Delta Kappan,* November, 1983, p. 167, 169.

(17)   Howe, Harold II, "The Unattended Issues of Recent Educational Studies," *The Education Digest,* May 1984, p. 2.

(18)   Schiff, A.I. and Botwinick, C., *op. cit.*

(19)   Schiff, Alvin I., "Funding Jewish Education: Whose Responsibility?," *Jewish Education,* Vol. 42. No. 4, Summer 1973, p. 5.

(20)   Rubin, Louis, "Formulation Education Policy in the Aftermath of the Reports," of *Educational Leadership,* vol. 42, No. 2, October 1984, p. 10.

− 17 −

ON THE NEED
FOR MORAL EDUCATION

Presented at Conference On
Moral Education
in The Jewish Day School
School of Education, Harvard University
February 9, 1986

The Jewish Day School Is Special

It is my pleasant task to set the stage for this conference on
Moral Education in the Jewish Day School. What started out as a
small consultation has become a major conference, and I'm delighted
that I was asked to initiate it. Whether or not we agree with Lawrence
Kohlberg's taxonomy, his sequence of stages of moral development,
his view of authority, his approach to pedagogy or his concentration
on the cognitive judgmental side of moral development, one thing is
crystal clear. Dr. Kohlberg has helped a generation of educators to
focus more knowledgeably and more effectively on the concept and
practice of moral education. This fact is the underlying significance of
such a meeting at Harvard University's School of Education.

When invited to make the opening presentation I asked myself, "Why a special conference on moral education for the Jewish day school? Moral education is moral education is moral education. American children are American children are American children. Teachers are teachers are teachers. Can't we treat moral education in the Jewish day school as we would deal with this challenge in other schools?

There is a difference — a uniqueness that characterizes the Jewish day school and makes this meeting different, special.

The Jewish day school is special because the children and teachers bring special baggage to their school setting. The day school environment is unique by virtue of its dual purpose, dual objectives, dual curriculum, dual language program, dual sets of teachers and principals, its dual role models and its pervading Jewish atmosphere. These distinguishing sets of characteristics justify a special conference on moral education in the Jewish day school.

To be sure, teachers in Jewish day schools share common responsibilities with teachers in other kinds of schools. It is not what teachers know, but what they do; not the content that they have acquired to transmit, but the way they behave in the classroom; not their pedagogical knowledge, but the way they teach that distinguishes all teachers as special influences on the lives of students in their charge. Yet, Jewish day school teachers are different. They may share many goals and objectives with teachers in other schools — public and non-public — and may face many of the same problems regarding the realization of these goals. Still, Jewish day school teachers, particularly instructors of Jewish studies, are different because they teach in special settings and have a specialized Judaic-American mission.

Reasons for Emphasis on Moral Education

A need for teaching morality in Jewish day schools derives from recent publicity about the unethical behavior of people, some of whom, in their youth, attended Jewish day schools. This is not to say that the Jewish day school bears any responsibility for the immorality of its graduates, or that unethical activity of day school graduates is a more acute problem than that of adults not exposed to a Jewish all-day school experience. I think that the opposite is true. However, recent extremely serious incidents of unethical business activity highlight the need for day schools to try to insure, no matter how difficult this may be, that such happenings will not take place in the future.

Recently, I received a letter from a leading litigation lawyer — himself a parent of Jewish day school children — who has become vitally interested in this subject. He writes, "In the . . . leasing case, [involving some of our most visible lay leaders] the most gripping point for me was . . . 's [the defendant's] testimony about his time at the Chase Manhattan Bank, how he rose in position in the international division, and how he turned down a post as a leader of a group because it would have required travel on Shabbat. . . . said that he thought that Chase was anti-Semitic, and he quit to join his relative . . .

"A second series of incidents which come to mind have to do with the phantom students in the Federal school feeding programs. So-called pious people find it acceptable to misrepresent in order to obtain money from the government. [The prime example of this is the well publicized summer feeding program in which many institutions of all religious denominations — Jewish and non-Jewish — and many institutions in the public sector were found guilty of fraud relating to phantom campers for whom they collected millions of dollars through the summer feeding program.]

"A third incident is a case which I have handled for a long number of years, . . . vs. . . . Here, devout Jews who dress distinctively and probably never miss a prayer were found guilty and convicted of criminal misconduct in connection with a very large-scale commodities fraud. The evidence showed perjured affidavits on the accounts, laundering of money to cheat on taxes, and reneging on a million dollar debt. This was as if to say that inside the community there's a different set of morals than those which pertain to the outside world.

"A fourth set of incidents has to do with the stealing of Regents examinations in a non-Orthodox day school. The stealing of exams is the result of student proclivity for cheating on tests, which occurs in all schools in the public and private sectors with scant adverse comment."

While the cases cited by this lawyer do not provide evidence that would indicate that Jewish day schools are at fault for that which happened, the schools have a role to play in helping prevent such occurrences from taking place.

The need for special instruction in moral development is interestingly expressed by Arthur Coombs in his delightful little volume, *Myths of Education.* "There are many good things about education today. We have beautiful school buildings, good programs, excellent materials, dedicated teachers and devoted principals. The problem is that the parents send us the wrong children."[1] Like all educational institutions, Jewish day schools have some pupils who are the "wrong" children with real moral dilemmas. Many of them find it very difficult to cope with the society around them. Many of them are the "wrong" children because their families do not associate themselves with the ideological goals of the schools which they attend.

Teachers have to learn to speak in the language of the "wrong" children. I'm reminded of an example which might not be far-fetched. When the General Motors car named Nova was exported to Latin American countries it did not sell because *Nova,* in Spanish, means "will not go." General Motors just wasn't able to communicate in the language of the people to whom it was marketing the automobile. Eventually, GM had to change the name of the car. One of our challenges is training teachers to communicate meaningfully with all our children.

Can we teach morality in the Jewish day school without regard to the goal of the Jewish home? Can moral education be wholly effective, independent of an approach involving the homes of the children in the school? James Coleman,[2] Christopher Jencks[3] and David Cohen[4] in their trailblazing research in the 1960's, clearly demonstrated the necessity for home support in order to achieve educational effectiveness. This is certainly the case in the area of moral education. Family involvement is vital in making the connection between learning and behaving, between knowing and doing.

Another challenge has to do with the relationship between knowing and doing. An outstanding personality who personified morality and ethical behavior was the first chief rabbi of Israel (then Palestine) — Rabbi Abraham Isaac Kook. His commentary on an interesting passage in *Ethics of the Fathers* is instructive in this regard. Commenting on the statement of Rabbi Shimon ben Gamliel, who said: "All my days I have grown up among the wise, and have found nothing of better service to myself (literally, nothing better for my own body) *me-sh'teekah* — than silence."[5] Rabbi Kook noted that the term *me-sh'teekah* is universally interpreted wrongly.

It does not mean *"than* silence," rather *"from* silence." Rabbi Shimon's statement should read: "I found nothing good for myself by keeping silent." We have to bring our youth to the level of articulating moral values and acting accordingly, standing up for what is right and just, even if doing so is not very popular. This would be a high stage of moral development.

Mentioning Harav Kook brings to mind the fact that Jewish tradition places much emphasis on teaching by example. And, fortunately, there are numerous models of moral behavior upon which we can readily draw. There are many personalities whose ethical life-styles are paradigmatic including Biblical, Talmudic, Gaonic and medieval figures and contemporary luminaries such as the Chofetz Chaim and Reb Aryeh Levin. Their lives provide a wellspring of insight as to the meaning of *hesed.* Moreover, each of us can point to numerous examples of how *hesed* was lived and practiced.

In addition to transmitting knowledge of ethics from Judaic sources and citing examples of moral individuals, it is necessary to develop vehicles for transmitting the concept of ethical behavior in an experiential and visceral way to our children. Schools need to build moral development into the warp and woof of the everyday school environment by providing opportunities for students to practice *hesed.*

This brings us to another reason for emphasizing moral education as a special subject in Jewish day schools — the larger society's relationship to the Jew. To paraphrase Rabbi Yehudah Halevi, one might say that problems which affect the larger society affect the Jews more. "When the world deals with Jews," Abba Eban once said, "It forgets humanity. When it deals with humanity, it forgets Jews." How do teachers in Jewish day high schools deal with the world's inhumanity to Jews, with the world's indifference to Jews, its baseless antagonism to Israel, the U.N. "Zionism is Racism" resolution? Moreover, how do we react to the revisionist historians of the Holocaust? What do we tell our children? Given these facts, should Jews be only for themselves? How do we interpret "If I am not for myself, who will be for me?" How do these questions relate to the development of moral judgment?

There is value to this conference for other reasons. It will help us focus on the great repositories of Jewish tradition and will motivate us to consider the more effective use of Judaic sources that deal with Jewish values and morality.

The problem is that in our daily lives we often compartmentalize Judaic teachings. For many Jews, the commandments or deeds that express man's relationship to God have overshadowed the role of the mitzvot between man and man. In this regard, once again, I come back to the letter from my lawyer friend.

He writes, "The distinction often made between ritual observance and moral conduct is without merit. It has to be done away with. The point should be made that everyone has base tendencies, and wrapping oneself in ritual and prayer is no guarantee that we will be able to resist the temptations of making money improperly. What to do about it is a different problem, and teaching cannot be satisfactory merely to extol appropriate precepts. I think it might be useful to develop a case method approach, with different extracts from the *Mishnah, Gemara* and *Responsa* that bear on the problem, leaving it to the students and their discussions to make appropriate applications. I think it might be useful to take some of the problem areas in the Bible and subject them to moral analyses. Close reading of the texts suggests, in many if not all the situations, that heavy penalties were ultimately paid by those who took advantage of deception to gain ends." These comments, made by a perceptive, committed Jewish leader underscore some of the challenges at hand.

This coming week's portion of the Torah, which deals with the Tabernacle, the sanctuary and the priestly service, opens with God's statement to Moses, "Speak to the children of Israel and tell the Israelite people to bring me gifts and you shall accept gifts for me from every person whose heart so moves him."[6] How can we move hearts? How do we create the desire for children to share with others? How do we develop the ability to rise above self, and to help build or contribute to the building of a trust community? In the long run, responding effectively to these questions is the universal raison d'etre of moral development in all educational settings.

Another value of the conference is that it will help us focus on the relationship between Torah and *mada* — the confluence between general studies and Jewish studies, between science and religion. Developing moral judgment speaks to the dynamics of this relationship. We hope this meeting will help us to learn to use real life situations and analyze them in light of Torah values. At this moment, the tragic explosion of the *Challenger* poses obvious questions that beg for responses.

Reservations about Potential Effectiveness of Moral Education

In preparing for today's assignment, I polled the principals of several day schools and several BJE staff members who work with day schools about their perceptions of moral education and the Jewish day schools. This poll of some thirty Jewish educators demonstrates unanimity of feeling about the need for moral education. Yet, some expressed doubts about its potential success. For example, one principal noted, "We really are not concentrating on this area, but perhaps we cannot just compete with society." Another said that the challenge to Jewish education in light of violence and immorality on TV, in the movies, newspapers, and "in the air we breathe" is to find ways to educate teachers and parents regarding societal problems — drugs, stealing and sexual behavior. But, given today's societal norms, "It may be virtually impossible for the *school* to deal with such issues. We must first reach the family."

In a similar vein, another principal said, "There used to be a time when the Jewish community was insulated from societal ills. At least the children were. Today, however, everything is out in the open, we have absolutely no control. Nevertheless, we must try to do our best." Said another principal, "There are very few role models for children. Teachers are not respected in the community. This condition in turn, affects the perception of pupils."

Despite these observations and other similar comments, all the principals agreed that special attention to moral education and curricular materials on moral education are desperately needed.

Focusing Religious Instruction on Moral Values

As we prepare for the various phases of this conference, one of our challenges relates directly to the role of Kohlbergian thought in the Jewish school. How does one resolve moral dilemmas from a religious or halachic point of view? Can one break a Judaic tenet to reach a higher moral stage in life? Is that halachically possible? Is there an internal inconsistency between Kohlbergian theory and Judaic thought and tradition?

Some time ago, I learned from one of my Catholic colleagues about three stages of moral development developed by a Belgian Catholic theologian: the taboo stage, the ethical-moral stage, and the religious-spiritual stage. According to this theologian, the third stage integrates and internalizes the ethical moral stage. It brings people to the understanding that religious, spiritual values elevate a person to the highest possible stage of moral behavior. In Judaism, the ethical-moral and religious-spiritual are integrated willy-nilly. How does that theory square with Kohlbergian ideas? Responding to this question is one of our challenges at this conference.

Last year, at the New York State Board of Regents and State Education Department Bicentennial Convocation, Jacob Lawrence, a black artist and one of the awardees of the convocation, told me: "You know, many of us look; few of us see. Many of us see the vast expanse of the lawn; few of us appreciate a blade of grass."[7] This seems to express the real meaning of the Aggadic discourse of Rabbi Yochanan who said, "Every place you find the greatness of God there you find also his humility."[8] Reaching this stage of understanding — appreciating the blade of grass — is the goal of moral education.

And now back to the question with which I began my remarks. In approaching the topic of this conference, I had a dilemma. On the one hand, moral values have been taught directly and indirectly in Jewish schools for centuries. Currently, teaching Jewish ethics is part and parcel of the curriculum of most educational institutions. In fact, many schools provide significant blocks of time for the study of *musar*. Values instruction in the classroom is generally indirect — deriving from Judaic textual study: *Humash, Mishnah, Gemara* and their respective commentaries. What teachers attempt to do is to stress "the light of the Torah" — the particular Jewish values and moral concepts emanating from the text being studied. In addition, many informal educational experiences relating to moral education and the development of ethical personalities are provided in most yeshivot.

If this is the case, if the inculcation of moral values and education for ethical conduct is part and parcel of Jewish day school and yeshiva education, why the need for a conference? In the first place, in addition to the reasons I have already given, it is clear that there is a need to heighten the focus of Jewish all-day schooling on the challenge of improving the methodology and content of moral education. Secondly, we can learn much from what has been going on within Harvard's hallowed halls and elsewhere that can be helpful to the Jewish day school movement. Thirdly, there is much we can learn from each other. The process of sharing at this conference is important for all of us, and will help each of us in our respective work settings as we deal with the challenges of moral education.

In this regard, I am reminded of the child who was trying to lift a very heavy box to no avail. He just couldn't lift it. His father, who was watching him, said: "Son, are you using all your strength?" The son replied, "Yes." The father asked, "Are you sure?" The son said, "I'm sure." The father continued, "Think about it once more. When you tried to lift the box did you use all your strength?" The boy said, "Yes, I'm positive." The father retorted, "No, you're not using all your strength; you didn't ask me." Here at the conference we're asking each other, and asking the experts to help. And we're learning from each other. There are many challenges day schools face that relate to moral education about which we can learn one from another.

To respond to all the challenges we face in moral education requires teacher training. This means convincing school leaders that we need greater investment of time, effort and money for on-the-job in-service education to help teachers succeed in the instruction of moral values.

We know how tight our budgets are, how difficult it is for schools to keep their heads above water. I'm reminded, however, that when a former resident of this city, John Quincy Adams, advocated greater government support for education, he said that "whole people must take upon themselves the education of the whole people and be willing to bear the expense of it." As Jewish education leaders we have to communicate this attitude more forcefully to the community at large and to the lay leaders of our schools, underscoring that more support has to be provided for moral education programming.

And so, upon reflection, my dilemma was resolved because it is good moral judgment to learn more about how to improve the methods we use to help our students develop better moral judgment. In this way, we guarantee that they will be more ethical adults, combining the desire to fulfill equally *mitzvot bain adam lamakom,* "mitzvot between man and the Almighty" and *mitzvot bain adam l'havero,* "mitzvot between man and man."

REFERENCES

(1)   Combs, Arthur, *Myths of Education,* Allyn and Bacon, Boston, 1979.

(2)   Coleman, James, *Equality of Educational Opportunity,* Office of Education, U.S. Department of Health, Education and Welfare, Washington, D.C. 1966.

(3)   Jencks, Christopher, *Inequality, A Reassessment of the Effect of Family and Schooling in America,* Basic Books, N.Y. 1972.

(4)   Cohen, David, "Why Curriculum Doesn't Matter," *The New Leader,* November 15, 1971, p. 16.

(5)   *Ethics of the Fathers,* 1:17.

(6)   *Exodus, 25:2.*

(7)   Lawrence, Jacob, Statement made at the New York State Board of Regents and State Education Department Bicentennial Convocation, 1986.

(8)   Talmud, Tractate *Megillah,* 31a.

– 18 –

FIGHTING DECEPTION
FOR THE SAKE OF HUMANITY

Presented at
Jews for Jesus Rally,
New York City
July 27, 1987

I rise at this time to raise my voice in strong protest on behalf of hundreds of Jewish schools, thousands of Jewish educators, and hundreds of thousands of Jewish school children and their families.

We are all terribly concerned, greatly exercised and absolutely determined that the unscrupulous mind-twisting activity we have been witnessing will *not* continue.

It is beyond belief.

It is the ultimate exploitation of America's freedoms — freedom of speech and freedom of religion.

The question is: Will American society sit idly by as a group of scheming, self-appointed saviors ingeniously distorts the truth — the truth of the Bible and the facts of history?

Will we allow a bunch of clever, deceptive entrepreneurs to apply their genius for duplicity in the name of religion?

Our answer today is we must mobilize the Jewish and Christian communities to combat this affront to Judaism, to eliminate this indignity to Christianity, and to blot out this insult to humanity.

Jews for Jesus is *not* Jewish.
Jews for Jesus is *not* Christian.
Jews for Jesus is *not* American!

Making a young person lose control over his or her own senses is not in the spirit of Judaism.

It is not in the spirit of Christianity.
It is not in the spirit of American democracy.

Being irrational and duplicitous is not the Jewish way. It is not the Christian way, nor the American way.

In this age of insecurity, when so many young people feel rootless, when so many Jewish youth lack a sense of belongingness, Jews for Jesus preys upon their insecurity.

In our open society — unfortunately so full of social, communal, psychological and physical problems — Jews for Jesus feeds on the doubts and feelings of young people in search of a way of life.

The answer of American society to this scourge must be loud and clear: "We will not tolerate it."

The response of the Jewish community to this plague must be *Jewish education*. The study of the Jewish heritage—learning Jewish sources — is the most effective way to respond to the devious missionary tactics so harmful to unsuspecting, unknowledgeable young Jews.

Jewish education makes better Jews.
Jewish education makes better American citizens.

We must offset the threat of Jews for Jesus and other missionary groups and cults by providing as many opportunities as possible for *quality* Jewish education for all Jews — young and old.

We dare not rest until we maximize our support for yeshivot and Jewish day schools; until we intensify and improve Jewish supplementary schooling.

We dare not rest until every Jewish child receives an intensive Jewish education.

Our most potent weapon in doing battle with our modern spiritual Amalekites is Torah study. Our most effective defense against the onslaught of well-funded missionary organizations is Jewish family education.

We commit ourselves at this moment of heightened concern to reach all Jews — from toddlers to the elderly — from nursery school children and kindergartners to college students, and beyond.

As patriotic Americans and good Jews we know it is our responsibility to educate our youth and adults toward moral and ethical living, toward greater Jewish commitment, toward a better American society and a more humane world.

בכל דור ודור עומדים עלינו לכלותינו.

The Jewish people have faced great crises in every generation throughout its history. We have overcome our adversaries — our Pharaohs, our Hamans and Hitlers. And, as the Bible instructs us, מחה תמחה, with God's help and our own intensified efforts, we will defeat our present day Amalekites dressed in the garb of wholesome religion and personal salvation.

For Jews, real salvation will come only through quality Jewish education and good, honest Jewish living.

In Herzl's immortal words, אם תרצו אין זו אגדה "If you will it, it will become a reality."

Our motto has been, is, and will forever be "Judaism for Jews." "Jews for Judaism."

עם ישראל חי! — Long live the Jewish people!

— 19—

DECADE OF THE JEWISH FAMILY

Prepared as background paper
for launching the
Supplementary Education Action Plan
Board of Jewish Education
of Greater New York
October 1988

I. INTRODUCTION

In Jewish tradition, beginning with Bible times, the parent played a key role in educating children. The Bible, Talmud and rabbinic writings stress parental responsibility for the schooling of their offspring. The Jewish family provided the necessary environment where Jewishness was nurtured.

In our open society, the role of the parent in the education process has all but disappeared. As for Jewish education, the role of the parent has diminished to the vanishing point. Most parents do not provide the necessary home environment needed to nourish the Jewish education experience. Most Jewish parents are simply not able to help insure the effectiveness of their children's Jewish education.

Without parental involvement the Jewish school is an irrelevant cognitive experience devoid of the affective dimensions so important for fashioning a positive Jewish outlook and for giving meaning to Jewish learning.

For these reasons the Board of Jewish Education of Greater New York is declaring the 1990s — 5750 to 5759 — *the Decade of the Jewish Family.*

II. DECLARATION OF JEWISH EDUCATIONAL RIGHTS AND RESPONSIBILITIES REGARDING THE JEWISH CHILD AND JEWISH FAMILY

A. Children's Rights

Every Jewish child has the right to a sound Jewish education and a wholesome supportive Jewish home environment.

Every Jewish child has the right to learn Hebrew, to enjoy the study of Bible and post-Biblical literature, Jewish history and Jewish life.

Every Jewish child has the right to become a Jewishly informed and knowledgeable Bar or Bat Mitzvah.

Every Jewish child has the right to attend a Jewish school which helps develop the necessary skills for wholesome Jewish family living.

Every Jewish child has the right to study in a school where parents play an active role; and where teachers, principals, cantors and rabbis relate effectively to the Jewish needs of the Jewish family.

B. Jewish Communal Responsibilities

To insure that the Jewish educational rights of Jewish children are guaranteed and maintained, it is the responsibility of the Jewish community as represented by its Jewish institutions — synagogues, schools, centers, central Jewish education agency and central communal organization —

1) to help Jewish parents to provide a supportive Jewish home environment for their children;

2) to help Jewish educators acquire Jewish family education skills to meld formal and informal Jewish education strategies in reaching and teaching Jewish children; and to provide materials and opportunities for Jewish learning in the Jewish home.

III. PURPOSE OF THE DECADE OF THE JEWISH FAMILY

To enrich Jewish life through the Jewish family;

To bring Jewish families into the Jewish education system;

To reinforce Jewish schooling through home support;

To strengthen the role of the Jewish educator via family involvement;

To make Jewish education more effective through home-school partnerships.

To insure continued Jewish communal support of vital services to the Jewish community by Jewish families.

IV. METHODOLOGY

To achieve the goals of the Decade of the Jewish Family, BJE will heighten the involvement of BJE Centers and Departments in Jewish Family Education. BJE will:

1) Reach out to marginally affiliated and unaffiliated parents via strategies developed by the Informal Outreach Educational Center;

2) Provide guidance and support to school/parent groups through the Informal Education and Outreach Center;

3) Enhance Jewish parental involvement in the home through services to principals and lay leaders;

4) Enhance the ability of schools to involve families in educational process through services to principals, administrators, teachers and lay leaders;

5) Involve teachers in Jewish family education programs through the Teachers' Centers.

6) Enrich opportunities for Jewishness in the home through Media and Computer Center activities and materials;

7) Provide Jewish educational materials for the Jewish home through BJE's Curriculum Materials Development program;

8) Help parents of pupils with special needs through the Jewish Special Education Center.

V. THE JEWISH FAMILY
AND THE JEWISH COMMUNITY

It is clear that in our open society, to be effective, Jewish schooling needs the support of the Jewish home. Moreover, to be effective, Jewish fundraising needs an informed Jewish home. According to a recent national conference on "Jewish Philanthropy in Contemporary America," one of the key reasons for the current problems of Jewish philanthropy is "the weakening of Jewish identity that comes with each new generation a Jewish family has been in America . . .

"What was in the (Jewish) people's guts in the 1930's and 1940's when people heard Yiddish in their homes and lived through the Holocaust ain't there anymore. It has to be put back in the homes . . .

"Those most inclined to give to Jewish causes seem to be older Jews who have been raised in a more insular, more Jewish environment, or they may be younger Jews intensely imbued with traditional Jewish values . . .

"The transmittal of Jewish values usually determines whether young Jews will focus their giving on Jewish causes . . .

"American Jewish philanthropy is heavily dependent not on big donors, but on the transmittal of Jewish values.

"We have to raise the level of Jewish knowledge about their own traditions and history and, most importantly, about values."

The case for supporting the Decade of the Jewish Family is made crystal clear by the Jewish communal need for the Jewish family.

– 20 –

THE JEWISH FUTURE
AND THE JEWISH FAMILY

Presented at the
Jewish Family Education Conference
Jewish Education Services
of North America
September 17, 1989

Moshe Finkelstein, a ninety-five-year-old man, would always become animated about Jewish issues, especially about Jewish problems to which he could relate. Every day his long time friend, Mr. Rappaport, would visit him and they would discuss Jewish affairs avidly.

One day Mr. Rappaport did not show up. Finkelstein waited impatiently. After an hour he phoned Mr. Rappaport:

"Why didn't you come to visit me today?"

"I don't feel well," responded Rappaport.

"You must come!" said Finkelstein.

"Why?" asked Rappaport.

"You can't imagine," retorted Finkelstein. "There are so many things happening in the Jewish world. There are so many problems and I can't handle them alone."

Indeed, there is so much happening in the Jewish world and in the world of Jewish education. We're all grateful to JESNA for convening us to deliberate about the challenge of Jewish family education, so crucial to Jewish continuity. Each of us — individuals and communities — just can't handle this challenge along. And if we could, it is our responsibility to share what we know, what we think and what we plan with others.

In this spirit, I want to make my modest contribution to this important conference.

What do Rabbi Yose ben Kisma, a third century Talmudic sage and the early twentieth century secular Zionist philosopher Asher Ginsburg (known as Ahad Ha'am) have in common?

And what do both of these scholars have to do with the French Revolution, the bicentennial year of which we are currently celebrating? And how does all this relate to Jewish family education and Jewish continuity?

We begin our answer with an episode described at the end of chapter six of *Ethics of Our Fathers:*

> Rabbi Yose ben Kisma said "Once I was walking on the road when a certain man met me. He greeted me and I returned his greeting. He said to me 'Rabbi from what place are you?' I said to him 'From a great city of scholars and sages.' He said to me 'Rabbi would you be willing to live עמנו במקומנו *with us, in our place?* I would give you thousands and thousands of golden dinars, precious stones and pearls.' I replied, 'Even if you were to give me all the silver, gold, precious stones and pearls in the world I would dwell nowhere but in a place of Torah."

According to the Maharal of Prague, Rabbi Yose refused the position because, in the language of the man extending the invitation to him, Rabbi Yose was invited not only to live "bimkomenu" — in the town physically, but also "imanu" — "with us" — to be completely in unison with the town's set of values and ambitions. This, Rabbi Yose would not do. He would not take a position in which his Jewish lifestyle would be compromised in order to fit into the pattern of living of the townsfolk.

The outcome of the French Revolution — Liberté, Egalité, Fraternité — opened the doors of communication with the wider free world to the Jews of France and to Jews in other free societies. A great blessing indeed!

Ahad Ha'am, in a penetrating essay *Hikkui V'hitbolalut* — "Imitation and Assimilation" — while hailing the value of freedom enjoyed by post-Revolution Jewry — underscored the potential dangers that this freedom brought with it to the Jewish people.

All minorities in Western society, Ahad Ha'am demonstrated, have no choice but to imitate the larger environment in which they live. Yet, there are two ways to imitate; *Hikkui shel hitbatlut* — "absorptive imitation," and *Hikkui shel hitharut* — "competitive imitation."

The First kind of imitation — *Hikkui shel hitbatlut* — leads to total assimilation. Via the second form of emulation — *Hikkui shel hitharut* — the minority group — in this case the Jews — becomes stronger and competes with the majority culture as it learns to use the technical skills and know-how of the larger society in order to communicate and reinforce its own values.

Rabbi Yose ben Kisma and Ahad Ha'am came from totally different religious and cultural backgrounds; yet, they both feared the results of deculturation. In a real sense, these fears underscore the present challenge of Jewish Family Education.

To be sure, educating Jewish families to be Jewish or more Jewish should be the concern of the total Jewish community. Within this overall context there is a specific challenge.

Let me frame that challenge from a Jewish schoolman's point of view — from a Jewish socio-educational perspective. On the one hand, we worry about the viability of the Jewish family and agonize over the factors that contribute to its ability to endure and to thrive as a *Jewish* family. On the other hand, we are concerned about the relationship of the Jewish family to Jewish continuity. How can we guarantee that the Jewish family will contribute to the survival of the Jewish people and to the enhancement of Jewish life?

Jewish education has a vital role regarding both of these challenges. In the Jewish world, as in the larger society, the term "education" is a code word that signifies a process of schooling which involves children and youth. In bringing up our children Jewishly, there is *one* essential dimension of their training which goes beyond the four walls of the school and the classroom that is necessary to insure their eventual Jewish behavior. Simply stated, this dimension, without which Jewish education cannot be effective is: children need — children must have — imitable adult models, particularly in their immediate environment.

The environmental impact upon children — upon their identity formation, their childhood behavior patterns, their learning styles and their eventual adult behavior — comes from three sources: the family, the school and society.

When the influences from all three sources are in congruence, children grow up according to the confluence or combination of these influences. When they are in conflict — when the influences contradict each other — then children will behave according to the stronger impact upon them. It is obvious that *family* and *society* are generally more powerful influences on children than the school. Moreover, it is abundantly clear that the influences of our current society are not helpful in achieving *Jewish* behavioral objectives. Therefore, the more the goals of the home and school are similar, the more likely their combined influence will prevail over the counter-influence of society on their Jewish attitudes and behavior.

The impact of society upon the average Jewish family is not much different than its influence upon the non-Jewish home. We have more single parents then ever before, more "latch-key" children, more unwed mothers, more teenage mothers, more grandparents bringing up children, more blended families (by products of divorce and remarriage), more intermarried spouses and more homes with two working parents. Children of the 1980's have more freedom and are exposed to less adult authority figures in the home than ever before. Once upon a time, adults were adults and children were children, and parents said "no."

It has now come to the point where one hears about the mother who said to her teen-age daughter as she was going out with friends to an ice cream parlor, "Have a good time." The daughter snapped back, "Don't tell me what to do." Indeed, times have changed regarding parent-child relationship.

And, we are all beginning to see the results of the impact of our technological age.

Recently a group of children was asked to draw pictures of fish. Some of them drew rectangular boxes because the only kind of fish they ever saw was frozen fish.

Just think of the other ways that our technological age has affected our children's concepts of reality. Consider, also, the influence of TV. Upon graduation from high school, the average American teen-ager will have spent many more hours in front of the tube than in school.

Add up all the influences of our modern, value-free, open, technologically sophisticated society upon our children — and American *Jews,* like all other Americans, are faced with a challenge of huge proportions. But, the *most critical challenge* we face as a *Jewish* community results from the changes in Jewish living styles, best described as deculturation.

Demographers call this phenomenon "sociological death," affected by the growing rates of intermarriage, apostasy and assimilation.

The effect of this phenomenon upon our children is very substantial. It constitutes a major reason for the failure of the Jewish supplementary school to transmit effectively Jewish knowledge and values to our children. Missing is the linkage of parents to our schools and schools to parents. Lacking is the Jewish home environment which nurtures an appreciation for Jewish schooling and reinforces the values taught in school. When the family, which Erik Erickson reminds us, is the "primary nurturer" of a child's weltanshauung, is not supportive of his/her schoooling, that schooling is in deep trouble. There is ample research in general education that strongly supports this notion.

To succeed, school must be a synergistic experience. Teacher effectiveness depends upon parental support, and parental effectiveness depends upon teacher ability and skill.

One way of viewing this synergism is the combination of an effective home experience with a cognitive school program. That was the way it was in the *shtetl.* Now each partner has to provide both experiences in partnership.

In a voluntary setting, like Jewish education, this synergistic relationship between home and school is absolutely critical. BJE's recent study of Jewish supplementary schools in Greater New York, demonstrates the absolute need of Jewish family background and support for Jewish schooling, if that education is to be effective.

A major challenge in Jewish education is reaching and teaching parents who do not fully associate themselves with the goals of their children's schools. In one sense, these parents are a captive audience. Yet, they are hard to reach and even more difficult to teach. For the children of such families, the Talmudic interpretation of the teacher role in terms of *ke'ilu y'lado* — whereby the teachers are considered like parents — is not sufficient. It is true:

כל המלמד את בן חברו תורה מעלה עליו הכתוב כאלו ילדו. (סנהדרין י״ט-ב׳)

However, the teacher in *loco parentis* simply cannot guarantee that the school influence will have a lasting effect unless parents are able to reinforce this influence. For Jewish education, this requires that parents have Jewish knowledge, be living examples of Jewish values and be strongly supportive of their children's Jewish schooling. That is what ושננתם לבניך "and you shall teach diligently to your children" really means. The Talmud (in tractate Kiddushin) emphasizes that this requires parents to be life-long learners of Torah. The Bible, Talmudic and rabbinic writings are replete with exhortations about the obligation of parents to teach their children, including statements such as: והגדת לבנך — "and you shall tell your son about the exodus," ולמדתם אותם את בניכם — "and you shall teach God's Commandments to your children."

Only if parents are unable to discharge this primary responsibility may it be delegated, in part, to others. However, parents are never freed entirely from this obligation.

The problem today is that the children who are most in need of parental tutelage and reinforcement usually have parents who are least able to help them. This challenge thrusts upon the school the task of educating parents to become partners in the day-to-day education of their children — a phenomenon that is now not only acceptable, but desirable in school systems throughout the country. This, then, becomes the synagogue's new educational role as it changes its thrust from Jewish schooling for children *only* to Jewish education for the entire family, including children *and* adults.

The new child-family focus means restructuring synagogue involvement in Jewish education whereby the rabbi, principal, teachers, cantor and youth leaders work as family educator teams.

It means turning the synagogue into a real community. It means working within a wholistic communal approach, together with JCC's, Federations and Jewish human services agencies. It means involving parents and pupils and giving them ownership of the program. Initiating Jewish family education programs will not be easy. It will stretch our imagination and pocketbook and try our patience. Planning and implementation will be a long process. It cannot be done at once for all schools. We will need to experiment with a variety of models in order to develop the most effective approaches. We need to study the variety of methodologies initiated by various communities and disseminate information about the effective programs. To be sure, this procedure will be very challenging. But, it can also be very exciting and extremely rewarding.

According to Jewish tradition, the school is an agent of the parents. For many schools, this translates into the challenge of teaching a growing number of parents what the substance and goals of this "agent" are. But what it really means is Jewish parent empowerment that can lead to pupil empowerment and enduring Jewish education for Jewish children and to enhanced Jewish living for Jewish families.

The time for Jewish parent empowerment is now!

To paraphrase the Almighty's charge to Gideon, some three thousand years ago, when the survival of the Israelites was endangered: לב בכוחכם זה והושעתם את ישראל "We will go forward with our strong resolve, unyielding commitment and special skills to insure the continuity of the Jewish people!"

God bless us in our efforts!

— 21 —

A PRO-ACTIVE DEFINITION
OF INFORMAL JEWISH EDUCATION
AND CULTURE IN
A JEWISH CENTER SETTING

*Presented at Task Force meeting
on Effectiveness of Jewish Education
in Jewish Community Centers; JWB
May, 1980*

"The functional scope of the Jewish Center embraces primarily informal education, health and recreation and its purpose is to make Jewish life meaningful in the area of its functional competence, namely, leisure-time activity." Oscar I. Janowsky. The JWB Survey, Dial Press, N.Y. 1948, p. 272-273.

"Making Jewish life meaningful" should be the primary goal of the Jewish Center. This objective can best be achieved by *informal* Jewish education — transmitting Jewish values and Jewish knowledge. At a time when no more than 70% of the Jewish child population will benefit from formal Jewish schooling it is an imperative of Jewish survival to utilize all possible means and resources for the promotion of *Jewish identification.*

There are two aspects to the process of Jewish identification: *Jewish identity formation* and *Jewish identity reinforcement.* For children, youth and adults having very little or no involvement with Jewish life the *formation* of Jewish identity is a *necessary* first level of Jewish informal education. For those having varying degrees of Jewish affiliation and knowledge, *reinforcing* their Jewish identity is the appropriate mode.

Opportunities for both Jewish identity formation and reinforcement amply exist in Jewish Center settings. Jewish Centers are unique entities as they embrace broad sectors of the Jewish community — from early childhood through older adulthood, spanning the spectrum of ideological affiliation and non-affiliation. Responding to the range of the Jewish needs of the *membership* requires a variety of educationl approaches. Learning takes place in various ways. Different things are learned best via different approaches. Learning outcomes depend on the nature of the learning processes. Essentially, there are two types of learning processes — *affective* and *cognitive.*

Affective Learning

The affective processes involve emotions, attitudes, interests, preferences and values. They are indispensable for efforts designed to 1) sensitize people to special concerns; 2) help them become receptive to new ideas; 3) develop in them a willingness to behave in special ways, and 4) instill in them a desire for and commitment to certain values.

While affective processes should be an integral part of formal instruction, they are the *sine qua non* dimension of informal education.

Affective education is especially important to the Jewish Centers as they strive to deal creatively with the Jewish continuity and enrichment needs of their members. Functionally, affective education in the Center comprises the experiential component of the program.

Examples of affective activities include Jewish family life experiences, Shabbatonim, trips, rallies, holiday celebrations and retreats. Jewish camping and Israel visits provide the best opportunities for affective education.

The effectiveness of affective education depends largely on *leader* and *peer* models, staff commitment and values, staff behavior and enthusiasm.

Cognitive Learning

The cognitive processes pertain to the acquisition of facts and the comprehension of ideas. They help the learner to analyze and articulate concepts and communicate information. Cognitive learning is the chief ingredient of formal education. It is also an important component of informal education — in early childhood programs, adult education and cultural enrichment activities.

Opportunities for cognitive Jewish programming include lectures, course offerings, discussion groups on a wide array of Judaic, Hebraic and contemporary Jewish subjects as well as Ulpanim in Hebrew and Yiddish language.

While we may identify the special features of the affective and cognitive processes, we must be aware of their necessary *interdependence* and confluence. They are not virtually separate domains or functions. Rather, for achieving particular educational outcomes, one set of processes may be more relevant or dominant than the other — but never to the exclusion of the other.

Environment

The environment is a major component of informal education. As a home reflects the identity and character of the family, the agency plant reflects the *raison d'etre,* goals and programs of a Center. The ability to transmit a sense of Jewish purpose via the creation of a positive Jewish feeling-tone and meaningful Jewish decor is a critical factor in the agency's proclamation of its self-image. An atmosphere which engenders comfort and pride in one's Jewish sense of self will go a long way in encouraging identity formation and identity reinforcement.

In Sum

Informal Jewish Education in Jewish Centers may be defined as the process of developing positive Jewish identity, socializing Jewish youth and adults into the Jewish community and transmitting Jewish knowledge and values.

The extent to which an agency achieves its Jewish educational purpose and goals can only be measured through an evaluation process which focuses on the quality, quantity and nature of Jewish programming throughout the agency. If informal Jewish education is perceived to be the agency's primary objective then it must be weighed in terms of the prominence, frequency and intensity in which it is offered and implemented.

Jewish Centers should be careful not to duplicate the formal Jewish educational services of the Jewish school and synagogue. However, a social planning approach involving the leadership of other local educational institutions can help define the nature and scope of the agency's role in offering *informal* education programs.

— 22 —

Rx For JEWISH CONTINUITY:
How to Keep Our Heads Above Water

Presented At The
Twenty-Fifth Annual Goldenberg
Scholar-In-Residence Lecture Series,
Talmud Torah of Minneapolis
May 9, 1991

In a moment of weakness I suggested the title "Rx for Jewish Continuity." To suggest that anyone has a patent on the Jewish future sounds like real chutzpah. To recommend such a prescriptive title might be the height of arrogance. Moreover, our rabbis in the Talmud taught us: מיום שנחרב בית המקדש ניטלה נבואה מן הנביאים וניתנה לשוטים ולתינוקות From the day that the Temple was destroyed, Prophecy was removed from prophets and given to fools and babies. It seems that I am about to delve into an area reserved for fools and babies. How can I get out of this undesirable position? How can I justify taking on such a task? The answer is simply that I belong to those who feel that the future of Jewish life is in jeopardy and that we must do everything in our power to vouchsafe it.

Creating public awareness of ways to insure Jewish continuity is not only not chutzpah. It is a mitzvah! And I'd like us all to share in that mitzvah tonight.

That explains the second part of the title — "How to keep our heads above water." כי באו מים עד נפש cries out the Psalmist. (Psalms 69:2)

"Keeping heads above water" is a term actually coined by King David, the sweet singer of Israel, some 3,000 years ago in the Book of Psalms: "Water has reached my nostrils" (literally, "my soul"), he complained when he was in trouble (deep trouble).

The challenge of being overwhelmed by our surroundings is 200 years in the making. It began with the French Revolution in 1789 when France achieved "liberté, egalité, fraternité." For many Jews this meant shedding the protective environment of the *shtetl* and the *yiddish gass* as they tried to adjust to their newfound freedom.

Our challenge in a modern open free society comprises three goals.

1) To educate a generation of upright, productive, caring, American Jewish citizens in an era of unprecedented rapid change.

Life has always changed. But, never in the history of the world has it changed with such rapidity as it does now. It was in this very vein, that scientist J. Robert Oppenheimer observed before his death: "One thing that is new is the prevalence of newness, the changing scale and scope of change itself, so that the years of a man's life measure not some small growth or rearrangement or modification of what he learned in childhood, but a great upheaval."

Schools must educate children to be able to handle the great upheavals they will face in their lifetimes.

2) The second challenge is to imbue Jewish youth with moral values in the face of a valueless, value-"rein" society, plagued with the scourge of drugs, substance abuse, and promiscuity. Hardly a Jewish family is immune to the problems of our American society. Among other things, the Special Education Center at the BJE deals with education about substance abuse prevention. It is busier than one could imagine with problems on all levels of the Jewish community affected by the use of alcohol and drugs, particularly by teenagers.

3) The third challenge is to insure Jewish continuity — to develop proud, literate Jews who know Jewish, who feel Jewish and

who act Jewish — who when they become adults will be able to enhance their family life Jewishly, and who will be in the forefront of Jewish leadership for Jewish causes here in the United States, the world over, and in Israel.

The immediate, more direct challenge of Jewish continuity to individual Jews is exacerbated by the problem of intermarriage. The Jewish Population Study underscores the accelerating decline of Jewish life through intermarriage. Dr. Seymour Lachman, University Dean, City University of New York, punctuates the pervasiveness and the spread of this problem by demonstrating the growth of intermarriage. In 1900 there was 4% intermarriage; in 1940 — 6%; in 1960 — 12%; in 1970 — 28%; and in 1990 — 50%. Currently, only 46% of Jewish children are being raised completely as Jews. thirty-eight % are being raised with mixed religions. And 16% are being raised with no religion at all.

Listen to the President of the Conservative Rabbinical Assembly as he warned his constituency that its failure to deal with intermarriage and its aftermath threatens "the future of the Jewish people."

"Speaking at the RA's annual convention at the Concord Hotel in Kiamesha Lake, Rabbi Irwin Groner told his Conservative Colleagues that '*even if* the Jewish partners in interfaith marriages retain their Jewish identity . . . the likelihood of that identity being transmitted to children and grandchildren has been catastrophically reduced.' (*Jewish Week,* May 4, 1991)

Another way of looking at the Jewish condition is considering the bi-polar state of Jewish behavior. We are the "more" and "many-more" generation. / *More* Jews pray every day, three times a day; *many more* do not pray at all. / *More* Jews eat glatt kosher; *many more* do not eat kosher at all. / *More* Jews drink halav Yisrael; *many more* drink intoxicating beverages to excess. / *More* adult Jews learn Talmud — daf yomi — each day; *many more* have no contact with Jewish learning at all.

The "many mores" represent the majority of Jews, best described as products of the acculturation-deculturation syndrome, as they became integrated comfortably into American society. This condition has had a threefold effect upon their Jewish identity and involvement. It has lessened the quantity and quality of Jewishness in their daily lives; it has diminished the extent and intensity of their synagogue affiliation and Jewish communal activity; and it has decreased their level of home support for Jewish education.

The challenge to Jewish education is to educate our youth to withstand the forces of deculturation. Jewish schools need to produce students like Johua ben Hannaniah, one of the five outstanding disciples of the famed Rabbi Yohanan ben Zakkai. At the time of the destruction of the second temple some 1950 years ago, when he established *Yavneh,* the model academy of Jewish learning, he called Joshua ben Hannaniah, a חוט משולש בתורה, בחכמה וביראת שמים. "A threefold combination of Judaic knowledge, worldly knowledge and Jewish commitment and behavior." In using the term משולש "threefold cord", ben Zakkai was referring to the statement of the wisest of men, King Solomon, who proclaimed, Two are better than one, but "The *threefold* cord cannot be rent asunder" — a powerful reference to continuity.

The combination of Joshua ben Hannaniah's traits translated into modern context suggests that each Jewish child be educated to become a living synthesis of *Torah Umadah* — who integrates the world of science with the world of religion. A young person who feels at home in both Jewish and general students and is sensitive to the need of friends and relatives.

What kind of Jew do we want to educate? We need to produce many Joshua ben Hannaniahs. Historically, the Talmud Torah of Minneapolis has been the place where this kind of education took place.

Unfortunately, there are not many Jewish supplementary schools that can make this happen today. More and more, the American Jewish community is realizing this fact of life. For one thing, Jewish supplementary school enrollment has declined precipitously in North America from 560,000 in 1962, the peak year of Jewish school enrollment, to 260,000 in 1990, a 55% decrease. This compares to a 375% increase in Jewish day school enrollment during the same period — from 40,000 to 150,000 pupils.

Our worst fears about the Jewish supplementary school were confirmed by The Board of Jewish Education of Greater New York's landmark study (conducted between 1984 and 1987), which Harold Himmelfarb of the U.S. Office of Education who directs Research in Non-public Education, called the "most methodologically rigorous and most comprehensive study to date on the subject."

Compare the findings of the BJE Study with your knowledge of

Talmud Torah of Minneapolis. You be the judges. Obviously, there will be significant differences. Remember. Unlike the Talmud Torah of Minneapolis, 99% of all supplementary schools in this country are synagogue based. The findings and conclusions are presented to make you aware of possible problems and potential dangers to Minneapolis, if they don't already exist.

The overall increase in Jewish knowledge from the first year of school to the sixth year was *only 10%*. From the second year to the sixth year, Jewish knowledge scores increased *by only 4%*. In all subjects but one there was actually a *drop* in pupil scores from the fifth to the sixth year. Twelve-and 12-1/2-year-olds know less than eleven-and 11-1/2-year-olds. As one of the post-finding consultants said, "Their brains fell out during their pre-Bar-Bat Mitzvah year."

— There was a sharp increase in scores in all subjects by pupils who continued school beyond Bar/Bat Mitzvah and were in their seventh or eighth year of school.

— Jewish involvement of pupils is generally passive. It actually decreased from the second to sixth year of school (by 10%).

— Jewish attitudes of pupils are generally neutral. The Jewish attitudes also decreased from the second to sixth year or school (by 15%).

It is interesting to note that pupils did *not* demonstrate *negative Jewish involvement and attitudes*. All respondents' involvement and attitudes were pareve — passive or neutral — and went from high passive or high neutral to low passive and low neutral.

School size, ideology, geography and *even numbers of hours of schooling* made no difference in pupils' Jewish knowledge, Jewish attitudes and Jewish involvement.

Conclusions

The BJE Study concluded that the construct of Jewish supplementary schools seems to have a homogenizing, parevising effect upon pupils. The average knowledge score is 49%! Jewish involvement is passive! And, Jewish attitudes are neutral!

It is clear that schools do a poor job in increasing Jewish knowledge in all subject areas; they show no success in guiding children toward increased Jewish involvement and demonstrate an inability to influence positive growth in Jewish attitudes.

The Study showed that this condition is due to a combination of factors: *the most critical of which is the lack of home involvement and support to Jewish schooling.* The other factors are: irrelevant curricular goals; inappropriate school programs; and ineffectual professional personnel, given the needs of pupils and families in the 1980's.

Finally, the study emphasized that unless Jewish education of the entire family becomes the absolute priority of the synagogue; unless the parents become inolved in the Jewish education of their children; unless the program is geared to the needs of families; and unless *all* synagogue personnel are able to relate effectively to pupils *and* their parents, very little or no improvement in Jewish supplementary education can take place.

The Findings in the Context of General Education

While there are major differences between the Jewish supplementary school and the public school, it is instructive to consider these findings and conclusions in light of research in general education.

In 1966, Chicago University Professor James Coleman and associates completed their mammoth study *Equality of Educational Opportunity* involving some 600,000 people by saying that "schools bring little influence to bear on a child's achievement that is independent of his background and social contacts."

Several years later Christopher Jencks and his associates brought evidence that schools do "not make the kinds and magnitudes of difference which most observers has come to expect" and were not the vehicles of progressive social change which most people had thought. Other studies have supported the Coleman and Jencks thesis.

Arthur Combs asks "Why is urban education so bad? After all we have better facilities, more informed teachers, better prepared principals, better texts and materials then ever before." "The answer is," says Combs, "the parents send us the wrong kids."

However, *Effective Schools Research* during the last two decades seems to challenge these conclusions. This accumulation of research studies suggests that there are a variety of correlates of effective schooling. And, school-family relations comprise only one of them.

A voluntary system of education, like the Jewish supplementary school, must consider seriously the conclusions *of both of these schools of thought.*

Prof. Benjamin Bloom, famed Chicago University educational taxonomer, points emphatically to this *dual* need in a fascinating study on talented people. He found that there are only two features common to the backgrounds of all top performers he researched in the arts, sports, academia, and science. The first common factor is home support. "The parents (of the top performers)," he said, "were all genuinely concerned about their children . . . and willing to devote their time, their resources and their energy to giving each of their children the best conditions they could provide for them. Almost no sacrifice was too great if they thought it would help their children's (educational) development."

It is clear that to be successful, education must be a synergistic experience. Teacher effectiveness depends upon parents, and parent effectiveness depends upon teachers.

The second characteristic common to top performers is "time on task." Simply put, you can't really succeed in study unless you invest sufficient quality time in it. That means quality teaching and quality learning.

It is precisely because of these two factors — *family support and quality time on task* — that the BJE study makes four recommendations for the improvement of the Jewish supplementary school, the first two of which suggest that we transform the thrust of synagogue schools from supplementary schooling for pupils to Jewish family education including children, and maximize learning time through a combination of formal and informal education experiences.

These recommendations strongly point out the need to reorganize the entire synagogue and to mobilize the community to provide the necessary support to make the changes possible.

The challenge, in the first instance, is to insure that parents send us the 'right kids.' To get the 'right kids' we must have the 'right parents.' For this we need effective Jewish family education which, in turn, requires the presence of two facilitating options — two 'building blocks,' as The Commission on Jewish Education calls them.

ISSUES AND CHALLENGES   153

The first building block is *personnel.* This means making more qualified personnel available through better training, better recruitment, better compensation, better supervision, better growth opportunities for teachers and principals. The first building block is dependent, in a large measure, on the second building block which is a significantly higher level of communal involvement in and funding for Jewish schools.

When one observes the American Jewish scene today, it is crystal clear that there has to be more support for Jewish education — particularly for the teacher. Teachers function so often *in loco parentis.* They must be acknowledged as such. An anonymous poem beautifully captures the role of teachers.

No written word nor spoken plea,
Can teach young hearts what man should be,
Not all the books on all the shelves,
But what the teachers are themselves.

Jewish schools need effective classroom teachers. I'm convinced that the Talmud Torah of Minneapolis excels in this respect. Now as we enter the last decade of the twentieth century, Jewish schools need Jewish family educators as well. Teachers in each school, including the Talmud Torah of Minneapolis, must be helped to become effective family educators. This idea is taking hold throughout the country, but it cannot succeed without increased Jewish communal support for Jewish education.

These are tough economic times. Particularly now, the Jewish school must be the *number one local funding priority in every Jewish community.* Certainly the Talmud Torah of Minneapolis deserves maximum communal support to help it continue its record of excellence as it responds to the emergency needs of our times.

Will we meet the challenge?
Will we keep heads above water?
In Minneapolis, will we continue to succeed in our mission?

The answers to these questions lie in the response Chagall gave to the query, "What do you consider your greatest masterpiece?" The answer came after considerable thought. "The next one," he said.

B'hatzlahah! More power to you in the years ahead.

ON

PERSONNEL

— 23 —

TEACHER PERSONNEL

Memorandum submitted to
Dr. Azriel Eisenberg,
Executive Vice President
Jewish Education Committee of New York
August 19, 1960

As you requested I am submitting herewith some of my thoughts on teacher recruitment and teacher retention.

Jewish educational literature is replete with the subject of the current shortage of Hebrew teachers. Numerous educational meetings, conferences, conclaves and committees have been convened with the express purpose of helping find solutions to this vexing, aggravating problem. The American Jewish community is becoming aware (alas, quite late — one hopes not too late) of the conditione sine qua non for the success of the American Jewish educational venture — the classroom instructor.

In reality there is no actual teacher shortage. At worst the shortage of teachers is not great. What with the influx of Israeli students and visitors (many of whom do not return to Israel or overstay their intended visit by one, two, three or more years); what with the many young people, particularly students with some Jewish knowledge who are looking for a part-time job; what with housewives and small business men and even young professionals who are seeking ways to supplement their income; and what with the young men possessing intensive Jewish background — usually yeshiva trained people — who by default, or because of lack of preparation or inclination to enter other more lucrative professions, choose to become Jewish teachers; what with all these "teachers" replenishing the diminishing ranks of the permanent Hebrew teaching personnel in American schools there is no teacher shortage. However, a critical shortage does exist, and that is the shortage of *qualified* career teachers.

Schools in rural areas and small towns far from the larger U.S. city centers which have no university or college in the vicinity, experience the severity of the teacher shortage to a much greater degree than their sister city institutions. The available teacher candidates from the sources mentioned often refuse to go to these "out-of-the-way places." They would rather forgo the opportunity to enter or remain in the teaching profession than to take posts in out of town schools.

Stopgap teacher recruitment can no longer be tolerated. it would be unrealistic to believe that new Hebrew teachers colleges will spring up overnight in answer to the need. It would be foolish to assume that their graduates will make Hebrew teaching their career. Our experience during the past score of years has proven the contrary to be true. It would be folly to expect Israel to fill our teaching needs. Certainly no other country can do it for us. (We should really be in the position to help other countries with such personnel.)

Many theories have been advanced and recommendations made for attracting more young people to the Hebrew teaching profession. Among these are raising teachers' salaries, making the shrinking (in terms of hours of instruction) Hebrew teaching position a full-time job by the addition of related activites to the roster of teacher responsibilities, providing opportunities for professional growth and advancement, heightening the prestige and social status of the teacher, and so on.

One factor aggravating the successful induction of neophyte teachers into the Hebrew teaching profession is the reluctance and even unwillingness, particularly by principals of large well established city schools to engage young teachers without previous teaching experience. "But, I have to start somewhere," and "Why can't I begin in a good school and have proper guidance in my first years of teaching" are familiar sounds to the ears of placement officials. This attitude must be rectified if the following suggestions are to be carried out with any measure of success. Principals and school boards of the better established schools must help assume the responsibility of orienting new teachers. Bureaus must actively seek their cooperation in this matter even to the extent of financial assistance, if necessary.

My recommendations deal only with the recruiting and training of new young career teachers. These are essentially: 1) an introduction of basic student - teaching programs in our Hebrew teacher colleges; 2) the initiation of teacher fellowship or assistant teacher programs in our Hebrew schools (these require the cooperation of "host" schools and the active involvement of bureaus and educational agencies in pre-service selection); 3) and a third recommendation for consideration at some later date: merit rating and professional advancement to attract and keep young people with superior ability in Jewish education.

1: Student Teaching

Basic comprehensive student teaching requirements should be instituted in all the teacher training schools. Better and more practical preparation in teaching will lead to more satisfying initial teaching experiences and gradually to a larger percentage of Hebrew teacher college graduates who choose Hebrew teaching as a career. The student teaching program should be comparable in scope and hours to those instituted by the universities and colleges throughout the country. A minimum of 150 clock hours of observing, assisting and instructing under supervision should be required. To briefly outline this program and demonstrate its beneficial aspects I would like to bring your attention to the following excerpt from an article in the recent issue of *Our Teacher* about the student teaching program in Teachers Institute for Women, Yeshiva University:

"In the Teachers Institute for Women program, emphasis is placed on helping the individual student. A supervisor is available one evening every week to discuss students' plans and problems.

"Guidance is provided as early as the junior year. Each candidate for the Hebrew teacher's diploma is interviewed by the faculty Guidance Committee at the end of her third year to determine her specific student-teaching needs. At this meeting the student's school record is reviewed in order to discover special strengths and weaknesses. Another guidance conference is arranged before she begins her observation, at which time details of the program are spelled out.

"During the first week, the novice meets with the principal, visits various grades, observes school routines, and learns about some administrative practices.

"Then she is assigned to a class, often one of her own choosing. After a week or so of adjusting to the classroom situation, getting to know the pupils, and observing the teaching process, the teacher-student is ready to assist the host teacher. As an apprentice, she performs — first with the aid of her host teacher, then by herself — many teaching chores.

"During the next two or three weeks she plans and actually teaches a number of lessons under the guidance of the cooperating teacher. After having 'practice-taught' until she is sufficiently at home in the class, the student is observed in action by her TIW supervisor who later evaluates her work with her and determines the course of the rest of her student-teaching program. Some student-teachers continue in the same class for another few weeks; some visit with other teachers in the school; still others are transferred to another school.

"Generally, the supervisor visits each student-teacher at work three times, though occasionally it is necessary to observe her four or more times. Each visit is followed by an evaluation conference.

Some of the student-teachers work as teams. They 'practice-teach' in different classes yet observe each other giving demonstration lessons and appraise each other's performance.

"As part of the student-teaching and guidance schedule a continuing follow-up program of all teaching graduates is in effect. For several years contact is maintained in writing and via phone with each teacher's school. The TIW Director and student-teaching supervisors visit the teachers at their places of work and encourage their professional growth."

The program has brought favorable results. Principals have felt more confident in hiring these neophyte teachers, and the teachers themselves, in addition to being better prepared, have had a greater sense of competence in performing their first year's work. TIW boasts the largest percentage of Hebrew teachers college graduates who remain in the Hebrew teaching profession. This in itself is partial testimony to the success of its student-teaching program. Since inception of the new training course in 1955, ninety-tow young women have completed their studies. Almost all entered Hebrew teaching professionally upon graduation. At the time of the writing of this article, seventy-five were still in the field.

The cooperating schools are not without benefits from the student-teaching program.

In the first instance, the student-teaching program lends prestige to the cooperating school. It stimulates host teachers to "put their best foot forward" and contributes to their professional growth. It provides school and classroom with added adult supervision. (The student-teachers have proven themselves very helpful. They assume yard duty, assist in lunchroom supervision, lead groups within a class and prepare teaching aids.)

Student-teaching also provides the school with a supply of teacher prospects. A number of graduates are now teachers in the very schools in which they student-taught.

A feature recently introduced after successful experimentation is the intervisitation plan for host teachers. Before leaving a class in which she has practice-taught, the student takes it over for one full day in order that the cooperating teacher be free to visit other teachers in his own school or in other schools. Intervisitation is clearly recognized as an effective way of encouraging professional self-improvement. Many principals are happy about this phase of the student-teaching program.

2: Teacher Fellowships

The greatest source of potential Hebrew teaching personnel are the Yeshivot Gedolot (the metivtot and rabbinical seminaries) in most of the larger cities. These schools of higher Jewish learning succeed in "handing over" the *keter Torah* to generation after generation of students. They succeed also in inspiring their exponents to be devout, observant and dedicated Jews. Some of their graduates — musmachim — enter the rabbinate. The great majority do not. This is where the role of the Jewish community — particularly the Jewish educational community — must be assumed. In the first place, these yeshivot must be guided to encourage those "bachurim" who show promise of becoming successful Hebrew teachers to enter the teaching profession.

In this regard the influence of the Roshei Hayeshiva upon their students must not be underestimated. The Roshei Hayeshiva can be the key people in a pre-service selection program. They can help induct tens of graduates into the Hebrew teaching profession yearly.

Secondly, these yeshivot must cooperatively or individually introduce some fundamental courses in educational method, conversational Hebrew and even content courses in Bible, History, grammar, etc. The policies and procedures of the national and local boards of license should be re-examined in the light of the preparation of such students for careers in Jewish education. Although well intentioned some of the requirements of the existing boards are unrealistic, if not archaic.

Finally, arrangements should be initiated by the larger bureaus involving day schools, intensive afternoon schools and the Yeshivot Gedolot in a cooperative fellowship program whereby graduates or senior students, upon completion of student teaching programs or in conjunction with them, would work as assistants or teachers (part - or- full-time as the situation demands). These teachers-in-training would receive special guidance from the principals, teachers and bureau supervisors. They would be nominally remunerated for their services — about 50% of the current average teacher salary. At the end of the year of fellowship and after completion of the basic courses, etc., and graduation or ordination from the rabbinical seminary, these teacher- trainees would automatically become eligible for a license. They would be prepared also to assume full-time teaching responsibilities. The educational courses may be arranged through the Department of Religious Education of Yeshiva University, Teachers Institute for Men, or a local university. (Because of the religious persuasion of these teacher aspirants, other colleges, etc., would not be readily considered.)

The mechanics of such a program need to be spelled out in much greater detail. Moreover, it might call for considerable financial subvention. This responsibility the Jewish community councils and bureaus must be ready to assume.

3: Merit Pay Plan

The following recommendation for consideration at a later date is submitted here because of its pertinence to the issue of teacher recruitment and retention.

Not unlike conditions in general education, one of the serious shortcomings of the Hebrew teaching profession is that few, if any, young poeple with superior intellectual ability and academic background choose to become career educators. This situation severely handicaps progress in Jewish education and endangers the future of educational standards. Jewish education needs young able teachers who will eventually assume supervisory and administrative posts.

Community councils, welfare funds and bureaus must assume responsibility in helping to attract such people to Jewish education and increase the schools' holding power over them. Merit pay and possibilities for professional advancement are basic to any forward looking program for recruitment of superior talent. Outstanding performance should be given tangible recognition.

Proponents of merit rating argue that "equal pay for unequal performance is really a perversion of the idea of equality." Single salary schedules and automatic increases do little to encourage gifted teachers beyond satisfactory performance. In contrast to this, monetary acknowledgment of outstanding achievement has been proven in many cases to be a good way of motivating teacher growth. Merit rating, moreover, stimulates self-evaluation, a necessary element of teacher growth. It also facilitates recruitment of, and helps hold, superior teachers.

Teachers, like employees in other vocations, are human. Industry to which education often looks for guidance in matters of personnel management has experimented with ways of improving personnel practices. The value of a good program of human relations (with all its attendant features) and the importance of pleasant working conditions are clearly established with regard to all workers. However, for the excellent performers, for the superior workers, special incentives are provided to encourage outstanding achievement. These include promotion and monetary compensation. The holding power of a salary increase over and above the regular increments for the superior worker cannot be underestimated. The possibilities of promotion in a Jewish school are very limited. Salary betterment is the only way superior performance can be rewarded.

In discussing the advantages of merit pay systems consideration of the characteristics of the various operating plans seems helpful. A recent study of existing successful incentive pay plans reveals several common salient elements.

1. The great majority of plans makes use of *some definite evaluative tool* or set of criteria to aid in determining outstanding teaching service.

2. The criteria used to identify superior efforts are *developed cooperatively with the teaching force having a major responsibility* in this development.

3. Adoption of a plan is accomplished only after *careful consideration* and then with at least a *'let's try and see' attitude* on the part of a majority of the teachers.

4. At least initially, most *incentive plans are built into the basic salary schedule.*

5. *The incentive plan is subject to constant review and critical analysis* after its adoption.

Introducing merit pay plans which would incorporate these common elements would be advantageous to the Jewish schools. Incentive pay need not eliminate payment based on a set salary schedule. On the contrary, maintaining a basic wage scale is a desideratum. The merit system may be incorporated in some way into a wage schedule. Lieberman calls the combination of salary scheduling and incentive planning the "merit type plan." "Merit rating need not be an exclusive basis of compensation. Some school systems are experimenting with a combination salary schedule and merit rating plan. The salary schedule insures each teacher a minimum salary. Merit rating is superimposed on the schedule to provide additional incentives and rewards for outstanding teachers."

The Washington Conference on Personnel Policies made a recommendation to this effect. "Teachers should have a fair and equitable salary based upon reasonable competence. For salaries above the adopted schedule, however, some type of merit plan should be employed." Although opinion regarding the recommendation was sharply divided, this writer feels that its advantages greatly outweigh its disadvantages, particularly for the Jewish school.

The combined plan would, in effect, accomplish a two-fold purpose: a) it would encourage the establishment of salary scales where none exist, and b) be an incentive to superior teachers.

The challenge to superior teachers over and beyond an existing scale may be presented in a number of ways:

1. *Acceleration to the top salary* makes it possible to reward superior teaching within an existing schedule by moving the outstanding teacher more quickly from the minimum to the maximum.

2. *Supermaximums* do not attempt to increase salary with an existing schedule but instead provide payments for the "master teacher" beyond the established top salaries.

3. *Major divisions* within a schedule are frequently established with two or three "barrier points" which require certain achievements or evidence of superiority in order for a teacher to move into the next higher salary level.

4. *Full merit provisions* can be found occasionally where automatic annual steps are not provided even though there may be established minimum and maximum salaries. This is the ultimate in incentive schedules and requires an annual year's salary.

Institution of cooperatively developed incentive pay plans may have many residual advantages. It relieves the superior teacher of anxiety regarding the nature of his rewards and how they will be made, thus releasing his energies for his teaching. It gives all teachers an opportunity to participate in making crucial decisions. This will lessen their reluctance to accept merit pay plans. Learning to accept one's own status and live with one's own abilities is a by-product of cooperative planning. In all life situations some people will excel in individual or group enterprises. Their peers learn to acknowledge their colleagues' excellence and often find the means of rewarding them unbegrudgingly. So, too, it is with a school faculty. Given a chance to plan a merit system — once their own salaries are adjusted with current living standards — teachers will enhance the values of the merit plan by their participation in developing it and, in doing so, be encouraged to increase their own effectiveness.

In drawing conclusions about merit rating from studies by a California state-wide committee, one educator notes that even bad rating devices are useful if they are developed cooperatively with teachers.

The opposition of teacher groups which stems mainly from insecurity and lack of faith in the local boards of education must be overcome before introduction of merit rating is attempted on a large scale. This can be accomplished by school administrators via the employment of fair and considerate personnel practices. The key to successful implementation of all desirable employment procedures, merit-type pay not excluded, lies in the establishment of cooperative teacher-administrator relations.

– 24 –

TEACHER LEADERSHIP —
SOME PSYCHOLOGICAL
CONSIDERATIONS

Monograph prepared for European Conference of Jewish Educators, under the auspices of the European Jewish Schools Principals' Council and JDC European Sector

Paris, France, July, 1967

Are teachers born? Or are they trained? Is teaching skill inherited or acquired?

Educators, particularly those engaged in the business of preparing teachers, would like to think that training is essential to 'teaching' effectiveness. However, one must admit that there are some persons whose inherent personal traits fit them more appropriately than others for work in a social setting, for a profession in which successful performance depends on interpersonal dynamics. This simply means that some people are born with greater natural teaching ability than others. Such individuals are known to have "teaching personalities."

Notwithstanding any other element involved in the instruction of children, the personality factor is the most crucial one in the teaching-learning situation, particularly in the Jewish school. Psychologists underscore the "social stimulus value" of the teacher's role. While subject matter mastery and pedagogic skill are basic to instructional effectiveness, the personal qualities of the teacher, more than any other, help motivate continued interest in learning and affect the attitudes of pupils toward school and toward study.

Although people are born with certain innate abilities and qualities, they can modify their interpersonal behavior, even in adulthood. This is true for teachers as it is for adults in other professions. Most teachers can develop, in varying degrees, positive teaching personalities. Those who can't should not engage in any work that demands constant human interaction and socially-oriented decision making.

In this article, I should like to discuss briefly some factors basic to the devlopment of a positive teaching personality. These are: self-concept, attitude toward children, attitude toward effectiveness of Jewish education, potential for change and teacher's approach.

Self-Concept

To succeed in any challenging endeavor, an individual must *think* in terms of success. He must feel confident in his ability to fulfill the demands of the task at hand. He must feel competent in relation to other workers in his feild. He must feel a sense of pride and accomplishment in doing what he does. He must realize and appreciate the value of his vocation. And finally, he must consciously try to increase his potential for greater self-fulfillment from his work. He must be success-oriented in a personal sense. In a word, he must have a positive self-concept.

Unfortunately, many teachers in Jewish schools consider themselves second class citizens. (Often their financial position and social stuatus contribute to this feeling.) A negative self-image cannot yield the kind of enduring warmth and confidence needed for attaining excellence in teaching.

The best way to achieve a positive self-picture is by feeling one's worthiness — first, as an individual, and, second, as a professional. To be truly effective, a teacher must like himself and receive gratification from the work he does.

Attitude Toward Children

It has been demonstrated adequately in educational literature that children who like a subject generally do well in that subject. It is known too, that pupils who like a teacher perform well in that teacher's class. At least they are motivated to learn what the teacher instructs.

It has also been shown that pupils generally like teachers who like them. Pupils are apt to emulate teachers they like. They tend to identify with the values of their best-liked instructors.

The implications of these statements for the Jewish school are clear. In the first instance, the work climate in the classroom depends on the degree of pupil affection for the teacher. There is a high correlation between the 'likability' of an instructor and the conduciveness of the learning atmosphere in his classroom. Our sages recognized this fact when they stated, "A student who finds his study as hard as iron, it is (generally) because of his teacher who does not respond to him favorably."

Secondly, the social stimulus value of a teacher varies with the affection pupils have for him. The teacher who is liked is the one who, in all probability will be able to influence the attitude formation of his pupils. In an era when the teacher often has to replace the home as a father-figure and religious superego of the child, being liked must become a goal of every teacher — even if only the possibility of saving only "one soul" or "one out of a thousand" exists.

Is it humanly possible to like all children? In all group settings there are bound to be some instances where amicable relationships between certain individuals are difficult to establish. This is true between leader and group member as it is true for peer relationships.

In a classroom this becomes a serious problem. The teacher cannot afford *not* to like all his children, at least in the beginning. Frequently those pupils whom the teacher is prone to dislike — for obvious reasons — are those very youngsters who need his love most. Not to show love and kindness to them would be inconsistent with the challenge of the teacher's function. Not to try to show love to pupils — at least 'professional love,' as the social workers call artificial love — is to severely limit the possibilities of positive influence upon those children denied the teacher's affection.

Often 'professional love' will lead to greater understanding of the youngster who is the object of this artificial device, and even to genuine affection for the pupil. In a sense, this is an operational definition of the principle — מתוך שלא לשמה בא לשמה לשמה "from a non-puposeful act it becomes a purposeful act."

Attitude Toward Effectiveness of Jewish Education

The discussion of teacher self-concept and teacher attitude toward pupils remains incomplete without the addition of another dimension — the teacher's attitude toward the potential effectiveness of the Jewish school. A salesman who believes in the value of his product is motivated to succeed by a sense of purposefulness in addition to financial gain.

In Jewish life, what higher goal could there be than the cause of Jewish survival? What greater feeling of personal fulfillment could one get than the knowledge that he is making a major contribution to the perpetuation of his people? Yet, many teachers in Jewish schools — particularly in supplementary Jewish schools — enter their classrooms daily with a "licked before we begin" attitude. They feel unequal to the task of competing with an apathetic home and an irreligious environment. They feel powerless to compete with the secular and scientific forces that overwhelm their charges.

This kind of occupational defeatism affects the image a teacher has of his own worth and influences his attitude toward his pupils. The Hebrew teacher must be convinced of the potential value of his instruction. He must feel that despite all obstacles, no matter how great, he will succeed. He must be success-oriented in a professional sense. Otherwise, he *is* 'licked' before he begins. Having confidence in the ultimate effectiveness of Torah teaching is in the best tradition of our people. Moses faced difficulties and strong opposition. The prophets were challenged by a hostile environment. Our *gedolim* had to overcome much resistance. The recent history of Zionism demonstrates admirably the stubbornness of our people's faith.

Without unswerving faith in the spirit of "nevertheless, in spite of it all" that he shall overcome a teacher cannot ever hope to be truly effective.

Potential for Change

Underlying the development of a positive attitude toward the possible effectiveness of Hebrew teaching is the psycho-biological principle that the potential for change inheres in the behavior of every human organism. Tangible expression of this principle is everywhere about us: a person 'changes his mind'; a young lady outgrows a fad; a child begins to relate to many children at one time; a young boy loves, hates, loves, hates and then loves his friend again; a pupil changes his attitudes toward a subject or toward a teacher. It is the belief in the potential for change that is the real challenge to the biblical statement "for the imagination of a man's heart is evil from its youth." כי יצר לב האדם רע מנעוריו Without belief in the possibilities for change, there can be no hope for resolving human conflicts deriving from individual and group differences. Without the potential for change even minor problems of our society have no hope for solution.

Where there is growth, change is inevitable. Change in education is synonymous with the educative process. The degree and direction of the change depends on many factors not least of which is the teacher.

Children's attitudes can be changed radically in short periods of time. This is aptly demonstrated by the following anecdote told by Arthur Godfrey.

The parents of Robert, an only child, decided to take him on a two week vacation. Robert did not want to go because there was no one in whose care he could entrust his pet turtle while he was away. After much persuasion, the father convinced Robert to leave the turtle at home with an adequate food supply for the two week period. Upon his return home, Robert dashed down to the playroom to see how his turtle was faring. Lo and behold, it was dead on its back. Robert began ranting, screaming and literally "swinging away" at his father. In self-defense, the father quickly concocted a plan. "Poor turtle is dead. Let's make a real funeral for him. We'll line one of Mommy's old jewelry boxes with silk cloth and use it as a casket. We'll place the coffin on your wagon and harness Billy (the dog) to it. He will slowly pull the coffin in a real military funral. We'll invite all your friends to join in a funeral procession. They will bring their toy trumpets and drums and play solemn music as we all march. I'll be the grave digger and make a hole in our back yard, large enough for burial, etc; etc."

The idea caught Robert's fancy. He made plans for the funeral; drew up lists of friends to invite; took one of his mother's jewelry boxes and lined it with the silk material that his father provided. After the preparations were completed, Robert and his father went to the playroom to place the turtle in the coffin. Robert was truly excited about the prospects of the funeral.

Just as he was about to pick up the turtle, it moved. Robert quickly turned to his father and yelled, "Daddy, kill it, kill it!"

Attitudes can often be changed rather quickly. For sustained change there must be continued stimulus under appropriate conditions. These the teacher must try to create. Frequently, he will not succeed. Nevertheless he must try continually to affect change. Always his guidepost should be אין לך דבר העומד בפני הרצון "nothing stands in the way of the will."

Teacher Approach

Basic to instructional performance is the teacher's approach to classroom management. A classic study classifies the approaches to group leadership into three categories: autocratic, democratic and laissez-faire. Of these three approaches, democratic-type leadership has been shown to be most effective, and the laissez-faire approach, least effectual.

Autocratic-type management has one fundamental advantage. Teacher goals may be reached more quickly via authoritarian devices. Teacher-centered methods eliminate the need of time required for pupil involvement in the various stages of democratic operation. Since time is a crucial problem in the Jewish school, a modified teacher-centered approach for specific short-term projects may be justified. However, when one views the classroom against the backdrop of the total Jewish education of the Jewish child which involves the development of a value system via pupil identification with school goals and teacher goals, the significance of the democratic approach looms large.

The democratic way of leadership recognizes the worth of the individual, on the one hand, and charges him with responsibility to himself and to the group, on the other. It understands individual and group needs; yet, it requires optimum development of individual and group potential. It stimulates individual initiative; yet, it encourages behavior in consonance with the best interests of the group. To be sure, the democratic approach is in the spirit of Jewish tradition for these very reasons.

To be effective, the democratic leader must be skilled in the group process. This is where the importance of training is paramount. The ability to initiate and maintain group processes is not innate. Its acquisition is the product of careful study and experience. While the mechanics of group dynamics can be developed quite independently of the feeling-tone of the class, the intangible personality factors that contribute to the final outcomes of the process must be considered seriously.

Technology alone does not insure desirable classroom results. The combination of 'teaching science' (acquired technical skills) and 'teaching art' (personal teacher qualities) is basic to the success of the democratic process in the classroom. This kind of synthesis is important for all phases of the instructional program. The marriage of the heart and mind is indispensable for sound creative teaching in the Jewish school.

— 25 —

REACHING, RECRUITING AND RETAINING PERSONNEL FOR TORAH EDUCATION

Presented at Conference on Torah Education Convened in commemoration of the Twenty-Fifth Anniversary of the Community Service Division, Rabbi Isaac Elchanan Theological Seminary Yeshiva University, January 25, 1970

The 1960's in Retrospect

For Jewish education in America the past decade has just ended with neither a flourish nor a death knell. The Jewish school still survives but so do the perils and problems that threaten to strangle it.

Looking at Jewish education in this country — and at Jewish education under Orthodox auspices, in particular — Chaim Weizmann would have commented, as he did about another crucial phase of Jewish life in his times, "Some problems never get solved; they just get older."

This has been an age of tall challenge and tiny response, of sky-scraping demands and mini-hut answers.

How can we avoid concluding that the sixties have ended not with direction for future growth of Jewish education, but with the characteristic symbol of our times — the question mark.

Why was there a decrease in Jewish school enrollment?

Are good, exciting teachers and competent administrators impossible to recruit?

What about our day schools? Are they really meeting the challenge of a dual school program?

Must we continue to stand by and witness the continuous and growing onslaught of alienation upon Jewish youth.

Why are we so slow in solving the Bar Mitzvah dead-end problem? Can we solve it? How?

Why does the Orthodox community still abdicate responsibility for the supplementary school?

How can we raise the status of the Jewish education profession? raise the standards of Jewish schooling? and raise the needed funds to conduct viable programs?

The '60's have been a decade where *old* problems not only became older but came also into sharp perilous focus — the personnel shortage, the irrelevant curricula, the Jewishly disadvantaged adults, the no-interest-non-continuation syndrome of Jewish youth, the turned-off generation of Jewish adolescents and the ever-growing financial crises.

It has been a decade where *new* problems and challenges appear in *all* their fullness and boldness and make demands upon the '70's to provide appropriate responses and solid solutions. These challenges include questions about: the space age and the Jewish school program; the new technologies and Jewish pedagogy; the Jewish college student and the New Left; the role of Israel in the Jewish school; Aliyah as a viable American response; and the social revolution and the Jewish studies curriculum.

In light of these challenges it is entirely appropriate that today's historic conference which launches the National Commission on Torah Education concern itself with *Reaching, Recruiting* and

Retaining.

The three R's are a convenient rubric under which we may categorize the major educational challenges facing the Orthodox Jewish community. Indeed they form the basic three R's for the National Commission on Torah Education (*Nacote*). Interestingly, the Hebrew root verb *nacote* — has an important message for us today: *nacote* is both an intransitive and transitive verb. As an intransitive verb it means *to loathe* or *to be weary*. As a transitive verb it has an entirely different meaning: *to take hold* or, as Maimonides used it in the expression *nekitat chaifetz, to acquire.* The message simply states: To be effective, *Nacote* must be *transitive;* the Commission must be active; it must be the personification of forward and upward movement.

Permit me, first, to define the three R's and then proceed to pose the challenges.

Reaching

Reach, I take to mean in its very profound sense of reaching out, or straining after something not easily attainable, of making a supreme effort.

Robert Browning defines the term for us: "Ah, but a man's reach should exceed his grasp, or what's a heaven for?"

Using this definition as a frame of reference, the challenge to Orthodox educators and Orthodox schools must be viewed in terms of educational quality. It calls for *higher goals* of achievement, *higher* standards of instruction and supervision, *higher* levels of pupil performance and *higher* expectations of learning outcomes.

And this challenge holds true for all types of schools and all levels of schooling, notwithstanding the intrinsic differences between the various institutions of learning under Orthodox auspices.

Is it realistic to make the same challenge of dissimilar schools with dissimilar programs and vastly different levels of achievement?

The affirmative answer sheds important light on a double-edged problem in Orthodox Jewish education and brings the challenge of *reaching upward* into sharp focus.

The Jewish day school and supplementary school are

significantly different with regard to structure, hours of learning, auspices, lay and rabbinic interest, moral and financial support and expectations for accomplishment. Yet, they share the same need to "raise the roof" of their aspirations and performance.

On the other hand, the afternoon school suffers from abuse, abandonment and atrophy. By and large, the Orthodox community has made peace with the ineffectiveness of an afternoon Herbrew education and has allowed itself to slip into a posture of convenient lethargy. Well-meaning teachers and rabbis all too often assume the "we're licked before we begin" attitude when it comes to make real demands upon themselves and pupils. This fateful feeling of inability to "move the mountain" has been building up for a long time and I dare say that we Orthodox seem to be the least interested in reversing this tendency and providing an antidote to it. And, this is for one good basic reason — *we* have the day school. The yeshiva is our saving grace. But, the 70,000 children attending Jewish supplementary schools under Orthodox auspices can take little comfort in the salvation of their yeshiva counterparts.

The first challenge of the '70's is, therefore, a resolve not to let these children down. It is a hard challenge. It means retooling our thinking, redoubling our efforts and redirecting our energies — physical, mental and emotional. It means many more things, too — better teachers, more effective teaching, better supervision, etc. (These we will get to later.) But, essentially, it means raising our sights and hopes as a national community and pooling our efforts so as not to lose another generation of Talmud Torah kids.

The day school is another story. It is the apple of our eye, the epitome of our educational achievements, the realization of our dreams, even undreamed dreams. We bask in its glory, take pride in the contributions that this form of schooling has made to the American Jewish community, and make demands upon the community to support it generously.

And that's just the way it should be, except for one fly in the ointment. For lack of a better word, I would name this little insect — *complacency.* "We've made it," we say to ourselves and to our neighbors. To be sure, we *have* made it, — but *only* up to a certain point.

I view the major need of the day school at this crucial juncture in Jewish life as one of striving for something *more* than we have. With all its goodness, with all its effectiveness, with all the dedication and blessing it has brought to American Jewry, to Orthodoxy and to individual Jews, the yeshiva — the Jewish day school under Orthodox auspices — must look upward and gear itself toward meeting the ever-growing challenges of our day. This means achieving both *higher* cognitive and *higher* effective ends which can only be accomplished by raising our sights with regard to the essential quality of performance in our schools and the lasting results we hope to produce via the most appropriate instrument for assuring creative Orthodox living — the all-day school.

Above all, in our thrust for excellence we must be our own severest critics.

The same self-critical high-sight approach should apply to all other educational endeavors under Orthodox auspices — pre-school classes, educational and adult education.

So much for challenge number one. The commentary to the challenge will hopefully be given in the respective workshops.

Recruiting

The second major challenge to NACOTE is conveniently contained in the word *recruit*.

Here we are confronted head-on with the crisis in human resources. We are challenged to strengthen and replenish our schools with new personnel. In its very literal sense the challenge is quantitative. It says: recruit *more* teachers, *more* principals, *more* lay people. It suggests, too, increasing pupil enrollment.

Yet, I submit that the challenge of recruitment has a more vital dimension than fortifying Jewish schools with more lay and professional personnel. Recruitment is not an additive function or process of accretion. The idea of recruitment has clear and definite qualitative dimensions. (In fact, the French verb root *recoitre* from which it derives means *to grow, to motivate growth*.)

It is not sufficient to attract *more* teachers, *more* principals and *more* lay people. But, it is absolutely vital to recruit more *talented* teachers and more *competent* principals, to recruit more *top-level* lay people, more *visionary* lay leaders. And, that's what the National Commission is all about.

I don't believe that the personnel shortage — despite the annual estimated need approaching 1000 teachers and principals — is merely quantitative. Somehow, the bodies are always found to man the classes by the time school starts. The manpower approaches catastrophic proportions because it is a *qualitative* crisis. We are losing *good* people and we have not been able — with few exceptions — to recruit *gifted* personnel.

The reason given time and time again for the inability to attract new blood is the lack of financial security and economic growth opportunities and the low social status of the profession. These are important contributing factors. They are *not,* however, the only reasons, nor even the major causes. I submit — and here I lay my reputation and life on line — that the educational personnel themselves are responsible, in good measure, for the low status of the profession. What we need are exciting gifted teachers, and high caliber dynamic supervisors who will *command by their performance* and not demand by their presence better recompense and greater esteem for the community. Fortunately, we have begun to see some glimmer of light shining in this direction.

As long as the image of the *heder melamed* persists, as long as the job of teaching is pedestrian and unexciting we will fail to attract the talented and the gifted young people we so desperately need to revive a lackluster, dying profession.

The challenge of recruiting is two-fold: In the first place it cries out to NACOTE: recruit the *best* lay people in the synagogues, the most prominent and able *baale-batim* — who ordinarily do not sit on education committees. Fire them with a desire to change the image of the afternoon school. Taking a leaf from the black community, make them feel a sense of urgency regarding our Jewishly disadvantaged. Charge them with the responsibility of doing something about it. Give them guidance; and, the miracle will begin to happen.

The synagogue will have an active, knowledgeable board of education comprised of people who *care* and who *count.* The board members will make demands for excellence upon themselves. They will demand standards of excellence — vis-à-vis the congregational school — from the rabbi and principal. The rabbi and principal will make demands for excellence upon themselves and upon the teachers; and the teachers will follow suit with demands upon themselves and upon their pupils, who eventually will make demands upon their parents and the community.

The challenge of recruitment speaks out, as well, to the day school leaders — effective as they may consider their schools to be — to play a vital role in the upgrading of the yeshiva teaching profession.

The second phase of the challenge says, in effect, to the Commission: go out to your rabbis and recruit them for educational work. They are the greatest single educational resource for their respective congregations. The challenge says to the lay leaders of the synagogue; free your rabbis from non-educational work, permit him, encourage him, require him to give his best talents and efforts to *all* the educational activities under the sponsorship of the synagogue. Furthermore, the challenge says to the Commission: go out to the young talented people in the *Yeshivot Gedolot,* in the Hebrew colleges and in the high schools; go to the religious young people on the college campus. Use all the means in your power to bring them into Jewish education. In truth, our youth are searching for a calling. What greater challenge, what loftier calling is there than teaching youth, and opening up their minds and hearts to Jewish values. "B'shaot y'duot bayom yoshev hakadush baruch hu umlamed tinokot shel bet raban." Even the Almighty considers teaching a worthy vocation for Himself.

Recruit these talented youth and then provide them with the incentives and the wherewithal to prepare adequately for Jewish teaching. Forthwith, they will become the emulative models for new and old teacher alike. And, the Jewish teaching profession will begin to rise out of the doldrums of mediocrity toward its rightful place in Jewish life.

Retaining

Retaining is denoted as the third challenge of the seventies. This challenge, too, has double meaning.

At one and the same time, it refers to increasing (1) the retentive powers of the school, and (2) the retentive powers of the *children* in the school.

Accordingly, two sets of questions are raised. In the first instance, we are challenged by the following questions:

How can we keep elementary school children in our schools beyond Bar Mitzvah?

How can we retain adolescents through the high school years?

How can we encourage high school youth to continue their Jewish study even beyond secondary school?

How can we develop in our educatees the desire to be (in good Jewish tradition) life-long students of Torah?

The second phase of the challenge poses these questions:

How can we make learning palatable and desirable?

How can we motivate our children and youth to want to learn?

How can we best secure the *cognitive* ends of learning?

What shall we teach on each level of schooling? What shall we stress? What shall we delete?

How can we insure maximum understanding of the intellectual fare of the school diet?

How can we assure the greatest possible retention of knowledge?

How can we best achieve the *affective* goals of Jewish instructions?

What must be done to cultivate positive attitudes to Jews and Jewishness?

How can we reinforce desirable behavioral patterns and modify unfavorable behavior?

How can we develop maximum commitment to yiddishkeit — to Torah, to the Jewish people, to Israel?

While these two groups of questions may appear to belong to two separate challenges (they are, indeed, addressed to two different elements of the educative function, the school unit and the individual child), they are absolutely interdependent and interlocking facets of *one* challenge and require, in fact, the same response or *same* set of responses.

Retention — for both the school and the pupil — is a function of *the what* and *the how* of the educative process.

Simply put in the language of the challenge, schools cannot *retain* (for extended periods of time in a voluntary system of education) children who are not motivated to *retain* the cognitive and affective elements of their schooling.

What set of responses can be given to this difficult, dual

challenge of retaining?

1. First and foremost, the Orthodox educational enterprise needs well-formulated clearly stated goals for all levels and programs of the various formal and informal educational activities under Orthodox auspices. This includes the day school, the congregational school, co-curricular activities, youth programs, adult education and educational camping.

A statement of purpose would form the long-needed guidelines for individual schools and local programs.

2. Secondly, within the framework of traditional Judaism relevant curricula must be created for all schools and for all levels of schooling.

To the average Jew in the old *shtetl* the goals of the *heder* may have been clear. Certainly, the subject matter was clear-cut and circumscribed. However, today, we cannot be smug anymore about the explicit aims of Jewish education or about the most appropriate curriculum for a specific school.

What should pupils in Jewish schools study? What should be the relationship between the subjects of the Jewish school curriculum and the secular studies to which the pupils are exposed daily? What kind of interdisciplinary articulation might be established between the Jewish and general curricula?

These questions suggest the exploration of the areas of relevance between Jewish learning and the American environment, as well as serious study of extant Jewish school curricula.

Sound Jewish education is instruction in how to live as a Jew in whatever environment the Jew finds himself. Judaism, in this sense, begs to be relevant, to be made relevant. The relevance of the Jewish heritage to the child can be explored on two levels: (a) on the personal, pupil-to-parent, pupil-to-peer relationship, and (b) on the impersonal pupil-to-religious school and pupil-to-world relationship.

In essence, the developing of a viable relationship between Jew and Jew, and Jew and his non-Jewish surroundings was the aim of the German Jewish rationale-theologians like Hirsch, Hildesheimer and Carleback. By admitting modern knowledge and technology and the scientific search for truth to a place in the Orthodox scheme of life they were demonstrating the possbility of establishing a compatibility between religious and secular disciplines. *Torah im derech eretz* showed that each realm was meaningful to the other; and more than that, this philosophy claimed that each was an indispensable helpmate of the other. The Hirschian emphasis on worldly knowledge as an aid to religious outlook and observance might not be entirely acceptable today without acknowledging that Judaism has a role to play in worldly affairs. The current version of this 19th century western Jewish attempt at a combination of synthesis (depending on how we view the union of the disciplines) of the world of religion and the world of modern thought presents its point of veiw as a *do-or-die proposition.* The challenge of the Jewish community by the surrounding culture is, as Ahad Ha'am might have phrased it, to absorb it and come to terms with it, or to be swallowed up by it.

One aspect of relevance that must be introduced vigorously into school programs is the role of Israel in Jewish life.

3. Relevance alone is not enough to insure a viable education.

To be effective, the curriculum must be well-graded and well-articulated — both vertically, and horizontally. This means developing patterns of sequential learning for all subjects, and correlating, where desirable, the subject matter of the different grade levels.

Articulation of the various curricular offerings in our schools has long been an important need and requires the immediate attention of N A C O T E.

4. Given clear goals, relevant and well-graded programs, the challenge of retaining then says to the Orthodox Jewish school:

If you honestly desire to achieve your goals, you must establish a pleasant learning climate and provide professional guidance programs for your pupils. If personal and psychological guidance is found to be a need of the secular school, how much more so is it a necessity in the Jewish school where significant behavioral modification is sought.

5. The response to the challenge of *retaining* must have yet another vital dimension. Our times require that the Orthodox Jewish school undergo a major change of purpose and broadening of function and service.

The formal school — be it a *yeshiva ketanah* or a congregational school — must become a total educational center, an umbrella community of learning whose members are not only children, but also parents, teachers, supervisors and lay leaders.

This means viewing the parent not *qua* parent, but as a learner, as a person *to* whom the school has an educational commitment and for whom the school provides educational programs.

Similarly, on their respective levels, the lay leadership and instructional personnel must find in the school a place for their own Jewish and professional growth.

The implementation of this *community of learning* concept may require retooling of the school organization including the budget, the use of the building and the utilization of rabbinic and educational personnel. These operative changes, too, will have significant positive effects upon the school. For example, they will provide more full-time educational positions for the individual school units. They will motivate closer home-school relationships and make the community a real partner in the educative process.

6. Finally, the challenge of retaining demands that our schools consider new technologies of teaching and learning.

During the past two decades there has been a plethora of serious and significant research and experimentation in general education with new instructional devices and learning media: new forms of grouping for study, new patterns of individualized instruction, programmed learning, new educational hardware and software, language laboratories, teaching machines and educational television.

Not to be aware of these new developments in educational technology is unforgivable *ignorance*. Not to be ready to experiment with new techniques is *intellectual heresy*. Not to adapt new technologies of instruction and learning to Jewish schools is *suicidal foolhardiness*.

The question is — paraphrasing the challenge to general education by the Charles F. Kettering Foundation — "Can Jewish educators leave the static ways and static guidelines which have dominated the history of Jewish schooling in America and adopt the process ways — the ways of meeting new challenges — which must become the Jewish educator's ways if the Jewish school is to survive?"

In sum, the challenge of retaining — assuring the retention of pupils in school and insuring the retention of the benefits of their schooling — requires clear aims, meaningful sequential programs of learning, a pleasant educational atmosphere, total involvement of the school community and the use of effective teaching technology.

Summation and Resolution

Reaching, recruiting and retaining for Torah education are the *necessary* challenges for the 1970's.

Will the Orthodox Jewish community in America be able to meet them?

As individuals we cannot. As a united community we can. In face of the perilous alternatives we must act in unison. We must share our thinking, pool our talents, coordinate our efforts and synchronize our response.

The only way to provide a viable unified solution is to create a national instrument to spearhead the response. I, therefore, respectfully place before this historic conference the following resolution to officially launch such an umbrella organization for Orthodox education.

In light of the pressing educational needs of the Orthodox Jewish community in America, particularly during these times of great social change, disturbing moral turbulence and growing alienation of Jews from Judaism, be it resolved that a National Commission on Torah Education be established to promote effective Jewish education under Orthodox auspices. Koh Lehai!

— 26 —

FOCUS ON THE PRINCIPAL: ON BECOMING A CHANGE AGENT

Presented at
BJE Principals' Center Conference
University of Pennsylvania
June 21, 1987

While there is no unanimity about definitions of an effective school in general education, there is clear consensus about the importance of principalship. Effective School Research demonstrates that a limited number of organizational programmatic characteristics or *correlates* consistently obtain in effective schools and are absent, in whole, or in part, in the ineffective ones. One of the key correlates of effective schooling is strong administrative and instructional leadership.

Ron Edmonds, acknowledged by most as the father of Effective Schools Research, noted that "there are some bad schools with *good* principals; but there are *no* good schools with *bad* principals."

The other correlates — including a clear institutional mission, a positive learning environment, high expectations for pupil growth,

186

productive student time on task, careful monitoring of pupil progress and good home-school relations — are integrally related to or flow from instructional leadership.

Voluntarism and Potential Impact

One major difference between public education and Jewish education *informs* any discussion in Jewish school principalship. Jewish education, like all aspects of Jewish life, is voluntary. There is no district or state hierarchy of authority. While the system of volunteerism has serious drawbacks, there are potential advantages to Jewish school admininstration. The independence and autonomy of each institution increases the possible impact of school-based leadership.

Maximizing Impact of Principals

Findings of the "Study of the Recommendations of Major National Studies on Education to Jewish Schooling" *(Jewish Education* Summer 1984) demonstrate that next to increased funding, the recommendation most relevant to the 1100 respondents (including teachers, principals, parents and lay leaders) was "improving instructional leadership and supervision."

In reality, the Jewish community looks toward the principal to lead. The community may not always articulate this feeling or communicate it, but it's clearly there.

"Focus on the principal as a change agent" implies there is need for change. Indeed, the need for Jewish supplementary school (JSS) reform is unquestionable. The problems of part-time Jewish schooling are manifold. These are documented by the findings of a three-year study of the Jewish supplementary school just completed by BJE.

Everyone agrees that this system must be changed. Clearly, there is a special role for principals in initiating and implementing change in each school. Responding to the JSS challenges depends heavily on the leadership that the principal provides. Among all the actors in the JSS drama — rabbi, teacher, youth leader, pupil, parent, school board member and synagogue trustee — the principal will have the major responsibility to help initiate change.

Without lay support and leadership and without rabbinic involvement, change will not take place. But, the change agent will have to be the principal. The ways that principals will be able to initiate change will best be developed by principals working together to achieve common goals.

As *change agents* we first have to look to ourselves. Rabbi Abraham Joshua Heschel in *The Prophets,* notes that "The significance of Israel's prophets lies not only in what they said, but what they were. The prophet's task is to convey a divine view, yet as a person he *is* a point of view."

Maimonides stresses the importance of the personal attributes of the communal leader, the dayan, the educational leader, the *talmid hacham.* This emphasis on personal traits and personal influence is no less important for us Jewish educators as we approach the 21st century.

An applicant for the job of Shamash in a shul in the East Side at the turn of the century couldn't read or write. He didn't get the job. So, he started out with a needle and thread and gradually built up a thriving garment manufacturing business and became a multimillionaire. He needed a large loan for expansion and was invited by John D. Rockefeller to the bank's office and given an application to fill out. He said that he couldn't read or write. Rockefeller was dumbfounded. "You're such a talented person. Imagine what you would have been had you been able to read and write?"

"I'd be the Shamash of the Second Avenue shul," was the reply.

We must ask ourselves, the Zusha question: Are we all that we could be? Do we maximize our personal and professional potential? One of the attributes we need in order to respond effectively to the challenges we face is found in the Sidrah we read last Shabbat. It is about the twelve Israelites sent by Moses to spy out the Land of Canaan. The spies were all important people. This fact is conveyed literally in the Bible. "All of them men who were the heads of the children of Israel. Each was a prince." Their importance is underscored by many biblical exegetes and commentators. According to Ibn Ezra, they were all "famous heroes." Obadiah Sforno notes that each spy was "the outstanding leader of his respective tribe." Rabbi Chaim Ibn Attar suggests that they were the most "righteous of their tribes."

So what happened? Why did ten of the twelve leaders fail in their mission? The answer lies in a clearer understanding of the biblical text.

Moses was instructed to send a leader from every tribe — *kol nasi bahem*, translated generally, as "each one was a prince among them." Actually, the meaning of "kol nasi bahem" is "each man had the potential qualities of a prince *in* him."

Only two spies were able to realize their potential. When they completed their mission, ten of the spies reported, "We were like grasshoppers in our own eyes, and so we appeared in their eyes." Clearly, they had a very poor self-image. (They felt like grasshoppers.) They lost their self confidence. They were not able to rise to the occasion and were not able to fulfill their potential as "princes."

But, Caleb and Joshua were able to realize their potential. They did not lose confidence in their ability to settle the land. As Caleb insisted, "We should certainly go up at once and possess it, because we are able to overcome it."

The obstacles facing the Israelites were real. But they could be overcome. To most of the spies the size of the challenge was the problem. Their perception of the challenge created the reality of lack of self-concept and the reality of the inability to complete the mission successfully.

The perception of the challenge is a critical dimension of leadership. The principal, as change agent, must first believe in himself or herself. A healthy self-concept coupled with knowledge and skill is the necessary combination for responding to the daily challenges of principalship and initiating change.

Im tirzu ain zu aggaddah. "If you will it, it will be no legend." What was true about the miracle of Zionism reaching fulfillment in a Jewish State is true about all leadership challenges.

Beginning with belief in self, we will be able to create the miracles for which we all strive — better schools, better teaching and better learning.

— 27 —

THE PRINCIPAL
AND STRESS MANAGEMENT
IN THE SYNAGOGUE SCHOOL

Introductory Remarks,
Principals Center Conference,
Columbia University,
June 20, 1988

Several socio-educational conditions relate to the role of administration in Jewish school settings.

1) The first is the matter of voluntarism — the voluntaristic nature of the Jewish community, of synagogue life and of Jewish education. This includes the importance communal lay leaders and synagogue lay leaders attach to the function of Jewish education in the larger Jewish community and in the local school setting.

2) The second is the status of Jewish educators in the larger society, in the Jewish community and in the synagogue.

3) The third is the hierarchal arrangement of professional authority in the synagogue — particularly the relationship between the principal and the rabbi, assistant rabbi and cantor. In the Jewish day school, the levels of professional authority generally refer to the role of

190

the principal in relationship to the executive director.

These three features of Jewish schooling — voluntarism, educator status and role in synagogue — have direct bearing on lay-professional relationships. They relate significantly to the quality of support the principal receives in his/her work and his/her authority, responsibility, accountability and flexibility in the daily performance of his/her duties.

There are several other characteristics that bear on Jewish school principalship.

1) Requirements for becoming a Jewish school principal or being hired as a principal — Judaic knowledge, Hebraic language ability, pedagogic and supervisory training, knowledge of curriculum development — comprise another important factor relating to the principal's role.

2) In the synagogue, the part-time nature of school administration has direct bearing on principalship. Less than one-third of all supplementary school principalships are full time.

3) The nature of the Jewish school teachers — their general and Jewish educational backgrounds, preparation for teaching, perception of Jewish school teaching as a career, time commitment to the school — and the shortage of quality teachers are other important considerations.

4) The lack of a professional association of school administrators that can authoritatively speak on behalf of *all* Jewish school principals speaks also to the principal in the individual school setting.

These four features are important dimensions of Jewish school principalship *as a profession,* as they are indicative of Jewish education as a *career.* Jewish lay leadership perception of principals is influenced significantly by these factors.

5) Finally, the role of the Jewish family in the Jewish educational process has a strong impact on the effectiveness of the principal's work. The support that parents give to the Jewish schooling of their children and the quality of their relationship to the synagogue are critical to the functioning of the principal.

Research in general education emphatically points to the key role of the principal in maintaining effective schools and classrooms.

This relates to his/her ability to work with teachers and facilitate their involvement with the overall school program. Given the relatively small size of Jewish school and the fact that the principal is generally the sole educational administrator, the actions he/she takes or delegates to others to promote growth in student learning are even more critical.

In a recent study I conducted on the *Relevance of the Recommendations of Major National Studies on Education to Jewish Schooling,* "Improving academic leadership and supervision" was considered the single most relevant educational challenge by some 800 representative respondents — including principals, teachers, parents and lay leaders. While the vast majority of all respondents viewed improving instruction leadership as "absolutely essential" or "very important," the parent/lay respondents felt that the leadership recommendation is particularly crucial.

It is clear that the principal is the princi*ple* change agent within the school. The extent of his/her ability to initiate change and implement new programs and educational constructs depends on the communal, school-based professional characteristics of his/her job just outlined.

The principal's mission must be to try constantly to upgrade the educational apparati he/she operates, and to improve the level of school effectiveness and the level of pupil achievement. The problems that inhibit responses to this challenge are not an excuse for not responding to it at all.

All these factors form the frame of reference against which stress and stress management must be considered.

The psycho-social dimensions of stress and the principal's ability to manage stress cannot be dealt with without an appreciation of the baggage the principal brings to his/her job and without a clear understanding of the total environment in which he/she operates.

– 28 –

EXECUTIVES IN JEOPARDY

Presented at the Annual Meeting
of the Conference on
Jewish Communal Service
May 1983

1. How seriously is the executive in our field in jeopardy?

In Jewish education, one cannot generalize about executive jeopardy since the executives operate in different kinds of settings. Essentially, they serve in three types of educational institutions: all-day schools and yehivot, supplementary or congregational schools and central communal agencies for Jewish education.

    a.   In the all-day school setting, the executive relates to and works with the president, members of the board of trustees, the chairman of the board of education, members of the board of education; to parents and to donors. He relates also to professionals in administrative activity (the number of these people obviously varies with the size of the school), to Jewish studies teachers, general studies teachers, and non-educational personnel as supervisor and colleague.

b.   In the congregational school, whether it's of the one-day variety or an afternoon Hebrew school, the professional relates first to the rabbi as the top professional in the synagogal structure, then to a variety of lay people, particularly to the chairman of the lay Board of Education and its members; to the chairperson of the PTA and members of the PTA, if there is one; and sometimes, also, to the president of the synagogue and members of its board of directors. He obviously relates also to teachers as their supervisor and co-worker.

c.   The executive of the bureau of Jewish education relates to and works with the president, officers and members of the board of trustees; to staff members in management and functional roles; and then to the officers, lay leaders and staff of Federation, depending upon the size of the community and the particular relationship between the bureau and the federation.

I have served in each of these capacities as executive, and also as executive in a university setting. In each of these, the executive plays a decidedly different role, so one really cannot generalize. There are some 50 communal agencies for Jewish education. *The executive position in the these organizations seems to be rather stable — with relatively little jeopardy.* A prominent feature here is that the demand is much greater than the supply.

While the supply of qualified school execs cannot keep up with the demand, muscial chairs is a game played in the day school and supplementary school. To be sure, there is regularly, a 10, 15 and sometimes 20% annual turnover in school executive positions. *For the school executive there is considerable jeopardy.*

2.   What are the causes of executives in jeopardy?

Again, one can't generalize about the causes of executives in jeopardy, but I feel that the following are the most important in order of frequency:

a.   Executive incompetence.

b.   Incongruence of personal, professional or religious goals with the goals of the agency and/or lay leadership.

c.   Inability to solve strategic problems relating to personnel and program, and in the case of schools, pupil discipline problems that reach the office of the principal or administrator.

d.   Inability to relate to parents and parental needs and idiosyncrasies.

e.   Poor chemistry between professional and lay leaders. In the case of the supplementary school, this would refer to the relationship between professional executive and the rabbi.

f.   Lay leadership dominance, which conflicts with the self-image and work style of the executive.

g.   Lay leaders' perception of the level of knowledge of the ability of the exec and his status in the community.

h.   Inability to handle idiosyncratic needs of lay leaders.

i.   Inability to relate to senior veteran staff. This is particularly so, concerning young, new executives.

3.   Is there a relationship between executive jeopardy and the changing lay leadership of our field?

Absolutely. Years ago, the typical lay leader was the *philanthrop* who was essentially a rich *ba'al bayit,* whose participation was generally via financial contribution. "I will give you the means to do the work, and the responsibility of running the show is yours" was his concept of lay leadership. This has significantly changed over the past years. Now, we have young, involved leaders who are very busy but want to take an active part in setting policy, in understanding and assessing the effectiveness of their institution and developing modes of accountability.

Turning the challenge of the latter kind of lay leadership into a blessing requires time in working with laity and the ability to work with them. This includes knowing how to staff lay leaders — write speeches, help create agenda for lay committees, orient new lay persons to the policies and practices of the agency and work with them in solving strategic problems and responding to new challenges. It also requires the exec to be able to help new, young lay persons realize their full potential. In Jewish education, many execs are not comfortable with lay people — either working with them or being accountable to them. There is no greater executive satisfaction than knowing you have a warm, mutual and productive relationship with your lay board.

Of course, there can be no comfortable working relationship with board members and officers if they don't respect the knowledge and ability and creativity of the exec. In turn, the exec must respect the lay leaders for their volunteer role, their commitment to his personal and professional goals and for the time and energy they invest in pursuit of the agency's purposes.

4.   What steps can be taken to prevent executive jeopardy?

I guess the best way to prevent it is responding appropriately to question 2 — removing the causes of executives in jeopardy; and working on number 3 — helping turn the challenge of young involved lay leadership into a blessing.

– 29 –

SHARED IDENTITY
OF
JEWISH COMMUNAL WORKERS:
THE JEWISH DIMENSION

Excerpted from Address
as Scholar-in-Residence
at Annual Meeting of the
Conference of Jewish Communal Service
Philadelphia, Pa.   June 3, 1990

I am honored and most pleased to join a distinguished group of scholar-practitioners who have served as Sidney Vincent scholars-in-residence at the annual Conference of Jewish Communal Service. This forum honors the memory of a Jewish communal worker who, in his professional and personal life, served as a model of knowledgeable, creative, compassionate and forward looking Jewish communal leadership.

אין חכם כבעל הנסיון. The scholar-in-residence practice is in good Jewish tradition. That tradition informs us that wisdom, at best, is the accumulation of experience. Indeed, one interpretation of the Hebrew word *ziknah* (which literally means "old age" attained at age 60) is "the one who has acquired wisdom." This interpretation, I believe, is the justification for my role this year at our annual conference.

Accordingly, based upon my own experience, I would like to share some thoughts with you about a major challenge for Jewish communal workers. Each CJCS scholar-in-residence had a special reservoir of experience upon which he drew for his remarks. My particular background suggests that my comment should be introduced by a *dvar* Torah.

But, first, I was asked to tell about what motivated me to become a Jewish communal educator, given that there were other more lucrative and professionally satisfying opportunities available to me. The answer is twofold. On the one hand, I was brought up in a very positive Jewish home that nurtured a love for Judaic learning and an uncompromising love for Israel and the Jewish people. On the other hand, as a precollegiate teenager growing up in Boston during World War II, I was exposed to and suffered, with other members of my family, the consequences of anti-Semitism.

The combination of these factors fired me with the desire to do something to enhance Jewish life. As such, I chose Yeshiva University over other colleges and Jewish education over medicine. I've never regretted this choice.

This coming Sabbath, in the Torah reading, *B'ha'alotcha,* Moses was instructed to tell Aaron, his brother the High Priest, "When you kindle the lights, the seven lights should shine toward the front of the menorah."

According to Obadiah ben Yaakov Seforno, 16th century Italian physician and biblical exegete whose commentaries were usually aimed at inculcating a love for mankind, the peculiar sentence construction of this statement has special meaning. Seforno noted that *the language of the Torah instructs* Aaron to kindle the lights in such a way that the three lamps on the left of the center light and the three lamps on the right would both face the center. The center light — the most important of the lamps — was kindled only when the other lights faced it.

Seforno extrapolated from the menorah arrangement a message for the Italian Jewish community of his time. The three candles on the left, he said, represented the left-wing Jews or those involved in "this-worldly" aspects of life. Those on the right expressed the philosophy of right-wing Jews or those with a tendency for "other worldly" involvement. Unless the "leftists" and the "rightists" work together, the middle candle representing Jewish vitality and continuity, cannot be duly kindled or continue to shine, once lit. Seforno emphasized that continuity and vibrancy of Jewish life is endangered by the lack of mutual respect and cooperation between all elements of the Jewish community.

What was true for the 16th century Jewish community in Italy is valid for 20th century American Jewry and for world-wide Jewry as well. The Seforno message has particular application for the Conference of Jewish Communal Service in the 1990's.

To be sure, every individual, like each light of the menorah, has a *unique identity* and a *shared identity*. A person's unique identity is essentially his own self with its constellation of personality traits. It is a composite of individual needs and personal responses to those needs.

For example, an artistically talented person will seek ways to express his/her giftedness via personal and/or professional artistic involvement. A person endowed with attributes of physical strength and agility will capitalize on these charecteristics professionally or avocationally. A handicapped individual will try to address his/her needs through specialized forms of self-help.

While each of these people has a unique identity, together they share a common need for clean air, healthful food and good technology for effective communication. If they live in the same community they have similar communal goals for a safe, secure neighborhood and good, efficient local government. Their shared identities might also be expressed via common patterns of dress and similar religious outlooks.

Groups of people, societies and organizations also have unique identities and shared identities. Their unique identities are the result of the common group purposes they espouse and the common activity in which they engage. Oncologists acquire ideals and work habits unique to their profession. Faculty members of a given university have their unique academic needs and patterns of activity. Sanitation workers express their uniqueness through their common efforts to improve their work conditions and through their union activity to improve their economic security.

Besides being members of a special subset and having particular group needs and involvement, all of these people belong to larger societies. Oncologists are part of a medical profession and express their shared identity in many ways with all doctors. Faculty of Harvard University are members of a larger academic family. Sanitation workers are part of a larger governmental force of employees. Members of all three subgroups share in the common purposes and concerns of their overall vocational groupings.

The *unique identity/shared identity* concept is especially significant to the Jewish communal profession. It speaks to us in very special ways. All of us, whether we are group workers, vocational counselors, Jewish educators, Federation executives, community relations personnel or case workers, have our particular organizational/agency needs, which we express together with our co-workers via a unique identity. This is important for the strengthening of our respective professions and eventual contribution to the Jewish community and to the American society.

Over and above our immediate professional involvement, we all share common goals and concerns as Jewish communal workers and participate in common activities. The CJCS is a prime expression of our shared identity. However, there is one overriding commonality that unites us as we enter the last decade of the 20th century with its host of challenges to American Jewry. This is our shared *Jewish* identity. No matter what our professional orientation or involvement or our particular Jewish ideological preference or commitment, as Jewish communal workers we have a shared responsibility for Jewish continuity and the enhancement of Jewish life.

To be sure, until the 1970's this aspect of Jewish communal work, with the obvious exception of Jewish education, was not a major concern of Jewish communal service as it subordinated the Jewish dimension of our respective functions to the larger human service endeavor. Increasingly over the last several decades, the Jewish nature of our work has surfaced as a significant component of our professional involvement. Indeed, Jewish communal workers, by and large, appreciate the particularistic concerns of Judaism as they continue to value the universal Jewish dimensions of human services.

The Association of Jewish Community Organization Personnel membership application, for example, expresses this dual feeling when it states:

"We are men and women engaged in community organization work locally, regionally, and nationally, within and on behalf of the

Jewish community.

"We are dedicated to the development, enhancement, and strengthening of the professional practice of Jewish community service.

"We seek to improve the standards, practices, scope, and public understanding of the professional practice of Jewish community organization.

"We recognize the importance of supporting these efforts toward creative Jewish survival."

Working toward creative Jewish survival is our shared identity, our common purpose.

Vouchsafing creative Jewish survival while providing our respective professional services has a variety of ramifications. There are 800 Jewish communities ranging from a few families to 1,800,000 people in North America. With almost no exception, every one of these communities provides human services to respond to needs of its members. No other nation or people takes care of its own like Jews. This dimension of Jewish communal life in America, which has its roots in the *hevrot kehillot kodesh* of earlier generations in European and North African Jewish communities, is the most profound expression of the universal values of Judaism.

More specifically, helping insure creative Jewish survival has *personal* connotations for Jewish communal workers. These include Judaic study to increase our knowledge of Judaism. To be effective in transmitting Jewish values to others, requires knowledge of and commitment to these values.

Our shared identity will also involve each of us in activities on behalf of the State of Israel and in support of Operation Exodus and of Soviet Jewish acculturation in our respective communities. It will motivate us to support programs that combat anti-semitism on the one hand, and reduce assimilation, on the other. And, it will encourage us to more intensive personal Jewish behavior and practice. And, as we become more involved in the processes of our shared identity, we will appreciate the need to socialize our common Jewish interests.

In the long run, our involvement as *Jewish* communal professionals depends upon the continuity and vitality of the Jewish community. By strengthening our shared identity we help enhance Jewish life and subsequently help provide opportunities for continued growth of our respective professional endeavors. This mutuality of purpose is what Jewish communal work is all about in the last decade of the 20th Century.

As Seforno implies, the light of the Menorah — the sum total of the individual candles shining *together,* — is actually greater than the combination of the light derived from the individual candles. As Jewish communal workers, our impact on the Jewish community is all the more profound when we act in concert.

− 30 −

ON INITIATING A PROCESS FOR JEWISH FAMILY EDUCATOR TRAINING

Introductory Remarks made at
The Israel and Ida Berman Colloquium:
Toward a Model for Training
Effective Jewish Family Educators

Sponsored by the
Board of Jewish Education
of Greater New York

June 13, 1990

Shloshah shutafim yesh ba'adam — Hakadosh Baruch Hu, v'aviv v'eemo.

"There are three partners in (the creation of) a person — the Holy one blessed be He, and his father and his mother." *(Niddah,* 31a)

The threefold partnership mentioned in this Talmudic statement does not only refer to the birth of a baby. The term *ba'adam*, literally, "in a person," suggests that the partnership goes much beyond the instance of birth. Indeed, the Hebrew word for parent, *horeh*, is derived from the same root as teacher, *moreh*. Parent and teacher are one and the same in the home. Thus, Jewish tradition long ago recognized the overriding influence of parents on the maturation of their children from infant to "person" — *adam*. According to the sages of the Talmud, the partnership between God and the parent relates directly to the spirit and content of that maturation.

About two decades ago, we were informed by research in general education that school, at best, is a reinforcer of attitudes, behavior patterns and even skills acquired earlier in the home.

This condition brings us together today. Adding significance to our meeting is the two-page *New York Times* article whose sub-title is "The Home's Link to School Success — A Special Report." The essence of the report is contained in the opening sentence of the front page article dated June 13, New Haven, the home of Yale University: "For more than 20 years in this city of scholars and elms, school children and their parents have been studying a basic axiom: students in troubled schools learn better when families and educators work together." The essay notes that when concern about academic performance and a child's social and psychological growth are entwined, "the child feels better about himself and learns more." The Yale research process turns on a seemingly simple insight: "that a child's home life affects his performance in school, and that if schools pay attention to all the influences on a child, most problems can be solved before they get out of control" — shades of the James Coleman, Christopher Jencks and David Cohen studies in the 1960's.

While the Yale University school population is generally underprivileged, as were the populations of the Coleman, Jencks and Cohen research, the study has important implications for Jewish supplementary education, where the population is, by and large, Jewishly disadvantaged. I believe we can easily make the leap from economically underprivileged — i.e. the urban poor — to Jewish underprivileged — i.e. the suburban marginally affiliated or under-affiliated Jewish families. The landmark three-year study conducted by the Board of Jewish Education of Greater New York, from 1984 to 1987, recommends exactly what Dr. James P. Comer of Yale suggests as a result of his research: Teach the whole child as part of his family and, in the process, relate to all the family members, particularly, the parents. The BJE study stresses the importance of developing a synergism between home and school, not unlike Dr. Comer's prescription for effective public education.

To create this synergism, we have to have Jewish family education. And for Jewish family education to be efffective, the appropriate Jewish family educators must be in place. Since Jewish family education as a discrete, formal profession is a relatively new undertaking in the Jewish community, one of our first tasks is to train a cadre of Jewish family educators.

For that purpose we are convened today to help guide the development of a Jewish family educator training process. I am, therefore, pleased and privileged to welcome you to this colloquium which honors the memory of Ida and Israel Berman, who, in their lifetimes, were major benefactors of Jewish education.

The interdisciplinary nature of the colloquium participant is, in and of itself, an important occurrence in the process of Jewish educator training.

Here we are, heads of departments of graduate education of the Hebrew Union College-Jewish Institute of Religion, Jewish Theological Seminary and Yeshiva University; psychologists, family therapists and family life educators from the Jewish Board of Family and Children's Services and the Ackerman Institute of Family Therapy, Mount Sinai Hospital; social workers, group workers, teachers, school administrators, rabbis and several outstanding Jewish family educators. As we join BJE staff members in this trailblazing effort, I bid you "Shalom and Hatzlahah."

I see our combined challenge today as a three-step process.

The first step is exploring and defining the *Jewish* needs of *Jewish* families in relation to their social and psychological needs as parents in the 1990's. This will lead to the process of conceptualizing change and growth in Jewish family life.

The second step is developing the guidelines for strategies — individual, synagogal and communal — to meet these needs. This includes the development of instructional techniques, program methods and materials as well as evaluation processes.

And, finally, the third step is developing the procedures for creating a cadre of specialists to implement the strategies. This involves exploring models of professional training and giving serious attention to organizational and systems analysis of the network of synagogue, communal agencies and family structures needed to sustain Jewish family education and Jewish family educators.

As we engage in this effort, we must recognize that we are not working in a vacuum. Jewish family education is taking place all over the continent. Some of its most prominent practitioners are here today. We must learn from their experience which is essentially programmatic. Moreover, we must take a good look at programs that work and why they work, and try to find out what makes a Jewish family educator competent and effective. These facts are basic to our challenge — to participate in a scientific effort to guarantee the effectiveness of Jewish family education via careful study, research, training and evaluation. We are at the beginning of a historic effort, which, when concluded, can have a profound effect

1)   upon the Jewish school — it will make it more effective;

2)   upon the Jewish educators — it will increase their effectiveness and provide many more career opportunities in Jewish education;

3)   upon Jewish families — it will give them more purposeful activity and make family life more meaningful;

4)   upon synagogues — it will give them a new lease on life;

5)   upon rabbis — it will provide them with more meaningful roles vis-à-vis their congregants and make them more effective practititioners; and

6)   upon the Jewish community — it will enhance the quality of Jewish life and help insure Jewish continuity.

What a promise for the future of Jewish education! We're here to join in that promise by giving it our best shot as we combine theory and practice in Jewish family education.

FOCUS ON
THE BOARD OF
JEWISH EDUCATION
OF GREATER NEW YORK

— 31 —

ON THE HISTORY OF BJE

*Prepared as Introduction
to the BJE Self-Study Report
Board of Jewish Education
of Greater New York
June 1972*

The Board of Jewish Education, Inc. traces its history to 1910, when the communal Bureau of Jewish Education was founded in order to exert a total communal effort to support Jewish schooling. According to Samson Benderly, its founder, this could best "be accomplished by making the Jewish school a communal institution and part of a community system of schools."[1] Benderly stressed that

> each city with a fairly large Jewish population should have a single well-planned educational organization dealing with the Jewish problem in its entirety. This organization should be absolutely divorced from congregational management and from petty benefactors, but should depend on the total Jewish

populations of the place. It should be in the hands of a well organized, properly trained, and fully informed staff of salaried, responsible teachers, guided by an able superintendent whose entire time must be devoted to Jewish Education and whose ideal should be the advancement of Jewish learning.[2]

The Bureau came into being at a special meeting of the Executive Committee of the Kehillah on April 28, 1910, as a result of a survey of Jewish education, made by a team headed by Dr. Mordecai Kaplan and Dr. Bernard Cronson, a New York public school principal.

The development of the Bureau was based on Benderly's "lever" theory for the study and improvement of primary Jewish education in New York City. The Bureau initially had the following objectives:

1. To study sympathetically and at close range all the Jewish educational forces in New York City, including alike those that restrict themselves to religious instruction and those that look primarily to the Americanization of our youth, with a view to cooperation and the elimination of waste and overlapping.

2. To become intimately acquainted with the best teachers and workers who are the mainstay of these institutions, and organize them for both their material and their spritual advancement.

3. To make propaganda through the Jewish press and otherwise, in order to acquaint parents with the problem before them and with the means of solving it.

4. To operate one or two model schools for elementary pupils, for the purpose of working out the various phases of primary education, these schools to act also as concrete examples and guides to now existing Hebrew schools, which will undoubtedly avail themselves of the textbooks, methods, appliances, etc., worked out in the model schools, as soon as public opinion shall have ripened. These model schools, while devoting themselves to the solution of the problem of primary Jewish education, might also act as

preparatory schools, that is, as feeders to the Teachers Institute founded last year.[3]

To implement the above aims and to meet the needs of Jewish education of that period, the Bureau developed ten departments, described in 1910 by Benderly as follows:

1. Finance Department, to gather and distribute funds;

2. Textbook Department, to prepare, publish, and distribute textbooks and other school materials;

3. Department of Investigation, Collection and Attendance, to investigate the status of all new pupils, establish tuition collection routes, and monitor school attendance (such monitoring was much needed since in many Talmud Torahs up to 60% of the children enrolled left annually);

4. Department of Propaganda, to acquaint parents and the public at large with the problem of Jewish education and "with the means for its solution";

5. Department of Standardization, to watch results of standardization efforts in affiliated schools;

6. Department of New Schools, to inaugurate and supervise new schools as long as necessary;

7. Department of Extension Work to experiment with extension work;

8. Department of Preparatory Schools, to supervise the three existing preparatory schools and establish new ones;

9. Department of Teachers, to take charge of the morning classes in English and pedagogy for Talmud Torah teachers, and of seven classes for college men and one class for young women;

10. Department of Out-of-Town Schools, to keep in touch with seven out-of-town schools indirectly cooperating with the Bureau and possibly other schools.[4]

During its early years, the Bureau established a Board of License for teachers in Jewish schools, and developed pay scales for cooperating Talmud Torahs. To standardize curricula, the Bureau created a general Board of Talmud Torahs and Hebrew Principals' Association. In addition, it founded three new experimental schools for girls and four new communal schools for various sections of the city.

While the Bureau viewed itself primarily as a service agency, it rendered financial support to Jewish education via grants to schools which affiliated themselves with the Bureau. These grants were, in a sense, scholarship subsidies for indigent children. Among other things, the Bureau pioneered the idea of a Code of Practice for teachers, promoted the idea of *Ivrit B'Ivrit* in schools, developed camping experiences for children particularly through Camp Achvah, introduced visual aids in classroom instruction, and formed Jewish parents associations in Greater New York. After two decades of operation, the Bureau shifted its emphasis from elementary to secondary and pre-school levels.

In 1930, the Florence Marshall Junior Hebrew High School, came into being and later combined with the Hebrew High School, organized in 1913, under the name of Florence Marshall Hebrew High School. For the pre-school level, the Bureau published The Jewish Home Institute, a correspondence course for mothers. In the mid-1930's, as a result of a one million dollar bequest provided by Col. Michael Friedsam to promote Jewish education in New York, a survey of Jewish education was conducted by Dr. Isaac Berkson to determine how best to utilize these funds. The survey resulted in the establishment of the Jewish Education Committee in 1939.

The primary function of the Jewish Education Committee, Inc. was to improve the quality of Jewish education in Greater New York. According to the survey:

> If (the Friedsam Fund were) divided among the many
> Jewish schools, the Fund would not go very far and at
> the end of its availability the institutions would again
> be thrown upon their own resources. While some
> temporary relief may thus be obtained, a precious
> opportunity for utilizing the funds for constructive
> purposes of lasting significance to the development of
> Jewish education would be lost. It is, therefore, urged
> that the Jewish educational funds derived from the

Friedsam Foundation would be conserved for projects
designed to improve the quality of Jewish instruction.[5]

After much deliberation, Dr. Alexander Dushkin's[6] concept of a
service agency which would provide *educational guidance and other
services to Jewish schools* prevailed over Dr. Berkson's
recommendations

> that the principal function of JEC should be exercised
> through a Department of Educational Research
> Experimentation and Educational Materials which
> would be responsible for conducting a laboratory and
> model school and classes to develop suitable
> educational programs, new types of instruction and
> prepare texts and other materials growing out of
> experimentation.[7]

Functioning as an all inclusive agency, JEC, from its inception,
offered a wide range of educational guidance activities to meet the
needs of all types of schools of the community.

In the early years of JEC, the Talmud Torah or communal
school, which had provided intensive Jewish education to large
numbers of children, was on the wane, and the congregational school
was beginning to supplant it. Although there may be advantages to the
congregational school structure, the transition brought with it a
decline in educational standards. Many of the synagogue schools were
little more than "bar mitzvah factories." The JEC made a substantial
contribution in raising the standards of these schools as well as guiding
the existing communal schools.

In keeping pace with new needs and opportunities, new
programs were developed, among them: Jewish Education Committee
Press,[8] Yeshiva Department, Yeshiva English Principals'
Association,[9] In-service Programs, Summer Ulpan, School
Accreditation and Testing Programs for supplementary schools,
Metropolitan Commission on Torah Education, Ezra Academies,
regional school associations, United Parent Teachers Association,
School Board Chairmen's Conference, Leadership Conference,
Department of Guidance and Psychological Services, Jewish
Orientation and Training Seminar, and Incentive Grants and Loan
Programs.

In the fall of 1970, the Jewish Education Committee was

renamed the Board of Jewish Education, Inc., in order to reflect more adequately the nature of the central agency's consultative services and activities.

Objectives and Characteristics
of BJE

An awareness of the general objectives and basic characteristics of the organization as it has developed is essential for an understanding of its operation and the recommendations embodied in this report. As indicated in the previous chapter, the JEC was envisioned as a community agency to provide educational guidance and other services to existing schools in order to upgrade the quality of instruction.

In order to carry out this basic objective, the JEC and now BJE has been giving considerable attention to educational guidance and supervision of schools. This emphasis does not rule out the possibility of innovative practices. It was envisioned by its founders that "Research projects and experimentation with new approaches would constitute a part of our overall service . . ." (Louis L. Ruffman, "The Jewish Education Committee of New York," *Jewish Education*, Spring 1965)

The BJE is a transpartisan, umbrella agency which endeavors to serve objectively and honestly all segments of the community which have a direct interest in Jewish education, without imposing upon any group a particular philosophy or point of view. It strives to help each ideological group to carry out its aims and objectives through improved educational practices. It strives to effect self-improvement on all levels and to offer a wide range of educational guidance activities which can meet the needs of all types of schools.

While working with each group and type of school according to its needs, the BJE strives to bring about a sense of unity within the diversity of schools and school groupings in New York. It provides activities designed to bring the various separate groups together on common ground where legitimate ideological differences are not directly affected.

The Board of Jewish Education is thus the central coordinating agency for Jewish education in New York. Working with all kinds of Jewish schools — communal, congregational, Orthodox, Conservative, Reform, Yiddish-speaking — it strives to offer more and better Jewish education to more Jewish children.

BJE carries on a six-fold program of educational service. It 1) helps formulate curricula; 2) promotes higher school standards; 3) provides pedagogic consultation services; 4) develops and maintains in-service programs for educational personnel; 5) publishes educational realia and teaching materials; and 6) conducts regional and city-wide activities for pupils, educators, and lay people.

Underlying BJE's function as a service agency is the principle of voluntarism. The nature of the Jewish community is such that the service of a central educational agency must be provided on a voluntary basis only. The agency becomes rooted in the community to the extent that its services meet the felt needs of the different types of schools in the community. Schools are not and cannot be pressured or forced into compliance. Acceptance of guidance and implementation of recommendations of BJE personnel are achieved on the basis of merit and the general confidence which has been developed. Cooperation in all BJE activities is on the same basis.

1. Samson Benderly, *The Jewish Community in New York City,* N.Y Bureau of Education, October 1910 Bulletin #1, Reprinted in *Jewish Education* New York, Summer 1949, Vol. 20, No. 3 pp. 110-112

2. Norman Bentwich, *For Zion's Sake, A Biography of Judah L. Magnes,* Philadelphia: Jewish Publication Society (1954) p. 77

3. Benderly, *Op cit.*

4. *Op cit.* p. 8

5. Louis L. Ruffman, *The JEC of New York: Profile of a Community Service Agency,* Reprinted from *Jewish Education,* Spring 1965, pp. 148-149.

6. Dr. Dushkin was Director of the Jewish Education Committee, 1939-1949.

7. Ibid. p. 149.

8. Publications activity was spearheaded and developed by Dr. Azriel Eisenberg, Executive Vice President, 1949-1966.

9. The Yeshiva department and the program of psychological services for Yeshivot were organized and developed by Rabbi Leonard Rosenfeld between 1951 and 1956. Rabbi Rosenfeld later served as Executive Vice President, 1966-1970.

– 32 –

THE ROLE OF
THE CENTRAL AGENCY —
THEORY AND PRACTICE

Excerpted from a Presentation at
New Board Member Orientation Meeting
Board of Jewish Education
December 14, 1988

There are four principles that guide the Board of Jewish Education of Greater New York: 1. Unity in Diversity, 2. Leadership, 3. Specialization, and 4. Leverage.

1.   Unity in Diversity

In light of the current problems of the Law of Return in Israel, this principle is critical. BJE's leadership and service are provided to meet the needs of each segment of our community — ideological, regional and chronological. At the same time, we provide the bulk of our services in transideological frameworks. All our *Centers* offer service to all ideological groups at any one time. While we provide for the specialized needs of our constituents, our communal approach serves as a unifying force while not compromising the ideological integrity of our clients and users of service.

2.   Leadership and Service

While BJE responds to needs of our constituents a key element of our activity derives from our leadership posture. An example is the Center approach. In establishing the *Media Center,* for example, we did not wait to take a survey of what schools thought they wanted or needed, but rather, we developed it at our own initiative. To be sure, many teachers and principals were threatened by the use of modern technology and we wanted to bring them into the 21st century. As a result of establishing the *Media Center* some seven years ago, the request and demand for this service has increased dramatically — to the point where last year we responded to 3700 requests for consultations and service. Our successful efforts create the demand for service.

Another example of our leadership answers the questions: "Does BJE serve what exists? Are we satisfied with what exists or do we want to change what exists?" The answer to this question regarding the level of enrollment in schools led to the *Survival thru Education Drive* from 1973 through 1985. This enrollment campaign recruited over 11,000 pupils into the Jewish school system in New York. It demonstrated clearly that leadership initiates new efforts in response to emergency needs, thus changing the current condition of Jewish education.

3.   Specialization

In this age of professional sophistication — of specialization in medicine and law — Jewish education cannot be less specialized. We therefore decided to change our service delivery from a generalist approach to a specialized approach. All our Centers were developed to respond to specialized needs. Examples of this approach are the *Special Education Center,* where our highly specialized group of professionals provide a variety of services to pupils with learning disabilities and special needs, the *Computer Resource Center,* the *Early Childhood Center* and the *Principals Resource Center.*

4.   Leverage

We will never have enough money to do what needs to be done

for Jewish schools and programs or what we would like to do as a central agency for Jewish education. What we must do, and do well, is help schools do what they cannot do alone or for themselves. No matter what level of our budget and availability of money we must leverage our services to provide the biggest bang for the buck. All our activities are based on this concept. The Teachers Center is a prime example of this principle. A relatively small staff of highly professional *teachers* — the best in the field — are available during specific hours and paid only for the amount of time that they spend in their "hands on" activity. This is a very cost-effective way of leveraging top talent for the benefit of the total Jewish teacher population.

— 33 —

IN SEARCH OF
EDUCATIONAL EXCELLENCE
Some Thoughts and New Directions
for Jewish Education

*Presented at the Leadership Conference
on Jewish Education
sponsored by the
Board of Jewish Education, Inc.,
at the Federation of Jewish Philanthropies
December 13, 1970*

Tradition of Education Endangered

Jewish education became an important problem in American Jewish life from the moment it was transplanted to the North American continent. Its task was monumental — relating the Jewish school to the development of American Judaism and to the larger American society.

The problem of Jewish education must be understood from the forces playing upon the *tradition* of Jewish education. That tradition

— an intensive one by any standard — was, it seems, doomed from the start in its open, free, untraditional American setting. In the first instance, it was threatened by the increasing diffusion of Jewish intellectuality — an imposing one by any criterion — among the various arts and sciences, and numerous academic and professional concerns. Secondly, its existence was endangered by the theory and practice of voluntarism in American Jewish life.

In our society, the function of Jewish education has been relegated to the Jewish community. Although there has existed in the American Jewish community — with some notable exceptions — a recognition of the value of Jewish schooling, the organized community never really assumed the responsibility *in loco parentis.*

As a result of these two conditions — the transposition of intellectual and cultural interest by a large majority of Jews, on the one hand, and the lack of real organized community support on the other — the institution of Jewish education was left to the rather meager resources and designs of individual Jewish and small groups of concerned leaders. For the Jewish school, the combination of an open, free society with the concept of voluntarism in American Jewish life has been, to use a Shakespearean phrase, a "precious bane" resulting in a multitude of patterns of educational practice and financial support.

Quantitative Dimensions of Jewish Education in New York

And so here we are, in these turbulent, critical times, faced with ever-growing problems in Jewish education — not really the making of the Jewish educational establishment. Essentially, these fall into two categories: problems relating to the educational community, and those pertaining to the educational program.

Before discussing each of the categories and proposing new directions, let us set the stage by examining briefly the parameters of our subject. When we speak of Jewish education in Greater New York, we are, in essence, addressing ourselves to a large variegated population of schools, pupils, parents, teachers, rabbis, school board chairmen, lay leaders and critics. We are, indeed, speaking of 704 schools: 168 day schools and yeshivot, 393 weekday afternoon schools, 109 one-day-a-week schools, and 34 separate nursery schools. Ideologically, there are 361 Orthodox schools, 180 Conservative institutions, 100 Reform religious schools, 30 Yiddish and Labor Zionist schools and 34 communal or unaffiliated institutions. The schools, varying in size from 30 to 2,000 pupils, represent a variety of educational objectives and a variety of curricula and subjects from elementary Hebrew and simple Bible stories to the advanced study of Talmud.

And, we are speaking of 130,000 pupils: 46,000 or 35% of whom are in day schools; 51,000 or 39% in weekday afternoon schools; 31,000 or 24% in one-day-a-week schools; and 2,400 or 2% in nursery schools. About one-third of the Jewish child population of school age is in a Jewish school during any given year and approximately three-fourths are exposed to some kind of formal Jewish education during their lifetime.

We are also speaking of 5,000 teachers: qualified and unqualified; licensed and unlicensed; European trained, Israeli and American born instructors. About 2,000 of the instructional force are full-time; the rest teach from three to fifteen hours a week. (For most teachers, *full-time* means two school positions — a morning post in a day school and an afternoon Hebrew school job.) In addition, there are approximately 1,500 general studies teachers in the day schools, about 200 of whom are full-time employees.

At the helm of the schools are 1,000 supervisors and administrators — about half of whom are full-time. A significant number of these are rabbi-educators. Less than 50% of the supplementary schools employ full-time principals. The typical day school, on the other hand, has two educational supervisors and one administrator or executive director.

In addition, there are 400 pulpit rabbis not directly involved in the day-to-day functioning of their congregational schools but nevertheless associated by virtue of their positions with the destiny of their synagogue educational enterprises.

We're also talking of 10,000 active lay leaders of the respective schools, and, during any given year, of 100,000 Jewish families directly receiving the services of Jewish education.

We are speaking of six ideological groups and their respective educational departments and of eleven regional lay associations and several teachers' and principals' associations and councils.

Finally, we speak also of Federation of Jewish Philanthropies and the Board of Jewish Education, Greater New York's central agency for Jewish education.

Jewish Education Challenges

I mention all these components of Jewish Education in Greater New York not for the sake of recital, but to underscore the scope of the education enterprise and the dimensions of the problems and challenges relating to and deriving from the two categories: the *educational community,* and the *educational program.*

The educational community must be understood in terms of its bifocal communal aims and common purposes on the one hand, and individualized goals and individual philosophies, on the other.

What we need in this metropolis of ours is a new alliance — an alliance of all Jews conjoined by a common purpose — to involve *all* elements of the Jewish community who believe in the survival of the Jewish community. It must be based upon respect for the differing needs of individual schools and school groups and upon the desire to meet the requirements of each group in appropriate ways. There cannot be a monolithic approach to solving Jewish educational problems.

This alliance also means, however, working cooperatively via communal structures and resources. Our common destiny as Jewish should unite us even as we endeavor to respond to our individual needs. Our *shared identity* must be ever reinforced as each group strives to strengthen its *unique identity.*

The Jewish community's response to crises demonstrates adequately its ability to transcend differences for the common good. Certainly, the present situation is severe enough, the current challenge crucial enough and the task before us enormous enough to elicit *real partnership* in resolving our problems — in turning prospect into promise and in propelling promise into reality.

The BJE stands solidly for such an alliance. In all its undertakings and services, it is keenly sensitive to the ideological needs of each school. BJE's philosophy "unity in diversity" guarantees that every school and school group be helped according to its particular requirements without imposing upon its educational or religious orientation. This sensivity is actualized by engaging professional staff who either identify with, are committed to, or are in empathy with the ideology of the schools they serve.

In viewing Jewish life in Greater New York against the backdrop of rapid social change in the larger environment, one is struck by the static of the Jewish community — by its apathy and slowness in meeting new and growing educational needs. Specifically, I am referring to the exceedingly slow movement toward support of Jewish schooling. The underlying reason for this surprisingly slow transformation as well as the lack of meaningful change in education is that the Jewish community does not feel a sense of urgency about its failures and problems in this area. It does not feel about its Jewishly disadvantaged children as does the Black community, for example, about the need for more effective education for its disadvantaged children. Neither does the organized Jewish community express the desire for initiating new vital programs in Jewish education as have the federal, state and local governments and other public and private establishments via the various antipoverty programs, antidrop-out programs and remedial programs.

There is a direct relationship between America's prosperity (notwithstanding our present economic crisis) and its educational growth. While the United States is a consumer oriented society, education, since 1957, has been considered not as a consumer good, but as an investment in the future. In fact, the current financial plight of higher education was partially induced by the government's inability to presently meet its commitment to the universities in the same grandiose manner it did during the last decade.

In contrast, the Jewish community, particularly in New York, views Jewish education almost entirely as a consumer service. To its credit, Federation leadership is increasingly aware of the need for massive support for Jewish education. Such support, to be sure, means either a major reordering of priorities or the uncovering of large new resources for the funding of Jewish schooling, or both.

It is indeed unfortunate that at a time when an important segment of its leadership is desirous of providing significantly greater support to education, that Federation should be the object of strong attack by the very groups it plans to help. Bluntly, it all adds up to the fact that in this age of the receiver, the potential recipients are impatient with the potential giver.

On another level, the community dimension of Jewish education reveals a lack of understanding or misreading by the community at large and its leaders of the state of Jewish education — its strengths and weaknesses — and the factors contributing to and the responsibility for whatever successes and failures may be its lot. The woeful lacunae of knowledge include serious misinformation regarding the role of the central agency for Jewish education and its relationship to and responsibility for the present condition of Jewish education in Greater New York. Here is where the factor of voluntarism is almost completely ignored.

As the pressure mounts for greater communal support for Jewish education, this misreading of the condition and the role of the educational "establishment" assumes critical proportions. What, in effect, is happening in reaction to the pressure in light of the current economic crisis is the unholy alliance — albeit unwitting — of the traditional detractors of Jewish education with the mis-informed well-doers for Jewish education.

The foregoing leads us to one convincing conclusion. The need for better communication and more effective public relations is vital and real.

A new program direction for BJE must be, then, to strengthen and, where necessary, to initiate *ongoing multi-level communication* with its various publics. The need for effective Jewish education on pre-school, primary, elementary, secondary and adult levels, and the need for and responsibility for adequate support for Jewish schooling must be communicated poignantly to the Jewish community and to its leadership. This communication must include reference to the problems and challenges of Jewish education and the conditions contributing to them, on the one hand, and a variety of program options and the viable educational constructs, on the other.

Second, and equally as important, is improving the image of Jewish education — of schools and educators — as the educational institutions and educative processes are themselves being strengthened and upgraded.

Jewish Education As It Is

In his utterly frank book, *Crisis in the Classroom,* Charles Silberman identifies the problem in public education as one of "visual mutilation of spontaneity, of joy in learning, of pleasure in creating, of sense of self." He bemoans how "intellectually sterile and esthetically barren the atmosphere" of the public school is. To be sure, while some

Jewish schools, in varying degrees, may share these unhappy traits, the reason for, and dimensions of this condition where it exists are significantly dissimilar.

Jewish school problems are different from public school problems because the schools are different. A comparison between the "full-time," "day-time" public school with the "part-time" supplementary Jewish afternoon school or one-day-a-week school will reveal most radical differences in setting, auspices, attendance requirements, instructional and employment practices and parental attitudes, to name a few aspects of variance.

In considering the programs of Jewish schools, differentiation between the dominant supplementary school pattern and the intensive all day school format must be made.

In broad general strokes, the differences might be portrayed as follows:

1. While enrollment in the supplementary school continues to decrease, all-day education becomes increasingly more popular.

2. While less than 10% of graduates of supplementary Jewish schools continue beyond bar-mitzvah for more than one year (and that for 2-4 hours a week), most day school graduates continue on to yeshiva high school for four years of intensive Jewish secondary schooling.

3. While the supplementary school must be intensified and available time put to better use, more effective use of time is the single challenge regarding the hours of instruction in the day school.

4. While curriculum *reform* seems to be the major curricular need in the supplementary school, more meaningful curriculum *articulation* is the most important curricular challenge in the day school. This does not imply that the need for program articulation is not an acute problem in the supplementary school nor that the day school could not benefit from curricular changes.

5. Finally, the all day school budgetary requirements are four and five times as much as the supplementary school.

With all their differences, the day schools and supplementary schools share many crucial problems.

1. Both are victimized by a severe shortage of qualified personnel.

2. Instruction in both types of schools requires significant upgrading. In both, teachers are terribly underpaid.

3. There is a dearth of appropriate texts, materials and teaching aids in both kinds of institutions.

4. Within each type there is a need to raise standards of achievement and to standardize administrative practices.

5. Both types of schools lack effective evaluation procedures.

6. Both need effective guidance programs.

Responding to Needs:
Premises for Educational Programming

As we move now to the area of educational programming, permit me to posit several premises upon which new directions must be charted.

1. It is the responsibility of the organized Jewish community to give priority consideration to *all* those activities which can best help maintain a viable Jewish community in Greater New York.

2. In our present society Jewish education is (or can be) the most direct and effective way of guaranteeing that viability. On the other hand, the Jewish school is not omnipotent in the cultivation of commitment to Jewish values and in the transmission of the Jewish way of life — a dominant notion of which we must disabuse ourselves.

3. All Jewish schools, in one way or another, can be improved and rendered more effective.

4. The respect for the ideological integrity of each institution receiving services and/or support is a cardinal principle of communal involvement in Jewish education.

5. The most orderly, effective and pragmatically sound system of providing guidance and financial assistance to schools is via a cooperative communal process — a central educational instrumentality.

Reaching the Youth

The common characteristics and differences between the all-day and supplementary school types have important implications for a central agency in Jewish education. In the first place, there must be a broadening choice of program options rather than single options. For the supplementary school an all-out effort to increase number of hours of schooling must be made. Simultaneously, new educational formats must be considered in addition to, and in many instances, in lieu of some of the formal educational experiences to which pupils are currently exposed. This means utilization of pupil leisure time for worthwhile educational activities; for example, using winter vacations and weekends for sensitivity retreats, utilizing summers for intensive Jewish camping and Israel-based tours and seminars; and free afternoons, evenings and weekends for informal activity — *all as integral parts of the school program.*

These types of programs are particularly essential for adolescents. For them, the creation of peer environments is absolutely essential. Values of high school and college students are not shaped primarily in the classroom but by their peer groups. It is the Jewish school's highest challenge — in this day of drugs, dropouts, turn-offs, and alienation — to communicate with Jewish adolescents via the development of stimulating peer environments. The more profound challenge lies in reaching the adolescents — "touching" the untouched youth — finding them in the community centers and in their public high schools, and providing them with imaginative, innovative programs and guidance.

Reaching Jewish youth in public school means, among other things, reaching them through their daily academic exposure. This seems most natural via Hebrew language and Jewish study programs in the public junior and senior high schools. Introducing and guiding the instruction of Hebrew in public high schools has been the function of the *Hebrew Culture Council* of the BJE. Now, the challenge lies in programming units on Jewish life via social studies, and more importantly, by taking advantage of the new emphasis on pluralism and stress on ethnic studies and developing programs in Jewish studies for the junior and senior high school levels. To the latter task the BJE must address itself during the next decade.

To make the instruction of the "schooled" adolescent more effective and to reach the unschooled, a *Department of Youth and Young Adults* has been planned as part of BJE's evolving program of service. Natural partners for providing informal Jewish education to Jewish adolescents are the Y's and Jewish Centers. A major thrust of this Department will be in the direction of the college campus. In this phase of the program cooperative efforts might be co-sponsored via existing programs and newly organized ventures such as the *Jewish Association of College Youth.*

Innovative Pedagogy:
Meeting Needs of Teachers and Pupils

For both types of schools new approaches to teaching should be introduced and tested: inquiry and discovery techniques, tutorial programs, new media and technology, video-tapes, televised instruction, simulation and computer-assisted instruction, to name a few. All this requires an understanding of the variety of factors in media application (for example, meeting specified objectives, adapting to learner characteristics) and selecting and producing effective media. To this end, a new *Media and Audio-Visual Center* is being planned.

Experience in general education has demonstrated that improvement or reform in the elementary and secondary school, must bring in the schools of higher learning and in the teacher in-service programs. This means establishing and strengthening relationships with teacher-education schools, improving the pre-service training programs and maximalizing the effectiveness of the BJE in-service course offerings and teacher-training programs. BJE's new Department of Instructional Services which focuses on teacher needs is, indeed, developing in this direction.

The future of Jewish education will be bleak, indeed, if it will not at once be able to attract bright, young talented people into the schools. Recruiting such teachers will remain a dream forever unless the economic and social status of educational personnel is drastically improved. For two decades this has been a clarion call of the Jewish education profession; and for two decades the call has fallen upon deaf ears. New directions, and even old viable programs, are but lofty thoughts if Jewish school personnel are not appropriately remunerated. Implied in this projection is the training of multi-skilled personnel for the supplementary school and the creation of "communities of learning" which will require the services of full-time teachers.

Revitalizing the Content
of Jewish Education

Accelerated erosion of Jewish life in the family and community, as characterized by the current identity crisis, clearly placed increased responsibility on the school as the major agent of the community to communicate Jewish life to Jewish youth. This responsibility is underscored by the current social upheaval and breakdown of moral values, and subsequent impact on Jewish adolescents. In effect, this implies a new vital response in curriculum terms. Needed is new form and content to effect Jewish identity formation.

The age we live in requires that parents, rabbis, principals and teachers become sensitized to the personal-social needs of our youth. To this end, the BJE has initiated a *Department of Guidance and Psychological Services.* A major thrust of the Department is an attempt to foster school involvement in mental health planning. Here, many of the other Federation agencies might provide vital services via BJE to schools and pupils. This possibility is currently being explored.

Without the total involvement and encouragement of the most important partners in the educational enterprise — the parents — schools cannot hope to be effective. Achieving this lofty yet absolute *sine qua non* will be the objective of the *Home Education Center* Which will combine the program and services of the *Parent Education* and *Adult Education Departments.*

Support for the Jewish Day School

The most positive development in Jewish education during the last three decades has been the growth of the Jewish day school. Originating as a modest, atypical Jewish educational establishment against a backdrop of acculturation and deculturation, it has captivated the attention of large segments of the Jewish community.

All Jewish educational movements publicly advocate all-day education as the potentially most effective kind of formal school experience. While more scientific evidence needs to be developed regarding the efficacy of the various day school programs, experience has demonstrated clearly that this type of educational constuct is infinitely superior to the supplementary school.

The growing, nagging problem of crisis proportions common to all-day schools is their financial plight. In light of the Jewish community's need for these schools and in view of the spiraling costs for this type of education during the past decade, it behooves the Jewish community to respond to the financial needs of the yeshivot and day schools. This requires an altogether new approach of funding including the use of public funds. Supporting all day education, maintaining it on a high level of effectiveness and improving it should be priority concerns of the organized Jewish community. To this challenge, too, the BJE has dedicated itself via its revitalized *Department of Yeshivot and Day Schools.*

Educational Appraisal

To consider, with absolute objectivity, the efficacy and achievement of Jewish school programs, and to provide comprehensive answers to the question being asked with increasing frequency and impatience — "How really effective is the Jewish school?" — an ongoing program of appraisal is needed. To this task, too, BJE must dedicate its future effforts. We must be ready to ask whether our concern for the cognitive domain, for the accrual of knowledge is indeed paying dividends. To this end, the current *BJE Testing Program* must be expanded significantly. In addition, BJE accreditation programs co-sponsored with the ideological groups must be reviewed and modified.

Looking Toward the Future

The desideratum in Jewish schooling is a Jewishly committed, ethical, goal-oriented and cultured personality sensitive to changing environmental conditions and able to meet changing personal-social needs. Achieving this purpose has been, historically, the greatest challenge to Jewish education in Israel and the Diaspora, and it remains the profound challenge of Jews in modren society.

Jewish education must be concerned with the problems of poverty and wealth, with the ways and needs of modern man, with social justice and social justice, with civil liberties and civil disorder, with the hopes of labor and the plight of unemployment. The Jewish school must speak to the problems of health and housing, of play and rest, of education and rehabilitation and of war and peace.

The Jewish school — whether it be of the all-day or the supplementary type — cannot afford ostrich-like concern for the ritualistic aspects of a pupil's behavior. Jewish tradition has much to say to contemporary Jewish society, and, in turn, can be enriched in and out of the classroom and contemporized via the "here-and-now" Jewish world and by recent Jewish experience. No contemporaneous Jewish school should be without significant instruction in the Holocaust, Soviet Jewry, contemporary American Jewish life and Israel. Materials and methodology beg to be prepared for these important study areas.

BJE has made an auspicious beginning in programming for the teaching of the Holocaust and Soviet Jewry via its recent All-Day Teachers' Institute and the initiation of a colloquium on "Teaching the Holocaust." It has initiated, too, a special series of seminars on the teaching of Israel. Study of Israel and Israel-based programs will be planned with the recently established Commission on Teaching Israel and Contemporary Jewish Life of the AAJE and with the Departments of Education and Culture and Torah Education of the World Zionist Organization.

The challenges of Jewish education to the Jewish education profession ring out loud and clear. To meet them vigorously and creatively we pledge ourselves — כשם שנטעו אבותינו "As our fathers planted for us we will plant for our children."

The challenges to Jewish education speak out to the lay community, as well. According to Judaism, one can have a meaningful life only if he is an active member of society, is concerned for the welfare of others and works for the benefit of the community. It is the view of Judaism that by performing acts of *tzedakah* — deeds of righteousness, justice and kindliness — we not only imitate God, but we also become His partners in the process of perfecting an imperfect world.

— 34 —

BJE 75: LAUNCHING BJE's SEVENTY-FIFTH ANNIVERSARY YEAR

Presented at the
BJE Board/Staff Annual Dinner
June 10, 1985

William Howard Taft was president — hand-picked by Teddy Roosevelt. Charles Evans Hughes was New York State's governor, about to be sworn in as a Supreme Court Justice; and little-known William J. Gaynor was mayor of New York City. The Model-T Ford was two years old. The Manhattan Bridge had just celebrated its first birthday. The year was 1910.

And, in far-away Palestine, Jerusalem and Eretz Yisrael were still under Turkish rule, a condition which began in 1517 and was ended in 1917 by the Brititsh. Tel Aviv observed its first anniversary as the first modern, all-Jewish city. Shmuel Yavne'eli departed on a mission to Yemen to explore its Jewish community and promote *aliyah.* As a result of his mission, a group of Yemenite Jews arrived in Eretz Yisrael before World War I.

In Europe, it was just seven years after the Kishinev pogroms and three years after the Bialistok pogroms, both of which brought thousands of Eastern European Jews to New York. And, it was the year that the Polish boycott was instituted against Jewish business establishements in that country, and the year Jews were expelled from Kiev.

And, here in New York, there were the teeming tenements on the lower East Side. One million, one hundred thousand Jews lived in New York City in 1910. They constituted 23% of the total population of 4,800,000. Yiddish was the lingua franca of the home and street. And, the public school was the gate to acculturation — to Americanization. Jews had just established themselves as pre-eminent in the garment industry, most of them spending 15 to 18 hours a day in the sweat shops.

The struggle for a livelihood was all-consuming. Jewish education suffered as a consequence. Seventy-five percent of Jewish children received no formal Jewish schooling at all. Of those who did, 20% were in organized communal Talmud Torahs. The rest attended improvised hadarim — shabby one-room schools — or were tutored by itinerant siddur peddlers.

In 1910, the Bureau of Jewish Education was born out of a critical communal need to upgrade Jewish education — to introduce modern texts and teaching materials, graded curricula, appropriate pedagogic methods, improved preparation and remuneration of teachers, and better supervision and administration of schools.

The Bureau was established as part of an effort to create a *kehillah* in New York. The kehillah experiment was short-lived. But, the Bureau of Jewish Education lasted, even flourished. And, here we are today, celebrating our 75th anniversary. And now, 75 years later, BJE is ever so important as it responds to the Jewish survival needs of the 1980's and beyond.

We Jews have been called an "ever-dying people." In every generation there are Jewish leaders and Jewish scholars who predict that the end is near, that assimilation will eventually lead to our demise as a people. To be sure, we are not about to vanish — witness the vibrancy of Jewish life and Jewish education in many quarters of our community. But the challenges to our continuity and to the quality of Jewish life are so real, so serious, so overwhelming, so immediate. All we have to do is look around us at the threatening, growing signs of erosion.

These are the reasons that cry out "Jewish Education — Now — More Than Ever." It is no coincidence that this is the theme of our 75th Anniversary Year.

What does BJE 75 mean? To begin with, it means Jewish communal responsibility for Jewish education. We are ever grateful to Federation for increasing its commitment and support to Jewish education. But we continue to be the strong advocate and goad to the Jewish community to provide *more* support for Jewish education, to create greater awareness that Jewish education is the primary responsibility of the organized Jewish community.

What does BJE 75 mean? We are the living example of Maimonides' שביל הזהב, the golden mean. "הדרך הישרה היא מידה בינונית" says the Rambam. "The righteous way is the middle path." In truth, it is not an easy task being a *central* agency, serving the needs of the total Jewish community in all its ideological and geographic shadings; the right, the left and the center; the sectarian and the liberal; the affluent and the poor; the urban and the suburban; responding to the needs of the committed, the marginal and the affiliated. We serve each segment and interest in the community, and we serve them *well*!

Ours is a romance of contrasts. Indeed, we are an agency of contrast. That is our blessing and our challenge.

What does BJE 75 mean? It means leverage and leadership. It means utilizing a relatively small amount of funding to exert the greatest amount of influence on the quality of Jewish schooling. It means providing leadership through example — like the prophet of old whose task it was to convey a point of view, yet in his own life as a person, he *was* a point of view. We at BJE represent a communal philosophy and approach, in principle and practice. We listen; we field-base our activities; yet, we exert leadershp. We provide specialized guidance; yet, we are sensitive to the total spectrum of our constituents' needs. We are objective; yet, we are biased toward those programs which provide the best chance for insuring and enhancing Jewish continuity. As leaders, we are realists; yet, we are dreamers — always striving to improve the good and to perfect the excellent.

What does BJE 75 mean? BJE means resource and service. We help schools, principals, teachers, pupils, parents and lay leaders. We feel free to criticize them, even as we support them in their efforts. We do for schools what they cannot do for themselves. We are like the *tavlin* in the *cholent;* like the catalytic agent in the chemical reaction. We seek no special acknowledgment, only the satisfaction of helping improve the quality of Jewish schooling and the quality of Jewish life.

What does BJE 75 mean? BJE personifies the act of giving. Giving time, energy, intellectual vitality, expertise and personal substance, epitomized by the devoted lay leadership of our officers and board members of BJE — an unusual group of people selflessly dedicated to the continuity and enhancement of Jewish life. BJE personifies giving through our staff — the most talented and most devoted professionals in Jewish education. In giving, our lay volunteers and our professionals are enriched as we are rewarded by the satisfaction of seeing fruits of our labors.

And, finally, what does BJE mean? It means partnerships. Partnerships with Federation, with Israel, with the World Zionist Organization; partnerships with ideological groups, Jewish Community Centers and Jewish communal agencies. Partnerships with yeshivot, day schools and supplementary schools; partnerships with teachers, principals and lay leaders; and partnerships with pupils and Jewish families. Without supportive home environments, Jewish schooling cannot flourish. Without the cooperation of our partners, BJE cannot fully realize its own potential.

During the coming year, the theme of our conferences, meetings and workshops will be "Partnerships for Jewish Continuity." There will be a major city-wide conference at Federation, a variety of regional meetings and seminars, and a host of functional programs highlighting this theme.

Tonight, we honor our partnerships with those on the front line of Jewish education. We are guided by the words of Isaiah the prophet — "והיו עיניך רואות את מוריך", "Let your eyes look toward your teachers." Let us see our teachers; let us appreciate them; let us give them more status and adequate recompense; and make Jewish education the profession it was meant to be!

According to Talmudic tradition, "בשעות ידועות ביום יושב הקב"ה ומלמד תינוקות של בית רבן!" the Almighty, Himself, spends several hours each day teaching Jewish children Torah. Indeed, teaching is a Godly profession. And tonight we salute the teachers who, in the words of Plato, hold the torch and pass it on to others. To those who light the tapers of the Jewish child's heart, to those who light the way of the Jewish future in America and the world over, to our parents, the teachers — the guardians of Torah — we pay noble tribute.

And in the days ahead, we will pay honor to all our other partners as we join forces together for the continuity and enhancement of עם ישראל, ארץ ישראל ותורת ישראל, — the people of Israel, the land of Israel and the Torah of Israel.

May we go together מחיל אל חיל, from strength to strength!

– 35 –

CHARTING THE COURSE
FOR THE NEXT QUARTER CENTURY

*Presented at Board of Directors Meeting
Initiating the 76th Year of Service
Board of Jewish Education
of Greater New York
October 15, 1986*

INTRODUCTION

I appreciate this opportunity to share some thoughts with you at this moment in Jewish communal education history in Greater New York. To be sure, the current BJE organizational and programmatic thrust is the result of changes initiated in 1970.

It is appropriate at this time, immediately after the High Holy Day season, to talk about the future, to consider directions for the next quarter century. Unlike the secular society and the secular New Year, in Jewish tradition we do not make resolutions *per se*. Our commitments for the future are past-based. Personal resolutions require *haratah al He'avar*, "regret for the things we have done in the past," and *kaballah al He-atid*, "acceptance of new directions for the future."

The verb root of the noun *Haratah* means "to engrave" or "dig in." We literally have to "dig in" to the past and understand it; and on the basis of that understanding create directions and make resolutions for the future. This will be the pattern for my position paper — reviewing the esential developments in order to help project directions for the future.

My remarks are based upon four premises:

1) The first premise is *urgency*. Helping to guarantee the provision of quality Jewish education to Jewish youth is a most critical, urgent need, particularly in light of the current condition of Jewish life expressed so often by so many, in terms of apathy, alienation and non-affiliation, and exacerbated by the problems of parental permissiveness, single parenthood and intermarriage. To be sure, in almost every generation we have been called a "vanishing people," and, yet, here we are to disprove that oft-repeated prognostication. But, we dare not misread the danger signs today — despite what some optimists say and write about the status and prospects of Jewish life.

2) The second premise is *community*. American Jewry is a remarkably pluralistic entity — an expression of the freedom we enjoy in this country. A central agency for Jewish education helps preserve the sometimes fragile unity of our community. Witness the diverse elements of our constituency, our staff and our board. As we respond to the variety of demographic and ideological needs of our constituents we make every effort to maintain the principle of "unity in diversity" and reinforce the concept of *one* community.

3) The third premise is *leverage*. Maximizing the use and effect of available funding is a cornerstone of our agency operation. We are painfully aware of the limits of Jewish communal funding for Jewish education. No matter the sources or extent of our financial support, it will probably never be sufficient to meet fully the service needs of our constituents.

4) The fourth premise is *leadership*. The *raison d'etre* of BJE is to provide educational guidance to all levels of the Jewish community — to formal and informal educational institutions, to professional personnel, to institutional lay leaders and UJA-Federation. It is our role to innovate, to goad and to advocate on behalf of Jewish education.

SPECIALIZATION IN RETROSPECT

And now, to "dig in" for a few moments.

Specialization was the new thrust introduced in 1970. Let me illustrate how this concept worked in practice.

Programmatically, the idea of specialization spawned our *Center* approach.

1)   Our first Center was the *Early Childhood Education Center,* which now serves some 300 early childhood education programs, sponsors The Jewish Early Childhood Association, and provides continuing education to the overwhelming majority of nursery and kindergarten teachers and directors. One of the most sophisticated early childhood departments anywhere on the continent, last year it conducted some 250 workshops and seminars throughout the city.

2)   We transformed our small Jewish educational library, used by a few scholars and educational researchers, to an active *Pedagogic Resource Library* which responded to over 3000 requests for information this past year.

3)   Ten years ago we established our first *Teachers' Center* in a 10x10 room in a converted residence owned by Federation on Jerusalem Avenue in Wantagh. What was a small bedroom is now a large facility formerly occupied by the Mid-Island "Y." The Teachers' Center in this building was endowed last year by board member, Hon. Jack Kranis. We now serve the community with four vibrant centers — in Manhattan, Nassau, Suffolk, and Westchester, where hundreds of teachers come regularly to share, learn and prepare lessons and materials for classroom use. We will soon open a Teachers' Center in Brooklyn, made possible by a grant from UJA-Federation this year.

4)   With a modest grant from FJE, we established our *Media Center* in 1979, which now serves over 300 institutions, whose personnel borrow films and videotapes; participate in workshops; and learn how to use hardware and how to integrate software into the curriculum. Last year some 1200 films were rented and nearly 3000 guidance consultations were made to schools and other Jewish institutions.

5)   To respond to the needs of principals in supplementary schools, we emulated Harvard University which established the first

Principals' Center in general education in the United States, in 1980. At first, in 1981 and 1982, we sponsored a special in-service program for supplementary school principals with NYU. During the last two years our *Principals' Center* was conducted, at Harvard University, with the participation of its faculty and researchers, with three-day seminars for selected supplementary school principals.

6) In April 1984, our *Microcomputer Center* was established with a modest grant from Federation. The Center now houses a sizable collection of software in general studies and all the available software in Jewish studies. Since its formation, the Microcomputer Center has provided guidance to some 200 schools.

7) Last spring, we inaugurated the latest of our Centers, the *Special Education Center.* Initially established as a one-person department in 1981, it has become a major force in Jewish education in our community — serving some 150 programs in supplementary and day schools, and sponsoring and guiding a variety of services for children with special needs including the Jewish Heritage programs for Retarded Youth and Young Adults in YMHAs.

In retrospect, our specialized approach has made it possible for us to provide direct, hands-on service and guidance, on *an ongoing basis,* to —

- 1500   Early Childhood Education personnel;
- 1100   Yeshiva and Day School professionals;
- 1200   Supplementary School personnel;
- 400   Specialty teachers in Music, Art, Media and Microcomputer Education; and
- 700   Special Education personnel.

In sum, this represents about 5,000 educational personnel that *voluntarily* benefit from our specialized approach. By and large, this excludes the Hasidic and right-wing Orthodox institutions whom we serve essentially through the School Food Service, FJE and the Joseph S. and Caroline Gruss funded programs that we administer.

The recitation of these numbers may sound impressive. To be sure, it demonstrates the educational cutting edge and contacts we have. It shows, too, our ability to respond to the many variegated personnel and program needs in the community. However, we lack depth in almost every area of service. We are essentially a personnel-intensive operation and our staff is severely overburdened. Moreover, the clerical and program support we are able to provide to staff is very limited. This means that we often cannot respond adequately to the needs of our constituents and requests for service. It also limits our ability to lead and innovate.

CHALLENGES FOR THE FUTURE

1) Critical to meaningful innovation is assuring the continuity of that which has already proven effective. Our first challenge for the next decade is, therefore, to find ways to help *reinforce the staffing* of each of our programs that merit strengthening. In toto, BJE has only 41 full-time and 31 part-time personnel, down from 47 full-time and 33 part-time professional personnel in 1984. And the full-time staff figure includes executive, administrative and fiscal staff, as well as programmatic personnel.

2) Some areas of our activity require *special consideration during the next several years.* These are: curriculum materials development, research, Israel-oriented activities and outreach and informal education.

   a) The first of these will receive significant attention via our newly formed Curriculum Materials Development Committee.

   I would hope that we would be able to provide schools all the needed materials not available through commercial publishers. And, since materials often make the curriculum, it would be a boon to Jewish education if we could impact school curricula more directly by our leadership role in *curriculum materials development.*

   b) Our *research* activity is essentially a part-time staff effort. We issue annual pupil enrollment reports, annual school directories, and occasional reports on school personnel and expenditures. We are currently engaged in an ambitious ethnographic study of Jewish supplementary school education in New York, to be followed by a study on the day school. The challenge here is to become involved seriously, on an ongoing basis, in Jewish educational research.

c) For an agency our size, we are minimally involved in *Israel-based activities.* True, we sponsor, with the respective educational departments of the World Zionist Organization, Israel seminars and educational tours for early childhood education teachers and day school and supplementary school personnel. However, this kind of activity needs to be expanded greatly. And we have to get into the business of Israel-based programs for youth and families as part of our outreach and informal education efforts in the future.

d) We are at the beginning stages of establishing an *Outreach and Informal Education Center.* Despite the fact that we did not receive a grant from Federation for this vital new thrust, our Community Services Committee decided to go ahead very modestly, within our means, and start to develop a Center because outreach requires our immediate attention and active participation.

By and large, BJE provides services to and is a resource for formal Jewish education. Since some 40% of the Jewish child age population will not be attending any type of Jewish schools; since so many young people and their families are outside the pale of direct influence of Jewish schools; and since so many of the families of children attending our schools are marginally affiliated, we must help strengthen the ability of our educational institutions to become involved in outreach and informal education. Jewish education must become a synergistic activity between the school and the home, between the Jewish center and the Jewish family. It is only natural that BJE help reinforce this connection. BJE should become the major Jewish communal resource in New York for Jewish outreach in schools, Ys, Jewish Centers and other Federation agencies.

3)   *The Personnel Crisis:* No Jewish education services or materials can improve the state of Jewish education if we do not have effective personnel in the classrooms. The critical teacher problem has to be addressed with utmost seriousness. The gap between teachers' salaries and principals' salaries tells the story. The average full-time day school teacher makes $18,500 compared to the average principal's salary of $45,000 and the average administrator's salary of $50,000. No wonder the Jewish day school suffers from a severe teacher shortage.

The part-time nature of teaching and supervision in supplementary schools makes it impossible to attract young talented people into such careers. How can we develop full-time professional opportunities? Can we make some of the part-time positions into full-time jobs? One way to do this is to convert the classroom teacher into a Jewish family educator. Alternatively, how can we attract, on a part-time basis, the kind of personnel needed to make supplementary Jewish education more effective? Either we have to make supplementary school teaching a paying full-time profession, or reorganize it drastically to attract part-time people á la the Peace Corps. The findings and recommendations of the supplementary school study which we will complete mid-year will give us much food for thought and, hopefully, directionality regarding the whole issue of Jewish supplementary school education, including the problem of personnel.

4)   *Art and Music Education* have not been given priority attention at BJE, even though we conduct some successful art and music programs each year. And, drama and dance education have been eliminated altogether, due to financial constraints. Needed is a BJE *Jewish Education Arts Center* to spearhead and guide enrichment programs for formal and informal Jewish education. Our schools are all the poorer without such a resource.

5)   Finally, I propose the development of a *Lay Leadership Center* whose task it would be to strengthen the lay leadership of our educational institutions. The interview process of our supplementary school study clearly underscores the need for lay education leadership training.

Communal Support for BJE

Transcending the thrust of my remarks thus far is the challenge to utilize our agency as an advocacy instrument — to help reinforce Federation's growing awareness about the priority of Jewish education for Jewish continuity.

We are fully cognizant that Federation has come a long way in support of Jewish education; but, not far enough. In comparing New York Federation's annual allocation to its central agency with twelve largest United States Jewish communities that have bureaus of Jewish education, New York is woefully behind. As a percentage of

Federation allocations to local needs, last year, BJE in New York received only 5.7% of the Federation allotment while the average allocations to the other central agencies was 11% of all allocations — 100% more than New York.

Given the ongoing needs of New York schools; considering the large percentage of day school enrollment and the widespread demography of our services; our agency requirements are signifcantly greater than the other Jewish communities. Yet, our allocation is relatively much less.

This means that we have to approach the merger between UJA and Federation with a sense of heightened urgency via-á-vis our services to Jewish education. We have forcefully advocated for and have strongly supported direct aid to Jewish schools in our community. We were instrumental in initiating the Program Development Fund for Jewish Education, and now administer the Fund for Jewish Education and the Gruss Funds which provide direct support to schools and other institutions in New York. The problem here is that the establishment of FJE has given rise to a feeling among many Federation leaders (as the result of the annual UJA-Federation matching contributions to FJE) that they have acquitted themselves admirably — or even too much — of their communal responsibility toward Jewish education.

The unfortunate result of this feeling is that BJE suffers from a kind of communal leadership posture which says *dayenu* regarding the money spent by Federation for Jewish education. It seems to lessen the desire of Federation leadership to increase its support for communal educational service in New York.

We at BJE will continue to advocate for more support to schools. Unquestionably, the current $5 million FJE level of funding should be doubled, trebled, and even quadrupled. We must, at the same time, continue indefatigably to advocate for significant increases to BJE. This is the propitious time for UJA-Federation to make a greater commitment to Jewish continuity via increased support to its central Jewish educational agency.

BJE lay leadership has become increasingly involved in UJA-Federation activity. We must continue to find ways to enhance our partnership with Federation through the communal planning and distribution processes.

Federation appreciates our role, but it must develop an even greater sense of appreciation for the nature, scope and quality of our service. *Ain Navi B'iro.* Our sages note that a person is usually not considered a prophet in his own city — meaning that *local* personnel and institutions are often taken too much for granted. That is actually the case with Federation's view of our agency.

BJE is the unparalleled leader among Jewish central agencies for Jewish education the world over. During the last several months Federation presidents, bureau presidents, Federation executives, bureau executives and professional bureau staff from all over the world — from Los Angeles, Washington, Baltimore, Detroit, Southern New Jersey, Buenos Aires, London, Paris, and Johannesburg, — came to BJE to learn and be guided. In our international role, we have helped train European principals and top Israeli Ministry of Education personnel. This is an important dimension of our work. Among other things, it helps us sharpen our outlook on our own educational service, even as we gain satisfaction from helping others. And, it develops stronger feelings of self-worth and self-esteem — so important for morale building. All of those who visit BJE marvel at the level, scope and quality of our services. The challenge is to make Federation more aware and more appreciative of the central role we play in the educational life of our community.

CHALLENGE TO BJE BOARD

The critical education needs in our community coupled with the demands for our service and our current level of funding by UJA-Federation challenges our ability to develop an effective endowment program of our own.

What should be our own financial involvement and support of BJE programs? This will have to be spelled out more clearly and more significantly in the future — both for the ongoing budget and for special programs via endowments, about which we will hear more this evening, and later on during the year.

We have in place an effective organization which we worked very diligently to develop. We have the basic ability and essential skills to respond to the variety of educational needs in our variegated community and to provide effective leadership. Clearly, the role of the Board is to make sure that the organization it helped build is able to continue to respond effectively and continue to provide quality educational leadership in the future.

This meeting takes place two days before our autumn festival which has three names: the first — *Hag Ha-succot* — "the holiday of huts" or "tabernacles" — symbolizes the frailty of human life, the tentativeness of human existence. Within that framework, the other two names — *Hag He-assif* — "the festival of ingathering" — and *Z'man Simhatenu* — "the season of our gladness" have special meaning. Ingathering refers to achievement, which leads to genuine satisfaction and joy.

This, then, is the message for the next quarter century for BJE. Together, board members and staff will work to achieve our common objectives in partnership with UJA-Federation and usher in a long period of joyous fulfillment from our Jewish life-enriching leadership, service and support.

– 36 –

EXECUTIVE COMMENTS
ON RETIREMENT

Presented at
BJE Board of Directors Meeting
February 12, 1990

The central theme of the Torah reading next Shabbat — *Mattan Torah* at Mount Sinai — is a source of a plethora of Midrashic interpretations. One of the Midrashim on the transmission of the Decalogue is actually a commentary on one of the most famous statements in another section of the Bible — the Book of Ecclesiastes, written by King Solomon in a contemplative, philosophical mood at the end of his kingship. That statement is לכל זמן ועת לכל חפץ תחת השמים "To everything there is a season, and a time to every purpose *under the heaven.*" (Kohellet 3:1) Says the Midrash — "a time to every purpose *under the heaven*" refers especially to the time for the giving of the Torah to the Israelites.

אמר רב בבי:
זמן היה לאותו דבר שהיה נתון למעלה מן השמים,
ועכשיו יהיה נתון למטה מן השמים.
ואיזה זה? זו התורה.

Said Rabbi Bibi: "There was a time for a certain thing to be found above the heaven, and now it was to be found beneath the heaven. And what is it? The Torah!" (Midrash Rabbah Kohellet 3:1)

The Torah was not given to the Israelites immediately upon their exodus from Egypt proper. They did not receive the Ten Commandments until they were ready for them — until after a remarkable series of events that prepared them physically and spiritually for the Covenant.

Chronologically, these events were:
— the entrapment of the Israelites between the Egyptian army and the Red Sea after Pharaoh reneged on his promise to let them go;
— the miraculous crossing of the Red Sea;
— the difficult journey towards Sinai;
— receiving *Manna* from heaven;
— drawing water from the Rock at *Horeb;*
— the victorious battle against the Amalekites under the leadership of Joshua;
— the establishment of an elaborate system of judges and assistant judges to govern the Israelites as per Jethro's suggestion;
— the uniting of the tribes in allegiance to God at the foot of Mount Sinai; and
— careful preparations to receive the Covenant.

Only then — after this series of events — does the Bible tell us, "And God spoke all these words, saying: I am the Lord your god, etc." (Exodus 20:1)

The timeliness of the giving of the Torah — a Godly action — is symbolic for all time of the timeliness of all of man's actions. Hence, "To everything there is a season, and a time for every purpose under the Heaven."

To demonstrate this truism, the same Midrash expounds that there was a time for Adam to enter the Garden of Eden (Genesis 2:15); and a time for him to leave it (Genesis 3:23). There was a time for Noah to enter the Ark (Genesis 2:1); and a time for him to leave the Ark (Genesis 8:16).

This Midrash has much personal meaning for me. The current BJE version of the Midrash says there was a time for Alvin I. Schiff to come to BJE as Chief Executive Officer, and a time for him to consider leaving. For a variety of reasons, I have decided to retire as Executive Vice President on August 31, 1991, a year and a half from now. By that time I will be 65 years old and will have completed 30 years of full-time professional association with BJE — 21 years as CEO, and nine years as full-time educational consultant in the 1950's. In addition, I have given six years in part-time service to BJE.

In sum, this represents 36 years of professional relationship with this wonderful central agency for Jewish education.

Since my very first introduction to BJE in 1948 — when I spoke at a city-wide Jewish education assembly representing college youth (after which Dr. Alexander M. Dushkin, JEC executive vice president and dean of American Jewish educators, told me, "I have a feeling that some day you'll occupy my seat"), I have enjoyed immensely and profited greatly from my relationship with this agency. My 20 years as CEO have been particularly pleasurable and fulfilling. To be sure, BJE was my extended family. As I told the Executive Committee, Mimi claims that I practiced bigamy. I admit that investing intellect, energy and time in my BJE work has been a source of much gratification.

To me, BJE has been a calling, not a job. The challenge for me was to enhance the value of our agency by applying the concepts of leadership, service and specialization, while emphasizing the principle of "unity in diversity." This theme underscores respect for the role, special needs and ideology of every type of school and program we serve through a unified communal approach.

Much has happened during the last 20 years, the highlights of which include:

1) The confirmation of the importance, relevance and meaning of a central agency for Jewish education in Greater New York in light of opposition to this concept in some Federation circles during the early 1970's.

2) The development of eight BJE specialized resource/service centers — each expertly dealing with a critical area of educational/pedagogic activity.

3) The development and expansion of our School Food Services Department which annually channels up to $20 million in government subsidies, foodstuffs and services to Jewish day schools and provides BJE with income over and above our administrative costs for this program.

4) The "discovery" of Joseph Gruss and the subsequent establishment of the Program Development Fund (PDF), the implementation committee of which I was privileged to chair, 1973-78. PDF was the predecessor organization of FJE.

5) Developing grantsmanship capability at BJE which led to the establishment of a resource development program in 1977. Currently, hundreds of thousands of dollars of income are realized annually by BJE and by Jewish schools and informal Jewish education programs via proposals we generate and/or help develop.

And, now we look forward to implementing the $6 million, 3-year, innovative Soviet Jewish acculturation/education program which we developed and for which we were instrumental in obtaining matching funding from UJA-Federation and a group of philanthropists.

Together with you and staff, I'm proud of these accomplishments, among others, and will savor the warm feeling generated by these achievements for a long, long time. Now it's time for me, in the words of Samson Raphael Hirsch, 19th century German Jewish scholar and leader of neo-orthodoxy, "to gather up my experiences" — to utilize my academic, research, administrative and pedagogic experience in other ways to benefit our community.

As for the future . . .

On an organizational level, it is critical for us to maintain, enhance and expand current resource/service centers and programs we have developed during the last 2 decades. During the next 1-1/2 years, I plan to devote a significant portion of my efforts in helping BJE lay leadership to insure that these creative centers are fiscally secure, that they continue their innovative work, that they be reinforced and expand according to the needs of the field.

Together, during our 80th anniversary year which we usher in this spring, we will learn from our past, continue our vigorous efforts in guaranteeing the viability of BJE programs and build for future. That means insuring that BJE is able to respond to emerging educational needs.

When I initially projected the development of our specialized centers of service in the 1970's, I envisioned 10 centers of activity. Eight have been launched and are now fully and productively operative. Two centers yet remain to be established. Needed is a *Center for Lay Leadership in Jewish Education* — to facilitate the improvement of Jewish education and enhance its viability throughout the five boroughs and three counties we serve. Responding to this challenge is a must.

Needed also is the long-envisioned *Jewish Cultural Arts Center* whereby we will help integrate drama, music, art and dance into formal and informal Jewish education programs. This center must also be on our drawing board.

Another challenge to which we have not adequately responded is the personnel crisis in Jewish education. While it is not unlike the personnel crises in general education and Jewish communal work, the personnel crisis in *Jewish* education is especially critical for the Jewish community since it deals with Jewish survival.

Finally, there is the critical need to implement SEAP (our Supplementary Education Action Plan) . . .

During the next fifteen months I plan to devote much effort to these challenges.

בן שמונים לגבורה; "Age 80 for Strength" (Ethics of our Fathers). *"Strength and Triumph"* must be our motto during our 80th year as we celebrate the past and build for the future . . .

FROM
DEEP DARKNESS
TO
GREAT LIGHT:

ON THE HOLOCAUST,
SOVIET JEWRY
AND ISRAEL

— 37 —

REMEMBERING
MUST BE PERSONAL

Remembrance Day Address,
Board of Jewish Education
May 4, 1978

! זכור ! געדענק ! Remember !

Did you ever stop to think about this motto for Holocaust Day? To whom does it speak?

Remember ! געדענק ! זכור !

Is it addressed to the vast majority of Jews who are either too young to know about the Shoah or were far removed in other continents of the world and did not experience the Nazi onslaught in Europe?

They have nothing vivid, nothing personal, nothing real to remember about the Holocaust.

Does Zachor speak to those who were transported to crematoria or were made to live in death camps or in hellish ghettos in

255

outrageously primitive conditions and yet survived the Nazis' final solution? The survivors don't need any reminders to remember. Their bodies and their memories bear the eternal scars of the Hitlerian nightmare. What is more, most of the survivors want to forget that tragic period of their lives.

And yet we persist in repeating ! זכור   ! געדענק   Remember !

And for good reason.

בכל דור ודור חייב אדם לראות את עצמו כאלו הוא יצא ממצרים

"In every generation each person must look at himself as if he himself was saved from the bondage of Egypt."

To understand and to appreciate the holiday of Pesah each Jew must have a very personal view and feeling of Egyptian slavery.

And, in a similar vein, in our generation each of us must consider himself or herself as שארית הפלטה a surviving remnant of European Jewry that was wiped from the face of the earth.

Each of us must feel the torture of the Nazi war machine — smell the stench of burning bodies, and the piercing odor of the gas rising in our nostrils. Each of us must hear the SS men barking out their orders — left! right! left! right! — to the showers, to the gas chamber, to the gravesite, to the firing squad. Each of us must feel the butt of the Nazi rifle crushing our skulls and the bayonet piercing the swollen bellies of our babies and young children. Each of us must see our loved ones snatched away, never to be seen or heard from again. Yes, each must feel the unbelievable pain and indescribable suffering of the victims of the Holocaust.

Each, too, must *feel* the heroism of their lives and deaths, their קידוש השם, their hopes their dreams, their valiant struggle for life. Only then, can we understand the meaning of the Shoah, the most tragic period in Jewish diaspora history, and of modern mankind as a whole. Only then can we know the meaning of the words געדענק! זכור! Remember! And only then can we comprehend the monstrousness of the Nazi atrocities, the vicious terror, the sadistic, demonic barbarianism that defies description.

Only then will we understand the depth of the agony of Kristallnacht, the beatings and rapings, the burning synagogues, the Nazi deception, fraud and massacre, the tragedy of human guinea pigs and human soap, the feeling of crippled half-dead men and women transported from one death camp to another — of victims forced to dig a pit, undress and stand at the edge of the grave as they were mowed down in cold blood. Only then can we remember Treblinka, Auschwitz, Buchenwald, Bergen-Belsen and their masses of wretched humans torn between despair and hope. Only then can we remember the pride of the yellow badge, the heroism of the Warsaw ghetto fighters and the courageous partisans, the heroic feats of the Resistance movement.

And only then can we remember the following testimony submitted to the International Military tribunal at Nurenberg:

"I, Hermann Friedrich Graebe, declare under oath: From September 1941 until January 1944 I was manager and engineer in charge of a branch office in Sdolbunow, Ukraine, of the Solingen building firm . . . On 5 October 1942, when I visited the building office at Dubno, my foreman Hubert Moennikes of Hamburg told me that in the vicinity of the site, Jews from Dubno had been shot in three large pits . . . About 1500 persons had been killed daily. All of the 5000 Jews who had still been living in Dubno before the pogrom were to be liquidated . . . All these people had the regulation yellow patches on the front and back of their clothes, and thus could be recognized as Jews.

"Moennikes and I went direct to the pits. Nobody bothered us". Now I heard rifle shots in quick succession, from behind one of the earth mounds. The people who had got off the trucks — men, women, and children of all ages — had to undress upon the orders of an SS man, who carried a riding or dog whip. They had to put down their clothes in fixed places, sorted according to shoes, top clothing and underclothing. I saw a heap of shoes of about 800 to 1000 pairs, great piles of underlinen and clothing. Without screaming or weeping these people undressed, stood around in family groups, kissed each other, said farewells and waited for a sign from another SS man, who stood near the pit, also with a whip in his hand. During the 15 minutes that I stood near the pit I heard no complaint or plea for mercy. I watched a family of about 8 persons, a man and woman, both about 50 with their children of about 1, 8 and 10, and two grown-up daughters of about 20 to 24. An old woman with snow-white hair was holding the one-year old child in her arms and singing to it, and tickling it. The child was cooing with delight. The couple were looking on with tears in their eyes. The father was holding the hand of a boy about 10 years old and speaking to him softly; the boy was fighting his tears. The father pointed toward the sky, stroked his head, and seemed to explain something to him. At that moment the SS man at the pit shouted something to his comrade. The latter counted off about 20 persons and instructed them to go behind the earth mound. Among them was the family which I have mentioned. I well remember a girl, slim and with black hair, who, as she passed close to me, pointed to herself and said, "23." I walked around the mound, and found myself confronted by a tremendous grave. People were closely wedged together and lying on top of each other so that only their heads were visible. Nearly all had blood running over their shoulders from their heads. Some of the people shot were still moving. Some were lifting their arms and turning their heads to show that they were still alive. The pit was already 2/3 full. I estimated that it already contained about 1000 people. I looked for the man who did the shooting. He was an SS man, who sat at the edge of the narrow end of the pit, his feet dangling into the pit. He had a tommy gun on his knees and was smoking a cigarette. The people, completely naked, went down some steps which were cut in the clay wall of the pit and clambered over the heads of the people lying there, to the place to which the SS man directed them. They lay down in front of the dead or injured people; some caressed those who were still alive and spoke to them in a low voice. Then I heard a series of shots. I looked into the pit and saw that the bodies were twitching or the heads lying already motionless on top of the bodies that lay before them. Blood was running from their necks. I was surprised that I was not ordered away, but I saw that there were two or three postmen in uniform nearby. The next batch was approaching already . . ." (Jewish Encyclopedia, Volume H, page 287)

And today we remember —
And as we kindle the lights in memory of the "batches" of Jewish martyrs, we remember!

As we now rise for the traditional prayer El Moleh Rahamin for the departed, we remember!

In this mood of mourning and sadness, let the lights we kindle ignite in us the spirit of life as we approach the period of celebration in honor of the 30th Anniversary of the State of Israel. Such is the bitter-sweet quality of Jewish existence.

מעבדות לחירות — from slavery to freedom
מאפלה לאור גדול — from darkness to light and hope.
משעבוד לגאולה — from bondage to redemption.

And the black ashes and earthen graves of Europe gave way to the green plains and green hills of Israel! The bitter pangs of death gave rise to the sweet sounds of life of the Jewish state.

The poet said it best when he wrote:

> I saw a field and a grave
> And the field flowed with blood.
> A book came flying by
> And settled on the grave,
> Settled on the grave.
> And the book opened itself
> Like an eye after a long sleep,
> And in the open book
> Alef kissed Tov
> Alef kissed Tov.
>
> And tall from that grave
> Grew a man,
> Like a tree shadowed the book
> And said: I am once more.
> Amen! I am once more.
>
> And the man took the book
> And his voice became flame:
> I am the new Abraham —
> And from me will again come God's tribe,
> From me will again come God's tribe.

געדענק ! זכור ! Remember !
And Life and Peace will be the lot of God's tribe.

− 38 −

TESTIMONY BEFORE PRESIDENT'S COMMISSION ON THE HOLOCAUST
Friday, April 6, 1979

I deem it a privilege, honor and a responsibility, as a Jew and as an American, to testify at this Committee hearing on the Holocaust Memorial currently being planned by the President's Commission on the Holocaust.

First, on behalf of the Board of Jewish Education of Greater New York, the largest agency of its kind in America, representing 115,000 students and 6,000 teachers and administrators in 600 Jewish schools, embracing all ideological groups in Jewish life, I wish to congratulate the President of the United States and members of the Commission, on this long-awaited development.

It is four decades since the bitter, cruel, agonizing era of the Holocaust began. It is fitting at this time, when peace in the Middle East can become a reality that a Memorial be established on this continent, so that future American generations will be mindful of the sinister, barbaric, and ungodly acts that were allowed to take place without significant intervention of the free world.

In my remarks, I will deal with the Memorial idea from an educator's point of view. There is a need to sensitize our generation and future generations to the catastrophes of the past and to the

260

undying moral courage of humanity in the face of attempts to destroy free man and free society. It would be most meaningful that an American counterpart to the Yad Vashem Memorial in Jerusalem be established as a permanent exhibit of the Holocaust era. This Memorial should be both a fitting monument to the memory of the 6,000,000, and a resource center of multi-media material for research, meditation and viewing.

This center should be a place where generations of Americans could meet regularly to contemplate and deliberate on the Holocaust and its effect upon mankind, since the Holocaust stands alone in the annals of history as a paradigm of the extremes to which totalitarianism, racism, fascism and communism can ultimately lead.

In addition to the Memorial, and in connection with it, the following are appropriate ways of memorializing the Holocaust period:

1.   One day each year (preferably coinciding with the 27th Nisan) should be established as a day of remembrance. For practical purposes it should be a definite date on the secular calendar.

2.   Issuance of a Presidential Proclamation declaring the day of remembrance as an official action.

3.   Candlelighting ceremonies in Washington and in State capitals.

4.   Renaming public squares or plazas with appropriate local ceremonies.

5.   Commemorative programs in public schools should be encouraged.

Dissemination of background information, provision of information and press releases to the media and distribution of program materials to appropriate sources would facilitate the meaningful implementation of the Memorial idea. A national TV program would be a dramatic way to launch this new observance.

The federal government should provide funding to enable the States to launch teacher-training programs regarding Holocaust instruction. In this regard, the Office of Education should issue curriculum bulletins on the teaching of the Holocaust. Moreover, the use of creative arts — music, art, drama, dance and literature — should be stimulated to give expression to the invincibility of the human spirit.

To be sure, we must urge legislation that will permit prosecution for crimes against humanity without imposition of statues of limitation.

Needed on the American scene regarding the Holocaust is an adequate sense of reality orientation. Most of our generation has grown up with an incomplete, distorted view of history. Learning about the Holocaust will be helpful in building an historical base for moral and ethical teaching, and for character education. History itself will teach the lessons that need to be learned.

Some may feel that the Holocaust is too gory a subject for young children. However, in this day and age of exposure to all kinds of horror and killing through fictional movies and television programs it is absolutely essential to demonstrate that unbelievable barbarism actually did occur in the enlightened twentieth century.

In light of my opening remarks about the potential for peace, it is necessary to underscore the relationship of the Holocaust to the rebirth of Israel. The establishment of the Jewish State reveals the undauntable spirit that helped the Jewish people sustain themselves in the face of great adversity until they finally saw the rebirth of the State which now on the eve of its long-dreamed-for era of peace.

Thank you for this opportunity to express my views. I wish the Committee much success in its efforts. Please convey my own personal gratitude and best wishes and the heartfelt thanks of the Officers, Board of Directors and staff of the Board of Jewish Education of Greater New York and its Committee on the Holocaust to President Carter, for developing the Commission that, hopefully, will help enrich the soul, spirit and moral fiber of the United States of America.

— 39 —

KRISTALLNACHT

Presented at
Community Observance of the
Fiftieth Anniversary of Kristallnacht
Central Synagogue, New York City
November 6, 1988

Kristallnacht! They didn't believe it could happen, but, it did.

Here we are, Jewish children and youth, Jewish young adults and adults living in free America.

Imagine coming home tonight and finding wild hordes running through the streets of your community — here in Manhattan and in Queens — Forest Hills, Rego Park; and in Westchester — White Plains, Scarsdale; and in Brooklyn — Flatbush, Bensonhurst, Boro Park; and in Nassau County — the Five Towns, Great Neck; and in Suffolk County — Huntington, Dix Hills; or wherever you live. Imagine coming home this evening and seeing and hearing the windows of all of the Jewish homes and Jewish-owned businesses in your community being smashed — watching your synagogue burn to the ground, and seeing your father, your uncle, your brother, your grandfather, your neighbor being slugged over the head, humiliated, arrested, dragged away while you, your mothers, and sisters, stand by in shock, being held back by police. Imagine the horror of such a barbaric event!

While this is happening, imagine, too, that all the other people in your community just stand by and watch — some of them actually enjoying the grisly scene.

That's what it was like this very week 50 years ago in hundreds of communities throughout Germany.

Kristallnacht! Kristallnacht! We've heard about it today, and we'll hear about it more and more. The gory details require repetition to insure that the world will never, never let anything like this occur again.

Thirty thousand innocent people arrested and sent to concentration camps in Buchenwald, Dachau and Sachsenhausen; scores of innocent Jews killed; over 7,000 Jewish shops vandalized and looted; hundreds of Jewish homes ransacked; hundreds of synagogues set on fire or otherwise destroyed; a fine of one billion marks imposed on the German Jewish community; insurance policies of Jews confiscated; Jewish communal and cultural organizations dissolved; and Jewish youth barred from German schools and universities.

And the world stood by silently. Great Britain had the opportunity to support German Jewry in the months prior to Kristallnacht but, characteristically, refused. The United States refused to modify its immigration laws to permit entry of more refugees into this country. The Catholic Church did little else but call upon people of all faiths to send up a "holocaust of prayer for those oppressed in Germany and in other parts of the world in this time of great turmoil."

And, there were German Jews who would not believe the real meaning of these events, who felt that this would pass, at least for them, since they were so well assimilated into German society.

And here we are today in New York doing what we must — learning about the various aspects of this inhuman series of acts against a minority population which was lulled into believing that it was safe and secure. And here we are preparing ourselves to answer questions about the role of the Jewish community with regard to anti-Semitism and anti-Zionism. How do we relate to the larger American society when we hear about anti-Semitic incidents in America? How do we react to anti-Jewish and anti-Zionist activity in other countries? What can we do as individuals and as a community to guarantee that there will never be another Kristallnacht or another Holocaust? Had there been a Jewish State in 1938, what a difference it would have made! Doors and gates slammed shut to Jews of Europe would have been open. There would not have been a Holocaust — certainly not the extent of human destruction that took place.

Therefore, it is our sacred obligation to do whatever we can to vouchsafe the safety and security of Israel — the home of hundreds of thousands of Jewish refugees and the homeland of the Jewish people.

And here we are today, observing Kristallnacht as a community in mourning, recognizing profiles of courage and heroism like the little-known act of courage that took place in the darkest days of 1942 and 1943. The White Rose Movement — the only German opposition to the Nazis, organized by two medical school students, both graduates of the Hitler Youth Movement. While treating the wounded on the Eastern Front in the summer of 1942, they witnessed the Nazi atrocities. They could not turn a blind eye. Other students joined them to form the White Rose. They distributed leaflets to the public exposing the atrocities and urging passive resistance to the Nazi regime.

All these students were arrested. Many were tried, convicted and executed. A handful have survived, and continue to speak out. The White Rose Movement lives with them, as a shining example — and warning — to a new generation.

And here we are — in spite of the efforts of all the Jew haters over the millennia who tried to destroy us. Here we are — celebrating our Passovers, our Purims and our Hanukkahs, our Israel Independence Days and our Jerusalem Days.

Here we are, a free people in a free land, observing Kristallnacht in pain and in tears, but knowing, in the words of the Haggadah, that we have been brought forth

מעבדות לחרות, מיגון לשמחה, מאבל ליום טוב ומאפלה לאור גדול . . .

from oppression to freedom, from great sorrow to joy, from mourning to festivity, from darkness to great light.

It is our responsibility as Jews, individually and collectively, to insure freedom for all, to speak up for the oppressed, to help the less fortunate and to fight for freedom and justice — for the Jewish people, for Israel and for all people everywhere. And that is why I speak today on behalf of the Board of Jewish Education of Greater New York, together with Ambassador Lauder who so diligently invests his talents, energies and support to realize this goal.

KRISTALLNACHT NO MORE! FREEDOM FOREVER!
This is our holy mission as Jews and Americans —
. . . לכו בכחכם זה והושעתם את ישראל

Let us go forward from this observance strengthened by our resolve that we can make a difference! God bless our efforts!

— 40 —

MARCH OF THE LIVING

*Excerpts from a live radio program broadcast
from the Rappaport Memorial in Warsaw to the
State of Israel
On the Eve of Yom Hashoah
April 22, 1990*

Here we are, 3600 Jewish youth from 100 Jewish communities, the world over, assembled at the Rappaport Memorial on Saturday night, the 26th of Nisan — on the eve of Yom Hashoah.

Here we are, all living witnesses to the fact that Hitler was not able to fully realize his vile ambition — the eradication of the entire Jewish people.

So unique, so encompassing, so horrible was his plan of human destruction that a new term had to be coined for the Nazi atrocities — for the vicious, demonic, barbaric effort to wipe out a whole race — *genocide* — the genocide of the Jewish people.

Here we are to commemorate the 47th anniversary of the Warsaw ghetto uprising.

And here we are in a city where Jewish life once thrived — where

267

Jewish tradition flourished — where Jews lived and laughed, argued and played, worked and prayed, sang and danced, studied Torah and Talmud . . .

Here we are in solemn assembly — to remember.
To remember our glorious Jewish past.
Here we are together — united in grief — to remember.

To remember and to mourn the unbelievable tragic loss of human life in a country which became a death factory — one huge human slaughterhouse.

Remember! Zachor! Gedenk! is our individual and collective responsibility.

And here we are — young and old — present and future leaders of the Jewish people. Here we are to vow that we will never, never again allow a catastrophe like this to befall our people.

And here we are to pay honor to the heroes and heroines of the Warsaw ghetto uprising, to pay homage to the sacred memory of the brave souls of the resistance movement during the deep, dark days of the Holocaust . . . As we remember fathers and mothers, grandfathers and grandmothers and great grandparents, uncles and aunts, brothers and sisters who are no longer among the living, we light a solitary candle in their memory . . .

We light in memory of
>Aharon Kaplan — a Jewish teacher in the Warsaw ghetto who was slaughtered mercilessly while teaching a Hebrew class.

We light in memory of
>Adam Czernakow — head of the Warsaw ghetto who committed suicide rather than deliver Jews for deportation to death camps.

We light in memory of
>Mordecai Anielewicz — brave commander of the Warsaw ghetto uprising.

We light in memory of
>Rabbi Mordecai Schriebman, Rosh Yeshiva of the Tachkemoni Yeshiva, who together with his students was savagely murdered.

We light in memory of
> Yitzhak Gitterman and Emanuel Ringelblum — outstanding activists for Jewish self-help.

We light in memory of
> Chaika Grossman and Frumka Plotnicki — heroic girls who went — disguised from city to city on dangerous missions to save lives.

We light in memory of
> Rabbi Yitzhak Nisenbaum — a leader of the religious Zionist movement who inspired his fellow Jews to try to save their own lives and the lives of other Jews. He urged; "This is the time for the sanctification of life and not for the sanctification of God's name by death."

We light in memory of
> Tosia Altman, Yosef Kaplan, Yitzhak Zukerman and Tzvia Lubatkin, founders of the underground Jewish military organization.

We light in memory of
> All the heroes who perished while trying to save Jewish souls . . .

> And to these names we add the names of the young movements — whose members gave them lives for the sake of their people:

> Hehalutz, Betar, Akiva, Hapoel Hamizrachi, Hanoar Hatzioni, Hashomer Hatzair, Hashomer Hadati, Gordonia, Dror, Bnai Akiva.

> And, we light in memory of all the innocent children who were led like sheep to slaughter.

> In memory of all the Kedoshim we recite the Kaddish.

> Yisgadal V'yiskaddah shmai Rabbah.

. . . And in our deep grief, we take an oath in the language of the Haggadah which we recited on Pesah just one week ago. Let us reaffirm our resolve that as the Exodus from Egypt brought freedom and promise to our ancestors, we will continue to devote every effort so that our Ethiopian and Soviet brethren be brought from slavery to freedom, out of sorrow to happiness, out of mourning to joy, from deep darkness to great light, and from bondage to redemption.

— 41 —

EMERGENCY RALLY
FOR SOVIET JEWRY

Jewish Community Council of Oceanside
December 29, 1970

Sylvia Zalmonson Kuznetzov, 10 years of hard labor under Soviet terms; Yosef Mendelovitch, 15 years of hard labor; Yuri Federov, 14 years of hard labor; Alexander Muzenko, 14 years of hard labor; Leib Khanokh, 13 years of hard labor; Boris Pestner, 12 years of hard labor; Isaac Zalumcan, 12 years of hard labor; Anatoly Altman, 12 years of hard labor; Mendel Bodman, 5 years of hard labor; Mark Dymshitz, death sentence; Anatoly Altman, death sentence.

All because they wanted to be free or, as the Russians put it, they were guilty of *treason;* they were guilty of *plotting* their freedom.

For their sins we are here tonight — Jews, non-Jews, men and women, adults and children. For their grave transgressions of wanting to be free, to live freely and to bring up their families in the spirit of freedom, we join them in kindling the eighth light of Hanukkah.

270

For the record, they are all guiltless. On Sunday, I saw a letter smuggled out of the Soviet Union detailing the ridiculousness and farcity of the charges. "What do you wish to say before we pronounce your sentence?" Anatoly Altman, one of the Leningrad victims, was asked by Chief Prosecutor Rudenko as the farcical trial ended.

"I wish to send from this courtroom Hanukkah greetings to all my brethren in Israel." For that wish he was sentenced to 12 years hard labor in prison. For that wish we are here tonight, to send Hanukkah greetings to our condemned brothers and sisters.

The moment Altman made his statement, all of the accused and their relatives who were in the courtroom stood in unison, as if not to accept their fate, and burst out into song. "Am Yisrael Hai," they sang. As they were being marched out of the courtroom the innocent victims recited "Shema Yisrael."

We are here tonight with them in spirit, to sing with them and to protest the vicious barbaric sentences; to proclaim that all humankind must be free — that in the spirit of Hanukkah we will achieve speedily the victory of freedom over tyranny.

Tonight we join all free living people throughout the world in expressing our shock and chagrin at the cruel injustice being perpetrated in the Soviet Union against Altman, against Mark Dymshits, Sylvia Kuznetzov and all the other victims of Soviet "justice." We have it from good sources that the demonstration of concern all over the universe has influenced the Soviet decision to speed up the appeal hearings. The Soviet Union wants to end the world wide furor before the Communist Party Congress in March.

The designs and plots against Jews in the Soviet are continuing in full force. As we meet here, nine Jews are scheduled for trial on January 6th in Leningrad and twelve more are to be tried in Riga and in Kishinev. We must continue to speak out and let our voices be heard.

Tomorrow morning, American Jewish leaders will seek a meeting with President Nixon, who has seen fit to quietly put pressure upon the Soviet government. This is obviously a result of the expression of American concern for the fate of the innocent victims.

The outpouring of sentiment, we are informed by sources close to the administration, must continue *unabated.* Letters and telegrams must be sent to President Nixon and to Secretary Rogers asking them to intervene with Ambassador Dobrynin, asking them to demand the commutation of the death sentences and the prison sentences.

All freedom loving people in Greater New York must make it their business to pay heed to Mayor Lindsay's call for a mass meeting at the steps of City Hall tomorrow between 12:00 and 2:00 p.m. A work stoppage has been called for that time.

Church authorities have been requested to have church bells ring at that time. Special prayers are requested to be offered at home and in our respective houses of worship. Headlights should be on during the 12 noon-2 p.m. period of concern and solidarity.

We must continue as free people to speak out *for* life and against death, *for* free speech and freedom of movement and *against* imprisonment, *for* peace and good will and *against* injustice and tyranny.

And tonight, we send the following telegram to the President of the United States:

"We the residents of Oceanside and neighboring comunities, Jewish and non-Jewish citizens of the United States, elected state-wide and local officials, and clergy of many faiths, assembled here tonight, December 29, 1970, hereby express our dismay, shock and chagrin at the cruel injustice being perpetrated in the Soviet Union.

"We are grateful for the steps you have already taken on behalf of the innocent victims. We beseech you as President of our great democracy to intervene even more forcefully to free those guiltless souls enslaved by Russian tyranny.

"May our *deep* concern and prayerful hope as Americans and your active leadership help bring life and liberty, peace and goodwill to all freedom-loving people behind the Iron Curtain."

Dr. Alvin I. Schiff, President
Jewish Community Council of Oceanside

Friends all, freedom can be a reality for our suppressed brethren in the Soviet Union. "Im tirzu, ain zoo aggaddah" If only we will it, we'll help them be free!

— 42 —

40 YEARS AND FOREVER!

Opening Remarks
at the Salute to Israel Parade,
New York City
April 17, 1988

— The Israelites wandered for 40 years in the desert.

— During their 40 years in the desert, the Children of Israel were forged into a nation as they were prepared to enter the Land of their forefathers — Abraham, Isaac and Jacob.

— Moses spent 40 days and nights on Mt. Sinai.

— At the end of his 40 day and night stay on Mt. Sinai, Moses received the Ten Commandments — the written Torah — the lifeblood of Jewish statehood.

— And, the 40 years of statehood have helped transform the Jewish people of the 20th century into a vibrant, strong and proud nation.

— *Ben arba-im la-binah.* Yehudah ben Temma advises us in the *Ethics of the Fathers* that age 40 is the time for wisdom and understanding.

273

Indeed, in the wake of the Holocaust, these past 40 years of nationhood have taught Israel much. Its bittersweet experiences — four major wars, hundreds of terrorist acts, constant daily threats of obliteration from Arab neighbors, and through it all, a cold, unsympathetic, even hostile world — have had a sobering effect upon this young nation-state. Against this background, Israel's sterling achievements in the human, social, political, cultural, industrial, technological and agricultural areas are all the more remarkable.

Above all, Israel stands high and alone as a beacon of democracy and freedom in a sea of corruption, anarchy, hatred and violence.

Forty years and forever! *Am Yisrael hai! Long live Israel.*

There is no better way to usher in Israel's 40th anniversary year than by blowing the shofar accompanied by the traditional biblical reading in Numbers 10:9,10. "And on your days of celebration, on your fixed festivals, and your new moon days, you shall sound the trumpets over your burnt-offerings and your peace-offerings."

We know what the "fixed festivals" are — Succot, Pesah and Shavuot. We know what the "new moons" are every month. But, what are the "days of celebration"? Ibn Ezra, medieval Hebrew poet and biblical exegete, helps us understand this phrase. "The days of celebration," Ibn Ezra informs us, refers to a time in the future "when the Jewish people will return to Israel from lands of their enemies, and to a time when they will defeat the enemy that attacked them." At that time, he suggests that the Jewish people establish a joyous holiday and celebrate it like the festivals of Purim and Hanukkah.

And here we are, 40 years after the Holocaust, after the initial ingathering of Jews from so many countries where they were oppressed. And here we are, 40 years after defeating the enemies who would deny us the right of our homeland and the privilege of Jewish statehood.

So now, on Israel's 40th birthday, let us initiate our celebration with the blast of the shofar: Tekiah, Shevarim, Teruah.

— 43 —

ISRAEL AT FORTY

*Presented at the
BJE Annual Reception
June 6, 1988*

תורת ישראל, ארץ ישראל, עם ישראל

The Torah, the land of Israel, the people of Israel. The Torah — broadly interpreted as the cognitive and emotive dimensions of Jewish education — the Land of Israel, the birthplace of Judaism and the homeland of the Jewish people, are the pillars of Judaic civilization. Both are absolutely essential to the existence and continuity of the Jewish people.

Both — Jewish education and the State of Israel — make unique and vital contributions to the enrichment of Jewish life. In each, the more we become involved and vested, the more we benefit, individually and collectively.

Yet both — Jewish education and Israel — struggle to maintain themselves. Both suffer from the lack of adequate fiscal resources, among others.

In an age when Jewish life is at the crossroads, when there are powerful forces that would erode the vitality of each — both Jewish education and the Jewish State have their heroes.

In Jewish education we are blessed with lay leaders — in our schools and in BJE — whose commitment, dedication and support of Jewish life is legion in the Jewish community. And we are further blessed with gifted and devoted professionals, some of whom we honor this evening. As a group, the BJE staff is unparalleled in its dedication and contribution to the vibrancy of Jewish schooling.

And Israel — during its brief history of Statehood — has had leaders of every stripe whose personal commitment and sacrifice for the ideals of Jewish nationhood have been literally an אור לגויים "a light unto the nations."

And Israel has its unsung heroes — the average Israeli citizens, the soldiers, the business folk, the professionals, the students and scholars, and the homemakers.

Young and old — in the cities, in the Negev, in the Galil, in Yehudah and Shomron — they deserve our heartfelt recognition and resounding tribute in the 40th anniversary year.

Unfortunately, this anniversary is tainted with unrest and terrorism, and with indecision regarding steps to take in order to vouschafe the future of Israel.

וגילו ברעדה "Rejoice with trembling," advises the Sweet Singer of Israel in the Book of Psalms. Indeed, we celebrate this year with much trembling. But, celebrate we must the birthday of this little democracy anchored perilously in a vast sea of anarchy and violence.

We must celebrate Israel as a place of refuge, as a homeland, as a center of Jewish life and culture, as we observe the miraculous rebirth of our national destiny.

Not everyone agrees with everything its leaders do — and we often take sides in Israel's struggle to be and to live in peace — but גילו we must and show our pride in Israel's accomplishments during these 40 years in the face of the most unbelievable difficulties and almost insurmountable obstacles.

One example of these achievements strikes home to those of us whose major interests lie in the wholesome development of Israeli youth. And that is Youth Aliyah.

Despite the numerous difficulties it faced and the criticisms many of us may have of this system — imperfect as it was and still is —

its post-World War II record of absorbing young, orphaned, haggard, homeless immigrants out of the mouth of the European Holocaust and from the bowels of oppression in Arab lands, and its current program of dealing with the educational and human needs of disadvantaged youth is absolutely remarkable. Added to this are its recent heroic efforts to absorb young immigrants from Ethiopia.

Over 250,000 Jews currently living in Israel are graduates of Youth Aliyah Youth Villages.

To see how the young Ethiopians are helped to adjust to modern Jewish life in Israel is to behold a human miracle.

Last week I spent an extended Memorial Day weekend in Israel at the request of the Jewish Agency to help develop a research design to evaluate Youth Aliyah's current programs. The highlight of my trip was Shabbat at the Yemin Orde Youth Village near Haifa — with several hundred disadvantaged youngsters among them 150 Ethiopian teenagers. To observe the progress they made in two or three short years is to see life in the making. There I witnessed what caring hearts and souls can do to rehabilitate the lives of these unfortunate youngsters — many of whose parents died in front of their eyes during their long trek to Israel.

One vignette will remain with me forever. About thirty Ethiopian graduates of Yemin Orde now serving in the Israeli army, came back to spend Shabbat in Yemin Orde. The love between their former teachers and counselors was so evident — the way they kissed each other on both cheeks.

Erez, one of the graduates is now a student at Gush (a Hesder yeshiva where he alternates studying for a half year and serves in the army for a half year, for a period of three years). I asked him if he wanted to be a Rav in the Ethiopian Jewish community. "God forbid!" was his retort. His reason — "There is no Ethiopian Jewish community, no black Jewish community, no white Jewish community, no Oriental Jewish community, no Ashkenazic Jewish community — just *klal yisrael* — one Jewish community." And he said he learned this in Yemin Orde from its distinguished director, Dr. Chaim Peri, who served for three years as a shaliah — pedagogic specialist — at BJE from 1977 to 1980. What Chaim has done for these immigrant children is nothing less than fantastic, monumental.

His kind of accomplishment is what we celebrate. He, in turn, sends us warm wishes from himself and the youth of Yemin Orde as we practice a year of גילו.

— 44 —

JEWISH UNITY THROUGH
STUDY AND PRAYER

*Presented at the New York Persian Gulf War
Assembly of Jewish Day School Student Delegates,
Convened by the Board of Jewish Education of
Greater New York at Yeshiva University, New York*
January 30, 1991

Here we are on Tu B'shevat תשנ״א (5751), 1500
students and 100 teachers and principals from yeshivot and day
schools throughout Metropolitan New York representing some
130,000 Jewish school students and 8,000 Jewish educators.

We have been convened by the Board of Jewish Education of
Greater New York in cooperation with the Yeshiva Elementary and
High School Principals' Councils.

And, we're here to celebrate Jewish Arbor Day —
ראש השנה לאילנות — in a very special way, special because of the most
unusual, difficult and painful times in which we live.

We are here to declare in unison that what Saddam Hussein is
attempting to do flies in the face of Judaic tradition which holds

sacred the lives of human beings and mandates the care and protection
of the environment — all creations of one God.

Tu B'shevat is the Jewish way to express love and admiration of
nature. We are told by our sages *(Kohellet Rabbah* 7:28) that when the
Almighty created Adam, He took him to see the trees and vegetation
in the Garden of Eden and said to him:

> See my works, how fine and excellent they are!
> Now all that I have created, I created for your benefit.
> Think about this and do not corrupt or destroy the
> world, for if you destroy it, there is no one to restore it
> after you.

On Tu B'shevat, in 1949, the nations of the world witnessed the
historic opening of the Israeli Knesset with 120 members — the very
same number as the אנשי כנסת הגדולה — the number of leaders who
comprised the Great Assembly at the time of the Second בית המקדש
(Holy Temple) over 2,000 years ago.

Today, then, is the 42nd anniversary of Israel's Knesset which
represents the only democracy in the Middle East and stands in stark
contrast to the demagogy of Saddam Hussein. It is in honor of the
Knesset and the free State of Israel that we gather here today.

And we are assembled here today to cemonstrate our solidarity
with Jewish youth in Israel. While we are participating in a Shiur on
the meaning of Tu B'shevat, over 100,000 Jewish youth in the Greater
New York area are studying Biblical and Talmudic sources relating to
Tu B'shevat and ecology. And hundreds of thousands of Israeli pupils
were engaged in similar Tu B'shevat study seven hours ago. Dr. Yosef
Yonai — chief supervisor of this program — informed me in a phone
conversation about two hours ago that although students are not
allowed to congregate in large groups, all over the country they
studied in small groups. In the words of Israeli Minister of Education,
Zevulun Hammer, with whom I concluded the arrangement for this
simultaneous Learn-a-Thon:

> Dr. Schiff: Please convey my heartfelt wishes to the
> yeshiva students assembled at Yeshiva University. Tell
> them that we in Israel are proud of them, that we
> appreciate thair participation in the Tu B'shevat
> Learn-a-Thon with students in Israel. Tell them also
> that most of Israel's 1-1/4 million Jewish students will
> be engaged in simultaneous learning about Tu B'shevat

and the protection of Nature.

In addition to learning together, as we read from the Book of Psalms here at Yeshiva University, over 100,000 students in Greater New York Jewish schools are reading the same Psalms. Hundreds of thousands of Israeli students have done the same thing at noon Israeli time on Tu B'shevat.

Moreover, as we read prayers for the Peace of Israel, for the welfare of Israeli soldiers and for the welfare of the United States and its military forces, Jewish students throughout New York are reciting the very same prayers as did the students in Israel seven hours ago.

When the first session of Israel's Knesset took place 42 years ago on Tu B'shevat almost all its members went to the Yeshurun synagogue in Jerusalem to *daven minhah* (recite the afternoon prayers). For them the words of the Tefillat Amidah השיבה שופטינו כבראשונה ("restore our judges and government as in the days of old") had very special meaning. For us, when we *daven minhah,* we will have special *Kavannah* (devotion) when we recite the words following in the very same *berachah* (blessing) והסר ממנו יגון ואנחה We hope and pray that *Hashem* will restore justice and remove sorrow, pain and anguish from our midst.

For all these reasons we have called our Tu B'shevat assembly today, "Jewish Unity Through Learning and Prayer."

All Jewish youth in New York are one in heart and mind concerning the well-being of our Israeli brothers and sisters. And, we are one with them in thought and feeling about the horrors of the Persian Gulf War. We pray fervently for the safety of the people of Israel as we anxiously hope for the end of the hostilities and the safe homecoming of all American Armed Forces.

A video tape of today's program will be made available to all schools in Greater New York as well as to the Ministry of Education in Israel.

At the end of this Assembly we will send to Israel a delegation of principals who will bring 18 tree saplings to Israel to be planted under the guidance of the Jewish National Fund in memory of the Israelis killed by the Iraqi missiles, and in honor of the Israel Defense Forces and the American military men and women serving in the Gulf. Our delegation will bring our message of solidarity to the Jewish youth of Israel and will bring back to all of us a message of *hope from Israel.*

— 45 —

ISRAEL-DIASPORA RELATIONSHIPS HOW CAN THEY BE MUTUALLY BENEFICIAL?

Presented at
the International Conference
on Jewish Communal Service
Jerusalem, June, 1980

At the outset, it seems appropriate to ask: Why does the topic of Israel-Diaspora education relationships surface annually? One would think that after 34 years of statehood, the patterns of relationships would be established firmly, and that all one would have to do from time to time is to modify and strengthen those patterns according to the changing needs of the Diaspora and Israeli scenes.

Although I speak solely from an American Jewish point of view, I realize full well that relationships between Diaspora and Israel will vary according to the differing needs and capacities of the Jewish communities throughout the world.

To be sure, various patterns of America-Israel relationships have already been set. Some intercontinental efforts, such as Tochnit Yud Gimel, the year-long Yeshiva study programs and several summer tour programs for youth have compiled a noteworthy track record. However, each time we approach the subject it is from a perspective of developing new, useful, mutually beneficial relationships. In a sense, it is like the almost eternal question of Israel-Diaspora relationships in the arena of government policy, where there are two opposing schools of thought. One suggests or demands Diaspora input and the exercise of authority. The other definitely excludes them.

Needed are cooperative effort to reinforce viable programs, eliminate or modify unsuccessful activities and initiate new appropriate projects.

To begin with, in discussing the development of closer relationships, we must understand that there are normal pulls and tensions between Israel and the Diaspora. One must assume that a Diaspora community of the size, status, wealth, and philanthropic and cultural development of the American Jewish community would expect to have primary input into the development of the relationships that involve it. In addition, as Rabbi Joseph Soleveitchik aptly put it, we live, "not in the age of the giver, but in the age of the taker." The recipient today helps determine, and is often the major or even sole determinant for the kinds of service he will receive. In the case of Israel, programs targeted for the American Jewish community — the very source from which the funds for these programs originate — this expectation is quite natural.

On the other hand, Israel views its own very special role in providing educational service to the Diaspora. To be sure, "From Zion shall come forth the Torah" is a goal to be attained by the Jewish State. However, its implementation at this time is premature. Israel has not yet developed into the kind of "cultural-spiritual center" for which Jews aspired throughout the ages.

Some Diaspora communities are almost entirely dependent upon Israel for materials, for teachers, even for administrators. They could not maintain their educational programs were it not for the help they receive from Israel via the Departments of Education and Culture and Torah Education of the World Zionist Organization. For these communities Israel-Diaspora relationships are basically a one-way street.

The North American situation is unique. American Jewry is not dependent upon Israel for the maintenance of its educational efforts. Yet, it should depend upon Israel for educational reinforcement and enrichment that uniquely emanates from Israel.

The American Jewish relationship, as spelled out in the guidelines of the Joint Education Fund, must be developed around three fundamental concerns of Jewish education: pupils, educators and materials.

In order to maximize the benefits of the relationships regarding Jewish education we must view them in the context of the atmosphere set by the pattern of annual American Jewish fund-raising programs for Israel, and by the America-Israel relationships in other areas of concern, including child care, health care, group work and services for the aged. In these areas, the American Jewish community is recognized for its know-how and expertise. And it is the American Jewish community that sets the tone for the relationships between Israel and America.

Jewish education differs from philanthropy, from social work, and health care. Israel has much to contribute to Jewish education just by its mere presence as a Jewish state, representing the implementation of a Judaic religio-national ideal. Moreover, it is the living repository of the historical and religious sites of the Jewish heritage.

There is a school of thought that suggests that American Jewry should rely on its own resources and create its own American Jewish culture with its own American Jewish institutions, and that it need not look elsewhere, not even to Israel, for reinforcement. This purist Diaspora philosophy overlooks the fact that with the emergence of modern Jewish statehood all Jewish communities throughout the world underwent a change. While not always articulated, a significant socio-cultural relationship has existed between Israel and the American Diaspora since 1948. Neither community can now exist without the other.

Indirectly, Israel enriches the Diaspora as it provides the Diaspora education with a sense of purpose and with programmatic opportunities otherwise not obtainable. The very presence of Israel has an influence on the American Jewish community and on the American Jewish school. Children are able to relate to a Jewish nation — the embodiment of the Zionist heritage about which they study. Ancient Israel, the Israel of the past, is a live and thriving place of the present. This fact has tremendous meaning for the educational process.

Directly, the Jewish education enterprise in America has received significant benefits from the World Zionist Organization via its Departments of Education and Culture, Torah Education, and *Hanoar Ve-Hechalutz* (the American Zionist Youth Foundation), the Ministry of Education and Culture, the various Israeli universities and yeshivot, and other Israeli institutions.

But the benefits that America receives from Israel would be multiplied if a true *partnership* were established. For one, Israel has never really thought in terms of being a recipient of benefits from the American Jewish educational establishment. This, in itself, is an error in judgment. Despite its problems and overwhelming challenges, the American Jewish educational enterprise and the American Jewish educator have much to offer to Israeli education. This challenge and opportunity have to be taken seriously.

For example, Jewish educators in America could help Israeli school personnel improve school administration. They could be most helpful in planning and implementing the activites like the recent Moreshet Bet Saba Conference. Just as American school personnel can benefit from an Israeli experience, Israeli teachers have much to gain from the American Jewish experience. To be specific, the Board of Jewish Education of Greater New York could be of invaluable assistance in helping Israel establish viable Teacher Centers for teachers in early childhood and elementary schools.

Regarding Israel's helping role, a careful assessment of Israel's capacity vis-a-vis the Diaspora is needed. This evaluation, I believe, should be conducted by the Ministry of Education and Culture. Hopefully, it will lead to a long-range plan which responds to the question: How can a relatively small amount of money (with the current inflation and fundraising problems the amount available is getting smaller and smaller) have the maximum impact upon the effectiveness of American Jewish education? In answering this challenge, several other questions have to be considered. Should Israel be more than a national presence? More than a locus where Jews recharge their batteries? Should Israel be an exporter of talent and materials? To all communities? How can this best be accomplished? The responses to these questions should form the basis of a master plan in whose development diaspora Jewry participates as a full partner.

On balance, the American Jewish community should evaluate its potential regarding the assistance it can render Israel in a variety of educational matters.

There are some benefits to the helter-skelter pattern which has epitomized the educational relationships between Israel and America until now. *Kin'at Sofrim*, as an operative principle, has value but also it has its severe limitations. Israeli agencies competing for the same clientele and for sponsorship of similar programs is detrimental to the effectiveness of ongoing relationships. Moreover, the lack of a master plan inhibits program implementation and expansion.

One community, for example, has conducted an outstanding summer program in Israel for its youth for almost two decades. Much communal effort, funding and professional guidance have been expended on this project. On more than one occasion, it received international recognition. Why should this community have to compete each year for summer headquarters for its students? In the words of its director, "We had to apply the necessary pressure to obtain adequate facilities." The process of finding a suitable place is time-consuming and often enervating. It underscores the need for an overall plan which would establish permanent summer places for the various programs, or a system of rotation, arranged *a priori*. Such designations should not be left to chance, politics, pressure or personal relationships.

Also, it is clear that the Jewish institutions in the United States, Canada, or any other Jewish community should not be used to help solve the problems of professionals seeking placement during their sabbatical years. It is creditable that Israeli academicians and educators are able to obtain sabbaticals so readily and so frequently. However, this should not be the reason for sending them abroad.

The American Jewish relationship must be developed around three fundamental concerns of Jewish education: pupils, personnel and materials, as spelled out in the guidelines of the Joint Education Fund sponsored by the Jewish Agency, the World Zionist Organization and the Israeli Ministry of Education and Culture.

In each of these three areas of concern — youth, educators and realia — clear objectives must be developed. In the first place, we need to know what is Israel's capacity for serving youth with intensive Jewish backgrounds. Similarly, what can Israel provide to a group of unaffiliated youth in order to help "turn them on?" How will these programs differ? In scope? In the planning stages? In implementation and follow-up?

Concerning educators, how should Israel relate to pre-service education? To the in-service needs of both neophyte and experienced teachers and principals? Many years ago, I proposed a plan to the Ministry of Education. I still think it is workable and can be mutually beneficial to America (or other Diaspora communities) and to Israel. Such a plan requires that the various partners in Israel — the universities, the WZO departments, the Ministry of Education of Education and Culture, and individual schools, participate together in designing the particulars of the program. The joint planning itself will provide a forum for meaningful interaction.

Briefly restated, the recommendation calls for a trimester, multi-level 13 month, in-service offering for Diaspora teachers. The program would start in the beginning of July with three months of intensive Ulpan activity and orientation to the land of Israel. October, November, December and January would be practice-teaching months, in which the American educator will serve as assistant teacher, co-teacher, or student-teacher with parallel course work to meet individual needs of the participant.

The third trimester, from February through May, would essentially be a service component in which the teacher would work according to his ability, either in an urban school or in a development town.

In addition, the last two months of the program (June-July) would be used to reinforce the Israeli experience with touring and university course work, as well as part-time work in informal Jewish education or camping. These months may also be used for meetings between the teachers completing their training and the new incoming group of teachers.

After 13 months of such activity, one can be sure that the teachers will return to their home base with new knowledge and new experience that will be helpful to them in their daily work. If they decide to stay in Israel, the Jewish State has gained an *oleh*. In this regard, however, the program should stipulate that the participants return to their home base for at least three years of teaching.

Candidates for this kind of in-service activity should be young people, not older than 35 years of age. America and Israel would have to cooperate and find ways to finance the identification and screening of the candidates, and their travel and placement.

Regarding the Israeli education system, Israel can benefit from the selective placing of small groups of teachers in special American Jewish school settings with concomitant education courses in local universities. This is often done individually by teachers. But it is not organized sufficiently to provide full impact. The American Jewish education community is not involved in helping to prepare and train these teachers. On a more profound level, a real exchange program for experienced teachers could be developed to replace the current limited, after-the-fact, one-way placement activity. A major component of the program would be a two-part orientation for both Israeli and American teachers. The first part would take place in their home country before they leave for their shlichut, and the second segment in their new communities prior to the beginning of their respective assignments. This kind of arrangement might be made for principals as well.

For the youth level, I propose the formation of an intercontinental consortium of a representative group of formal and informal Jewish educators who have had experience with year-long academic and summer tour programs. This consortium would meet bi-annually or tri-annually for a sufficient length of time to review all the Israel-based programs in depth and make recommendations regarding their continuation.

As far as materials are concerned, Israel has produced a plethora of realia, most of which cannot be used directly in American Jewish schools — even in intensive Hebraic day schools. Much has been said about adapting select materials for the American Jewish school. However, nothing of consequence has ever been accomplished. The Ministry of Education and Culture has been taking steps in this direction, initially with the Board of Jewish Education of Greater New York, and then with the American Association for Jewish Education, and several bureaus. As yet, the program has not gotten off the ground. The slowness of implementation is essentially due to the lack of proper funding and the politics within the American Jewish educational establishment. Genuine intracommunity activity in America would lead to increasingly expanding cooperative relationships between Israel and America in this area.

Finally, a crucial aspect of relationships is actual classroom instruction and school ambience. Here, the Diaspora schools can intensify efforts to incorporate Israel in the respective curricula. And

Israel can strengthen its attempts to emphasize *Klal Yisrael* in its school programs. From both ends greater effort should be made for cultural exchange between schools and pupils, including activities such as pen pals, stamp exchange, tape exchange on Hebrew and English language projects, and art exhibits. This kind of intercontinental programming requires a heightened measure of cooperation between the educational leaders of Israel and the Diaspora.

In order to heighten the effectiveness and efficiency in program relationships between the Diaspora and Israel, a structural change in the delivery of services to the Diaspora by the World Zionist Organization seems in order. This would avoid unnecessary duplication and competition between WZO programs. Ideally, the Departments of Education and Culture, Torah Education, and Noar Vehalutz should be consolidated into one overarching Department with specialized thrusts. However, because of tradition and political realities this is not a realistic expectation. Nevertheless, consolidation is a valid objective to be achieved and one that the WZO whould strive to accomplish no matter how long it wll take.

In sum, many beneficial Israel-American educational programs and activities have taken place in the past. With its relatively meager resources, Israel has made herculean efforts with respect to Diaspora education. However, the impact of these efforts has been limited by the lack of appropriate structure to maximize Israel's resources and manpower. The Israel educational establishment must learn to coordinate its efforts via-a-vis the Diaspora. Similarly, the American Jewish community has to devlop a suitable modus operandi in order to relate more effectively to Israel.

In tandem, the mutual education gains will be immeasurable.

In affection
and deep appreciation of

Harry Fleschner ע"ה
Helene Fleschner

the wonderful parents
of my *aishet hayil,*
MIMI
and the loving grandparents
of our children

for their exemplary devotion to
Yiddishkeit and Jewish peoplehood.